DANCE IN THE FIELD

Also by Theresa J. Buckland

ASPECTS OF BRITISH CALENDAR CUSTOMS (*co-editor with Juliette Wood*)

Dance in the Field

Theory, Methods and Issues
in Dance Ethnography

Edited by

Theresa J. Buckland
Senior Lecturer
Head of Department of Dance Studies
University of Surrey
Guildford

Published by PALGRAVE MACMILLAN
Houndmills, Basingstoke, Hampshire RG21 6XS and
175 Fifth Avenue, New York, N.Y. 10010
Companies and representatives throughout the world

PALGRAVE MACMILLAN is the global academic imprint of the Palgrave
Macmillan division of St. Martin's Press, LLC and of Palgrave Macmillan Ltd.
Macmillan® is a reistered trademark in the United States, United Kingdom
and other countries. Palgrave is a registered trademark in the European
Union and other countries.

Outside North America
ISBN 0–333–71913–1

In North America
ISBN 0–312–22378–1

This book is printed on paper suitable for recycling and
made from fully managed and sustained forest sources.

A catalogue record for this book is available from the British Library.

Library of Congress Catalog Card Number: 99–21778

Transferred to digital printing 2004

Printed and bound in Great Britain by
Antony Rowe Ltd, Chippenham and Eastbourne

For Elsie (1920–92) and Reg Buckland

Contents

List of Plates

1. An audience-oriented Samoan dance performed by the Samoan hosts at the seventh Pacific Festival of Arts. Apia, Western Samoa, September 1996. © Adrienne Kaeppler.
2. Researcher, Anca Giurchescu, interviewing a group of căluş dancers in the village of Stoiconeşti, Arges, Romania, 1994. © Colin Quigley.
3. Teaching and learning a couple dance *în două lături* during fieldwork conducted by the Sub-study Group on Fieldwork of the International Council for Traditional Music Study Group on Ethnochoreology. Village of Berchies, Cluj district, Romania, 1995. © Anca Giurchescu.
4. Egil Bakka solicits opinion on the dance tune from one of the local dancers, Birger Nesvold, who has just performed a *pols*, during a field trip to investigate dance/music relationships in Røros, Norway, October 1992. © Rådet for folkemusikk og folkedans.
5. An early example of the detailed photograph documentation of folk dances in Hungary. *Kanásztánc* (shepherd dance), Márcadopuszta (Somogy county), 1932. © Hungarian Ethnographic Museum H-1055 Budapest Kossuth ter 12.
6. Andreas Veda performs the *springar* in the farmyard with his daughter-in-law called out to help demonstrate typical motifs. The dance has now been revived for performance, based on subsequent film recordings and Veda's later teaching. Osteroy, near Bergen, Norway, 1966. © Rådet for folkemusikk og folkedans.
7. Example of field notes using Labanotation (written in real time) of the Korean dance, *ch'ôyongmu*. © Judy Van Zile.
8. Example of Japanese *bon odori (Hanagasa Odori)* notated in brief as field notes (A) and the final score (B). © Judy Van Zile. (Based on Van Zile, 1982, pp. 73–74.)
9. Susindahati rehearses *Bĕdhaya*, Yogyakarta, Java, 1987. © Felicia Hughes-Freeland.
10. *Ledheks* perform for the village spirit, Java, 1994. © Felicia Hughes-Freeland.

Acknowledgements

I would like to express my thanks to the Department of Dance Studies, University of Surrey for financial support in the preparation of this book; for permission to reproduce illustrations: the Rådet for folkemusikk og folkedans, the Hungarian Ethnographic Museum, Colin Quigley and Theodoros Stavrakas.

Thanks are also due to colleagues and students for constant reminders that such a text needs to be published and to Macmillan for continuing to champion publications on dance.

For continuous support, my father, Reg Buckland, and my partner, Tony Moore.

This project would never though have been realised without the patience, commitment and professional eye of Chris Jones in preparing the typescript for submission; I could not have wished for a more supportive and knowledgable colleague – nor indeed one who has made the process so thoroughly enjoyable.

Notes on the Contributors

Egil Bakka is Director of the Centre of the Norwegian Council for Folk Music and Folk Dance (Rådet for folkemusikk og folkedans) and Adjunct Professor in Ethnochoreology at the Norwegian University of Science and Technology in Trondheim. He has established film archives of traditional dance through extensive fieldwork in all parts of Norway, published numerous books and served as chair and member of several boards nationally and internationally within the field of dance research.

Theresa J. Buckland is Senior Lecturer and Head of the Department of Dance Studies, University of Surrey, England, where she is responsible for the Master's programme and for courses in dance anthropology. Her publications include *Aspects of British Calendar Customs* (co-edited with Wood, 1993), chapters on dance and oral history in *Dance History: An Introduction* (eds Adshead-Lansdale and Layson, 1983, 1994), and on dance and music video in *Parallel Lines: Media Representations of Dance* (eds Jordan and Allen, 1993).

Brenda Farnell is Assistant Professor of Anthropology at the University of Illinois (Urbana-Champaign). She trained at I.M. Marsh College (Liverpool) and the Laban Centre for Movement and Dance (London) prior to completing graduate studies at New York University and Indiana University. Her publications include *Do You See What I Mean?: Plains Indian Sign Talk and the Embodiment of Action; Human Action Signs in Cultural Context: the Visible and the Invisible in Movement and Dance* (editor); and a CD-ROM entitled *WIYUTA: Assiniboine Storytelling with Signs*. She serves as associate editor of the *Journal for the Anthropological Study of Human Movement (JASHM)*.

László Felföldi is the Head of the Folk Dance Department, Institute of Musicology, Academy of Sciences, Budapest. He gained his ethnographic training at Szeged University and his doctoral degree in 1984 with a thesis on the folk dance traditions at the lower course of the Maros river. His numerous publications mostly arise from over 20 years of extensive fieldwork in the Carpathian Basin with additional research in Bulgaria, Turkey and Moldavia.

Anca Giurchescu is a freelance dance ethnologist who worked for 26 years as principal researcher at the Institute of Ethnography and Folklore in Bucharest, Romania. Since 1980, she has lived permanently in Denmark, where she continues ethnographic work on minority groups. She has published numerous articles on dance and ritual (especially căluş), dance and structural analysis, and dance and identity. She is Chair of the International Council for Traditional Music Study Group on Ethnochoreology.

Andrée Grau, anthropologist and Benesh movement notator, is Senior Lecturer in Dance at Roehampton Institute, London and Associate Lecturer at the London Contemporary Dance School. She taught anthropology at Richmond, the American International University in London, between 1993 and 1997. Her doctorate on the dance of the Tiwi of Northern Australia was gained from the Department of Social Anthropology, The Queen's University, Belfast. She has published numerous articles and conference papers on dance and anthropology and is working on a book on dance and the embodiment of knowledge.

Georgiana Gore, PhD, is currently Maître de Conférences at the Université Blaise Pascal, Clermont-Ferrand II, France and has held positions in dance/anthropology in the UK and Nigeria. In addition to publishing in journals and conference proceedings, she has contributed chapters to *Dance History: an Introduction* (eds Adshead-Lansdale and Layson, 1994), *Dance in the City* (ed. Thomas, 1997) and *Sociopoétique de la danse* (ed. Montandon, 1998). Her research focuses on the mutual construction of bodily and discursive practices in dance and ritual contexts.

Frank Hall received a PhD in anthropology from Indiana University in 1995 with a dissertation on Irish dancing. In addition to his academic interest in dancing, he is a performer with Rhythm in Shoes, of Dayton, Ohio. He resigned artistic directorship of the company in 1986 to pursue graduate study in the anthropology of dance and human movement. He currently teaches at Indiana State University (Terre Haute) and lives in Bloomington, Indiana.

Felicia Hughes-Freeland is Senior Lecturer in Social Anthropology at the University of Wales, Swansea. She has conducted research in Indonesia for nearly 20 years and has published widely on different aspects of performance in Java, and on television and cultural transformation in Bali. She also makes ethnographic films, including *The*

Dancer and the Dance. She is currently completing a monograph on Javanese court dance entitled *Performance from a Javanese Palace.*

E. Jean Johnson Jones, MA, CMA, is a Lecturer in the Department of Dance Studies, University of Surrey, England, and Director of the Labanotation Institute. As a professional notator and certified movement analyst, she has recorded a wide range of dance styles. Currently, she is engaged in doctoral research on dance in South Africa at the School of Oriental and African Studies, University of London.

Adrienne L. Kaeppler is Curator of Oceanic Ethnology at the Smithsonian Institution in Washington, D.C. She has carried out field research in Tonga, Hawai'i and other parts of the Pacific. Her research focuses on the interrelationships between social structure and the arts, especially dance, music and the visual arts.

Maria Koutsouba, a dancer and teacher for ten years, graduated from the Department of Physical Education and Sports, University of Athens in 1989, specialising in Greek folk dances. She gained her MA in dance studies from the University of Surrey in 1991 and was awarded a doctorate from Goldsmiths College, University of London in 1997. She currently lectures in the School of Intercultural Education and is a lecturer in dance at the Military Academy, Athens.

Andriy Nahachewsky occupies the Huculak Chair of Ukrainian Culture and Ethnography at the University of Alberta, Edmonton, Canada. His research centres on the ways that dance expresses identity and ethnicity and he is currently preparing a book exploring the concepts of folk, character, national and ethnic dance. His field research focuses on Ukrainians in Canada and Ukraine.

Owe Ronström is Assistant Professor at the Institute for Folklife Studies, University of Stockholm and is a founder-member of Orientexpressen, one of Sweden's leading folk music bands. He has researched, lectured and published extensively on traditional music and dance in Sweden and south-east Europe. His doctoral dissertation was published as *Att Gestalta Et Ursprung*, a study of dancing and music-making among Yugoslavs in Stockholm, in 1992.

Judy Van Zile is Professor of Dance at the University of Hawai'i at Manoa, where she coordinates the dance ethnology programme. A certified Labanotation teacher and Fellow of the International Council of Kinetography Laban, she has published broadly on movement analysis and on Korean dance. Her work often includes Labanotation scores.

Drid Williams has conducted fieldwork in England, the USA, Australia and Kenya. She has taught anthropology of the dance and human movement studies in all four countries. She holds a DPhil in social anthropology from St Hugh's College, Oxford. In addition to numerous book chapters and articles, her publications include *Anthropology and Human Movement, 1: The Study of Dances* and the *Journal for the Anthropological Study of Human Movement (JASHM)*, which she founded.

1 Introduction: Reflecting on Dance Ethnography

Theresa J. Buckland

INTRODUCING FIELD RESEARCH IN DANCE AND MOVEMENT

Dance in the Field reflects the continuous growth and diversity of research and scholarship within the international arena of dance ethnography; it is, to my knowledge, the first book to address ethnographic practices in the study of dance and human movement systems. The contributors to this volume speak not only from different geographical but also intellectual positions. Thus my use of the term 'dance ethnography' is deliberate, since it both underlines the present focus on the study of dance through field research and it floats free of any existing disciplinary affiliations.

When the dance scholar Gertrude Kurath sought to establish the parameters of a discipline which she entitled 'dance ethnology' in 1960, she surveyed a voluminous but scattered international literature. Much of it had been written for compatriot scholars in languages other than English. Most of the authors to whom she refers – as in this volume – are drawn from Europe and north America, although Kurath does include publications by, for example, Indian and Japanese writers. This present volume attempts more than a panorama since, as a collection of specially commissioned essays, it aims to promote the field of dance ethnography further than has hitherto perhaps been possible, reliant as it has been internationally on conference proceedings and specialist journals of somewhat limited circulation. The upsurge in scholarly attention to dance and movement generally in the closing years of the twentieth century, however, has highlighted a wider forum in which dance ethnography may flourish and contribute to other more institutionally established cognate disciplines.

Ethnographic studies of dance are variously located in anthropology, sociology, folklore studies, ethnology, cultural studies, performance studies and history. The dominant disciplinary homes of the contributors to this volume are ethnology and anthropology, each

1

being, of course, by no means monolithic in its practice. Moving across Polynesia, Asia, Europe, Indonesia, North America, Australia and Africa, the contributors have each undertaken extensive field research, whether working at home or abroad. Because of the focus on the conduct of fieldwork on dance – how the field is conceptualized, how the data are gathered and for what purposes – it is hoped that newcomers and established scholars may gain a more accessible and current appreciation of the diverse trajectories of dance ethnography. Indeed, primary objectives in compiling this text have been to encourage greater understanding and discussion across those discourses in which ethnographic studies of dance have arisen, as well as to stimulate further reflection on the socio-historical and cultural circumstances of their geneses. This juxtaposition of writings on fieldwork on dance aims to reflect: the paradigms of the authors' training; influences upon them from other disciplines (where appropriate); the particularities of their field sites; and the individual inflections and innovations of their research. The scope of this initiative is thus to underline the specificities of dance ethnography as a mode of study and its affinities with adjacent ethnographic discourses. In this preliminary venture, the detail of each fieldwork enterprise is necessarily absent; but the collection affords an opportunity to identify the intellectual provenance of the themes, methods and issues which emerge and characterize the various approaches taken. This should not be a reductionist task for author, editor and reader but a means to effect greater understanding, thereby laying down a more solid foundation for subsequent research and exchange of ideas.

From the late 1980s, following the collapse of the Soviet bloc, the potential for international exchange of ideas on dance ethnography has widened, particularly through the interpersonal contact granted by the Study Group on Ethnochoreology of the International Council for Traditional Music and, more broadly, through virtual discussions via the Internet. The number of publications, conferences and research projects has expanded, yet has received little comment in late twentieth-century surveys which call attention to the changes and upsurge in literature on dance (see Morris, 1996; Desmond, 1997). The dominant focus upon western theatre art dance, with its accompanying methodologies and theoretical outlooks, within publications and university curricula expressly concerned with dance studies, has tended towards the exclusion of more fruitful dialogues taking place between other dance and movement specialists and dance ethnographers. Often the work of dance ethnographers is othered, even though its largest forum for dance analysis, the Study Group on Ethnochoreology, pre-dates many other international academic groups on dance being active from the early 1960s.[1] This situation of liminality is undoubtedly poised to change.

A new generation of students has emerged whose environments oscillate between the local and the global; whose enjoyment of cultural practices finds the modernist concepts of popular and high art a straitjacket irrelevant to their lives; and whose experiences and identities transcend those of mono-nationalism. For these students, the narrowness of the canon of western theatre art dance is being challenged; not to overturn it, but to gain a more balanced perspective on the practice of dance and codified movement systems in human society. In confronting under-investigated genres and cultural practices, dance ethnographers may document new texts for study through fieldwork which may result in the production of more scores, photographs and films to assist in analysing the moving body. In common with ethnomusicology and other social sciences, 'ethnographers derive from fieldwork their most significant contributions to the humanities in general' (Cooley, 1997, p. 4). Those contributions come from the encounter of people in the field. People make dances and it is this agency of production which has often been neglected in mainstream paradigms for the study of dance. Through its essentially humanizing approach, ethnography can redress the balance and remind dance scholars of the breadth and scope of dancing amongst a variety of populations. In tandem with that encounter with people, however, is a moral maze of responsibilities of confidentiality, power relations, issues of representation and self-knowledge, some of which are examined in Part III of this volume.

A growing number of courses in higher education specifically address the training of dance ethnographers in north America and Europe – the established Master's degree programmes at the University of California, Los Angeles, USA, the University of Surrey, England and newer developments at the University of Limerick, Ireland, the Rådet for folkemusikk og folkedans, Norwegian University of Science and Technology (see Bakka in this volume) and the annual Young International Ethnochoreologists Seminar launched in Budapest in 1997. There is certainly a case to be made that such expansion calls for prescriptive manuals on dance ethnography but, as been made apparent, this volume is not designed to serve this end, although, as the sub-title suggests, a number of chapters do provide practical information on how to conduct fieldwork (see especially Giurchescu and Felföldi) and on the means of documenting movement in the field (Van Zile). Guidelines on the conduct of field research on dance do exist (see, for example, Karpeles, 1958; Harper, 1968; Kealiinohomoku, 1974; and Lange, 1984 [1960]) but, as relatively early publications in dance scholarship, they reflect a positivist stance, pursuing ethnography before the impact of reflexive textualization which explicitly problematized representation and power relations between the researcher and the researched.

The division of the book into three parts belies the reflections of theory, methods and issues which criss-cross all the contributions. Each section may emphasize aspects of the ethnographic endeavour in dance and movement study, but the reader is invited to make links and comparisons throughout. Informed contemplation of theoretical perspectives, sensitized choices of techniques and strategies of documentation, and self-critical awareness of the moral dilemmas of social relations can no longer be evaded in print: they are a public part of every ethnography.

THEORIZING ETHNOGRAPHIC RESEARCH ON DANCE

Part I introduces the theoretical foundations of the fieldwork undertaken by major contributors to the ethnographic study of dance and movement, whether this has been on an institutional or individual basis. The opening chapters by Kaeppler and Williams are written from strictly anthropological perspectives, whereas those following reflect the legacies of European ethnology. Such a statement, which neatly pigeonholes the contributors' theoretical provenance, must immediately be qualified, especially in the case of Giurchescu, who explicitly seeks to integrate anthropological and ethnochoreological approaches and aptly demonstrates an increasing tendency for scholars to draw upon a variety of disciplinary approaches to illuminate their study. Nevertheless, as Kaeppler points out, distinctions between classic anthropological perspectives and other disciplines which employ ethnographic methods remain 'both qualitative and conceptual' (p. 13).

Kaeppler and Williams have pioneered and sustained systematic anthropological approaches to dance. Alongside Kealiinohomoku, who has perhaps a higher profile of publication in mainstream dance studies,[2] at least in Britain and north America, they have repeatedly criticized ethnocentric modes of thought endemic in academic studies of dance. By destabilizing western assumptions of dance as a universal activity, long before the impact of postmodern writings on this matter, their work has established theoretical foundations for the study of human movement as culturally codified and conceptualized.

The mode of fieldwork for the anthropologist of dance and movement is essentially that of the lone participant-observer who aims, in true Malinowskian fashion, to become totally competent in the culture under investigation. Through the performance of human movement systems which has been acquired through long-term immersion within the culture and which is other to that habitual to the researcher, the anthropologist strives to comprehend the conceptualization of movement systems through the society's own eyes. Such a strategy is intended to reveal more about that society itself.

The choice of anthropology as a theoretical home and starting point is often, even today, erroneously conceived by the non-specialist as a paradigm for studying all dance and movement activities which stand in opposition – are indeed other – to western theatre art dance. This populist view, itself a cultural survival and one which I continue to meet in my professional life, maintains that anthropologists of dance must of necessity find a postcolonial field site. Such a belief reflects a flawed and outdated notion that theoretical perspectives can *de facto* be equated with the choice of field site.

If the methodology of the anthropologist can be characterized as that of the lone fieldworker, the ethnographic practice of east European ethnochoreologists is that of the team. The chapters by Giurchescu and Felföldi illustrate the field aims and techniques of the research institutes associated with the Academy of Sciences in Romania and Hungary, respectively. This long tradition of scholarly research mostly nurtured within the context of nationalist ideologies over the past two centuries has resulted in state-funded archives and the employment of specialist dance researchers.

Working within their own culture, European researchers have no prior imperative to make manifest the underlying definitions of dance within their society. Propelled by the concept of tradition, most European studies of dance have an historical dimension infrequently found in classic anthropological treatments of dance. The search, as Bakka's personal narrative makes clear, is to find older performers in order to restore past dances for revival performance: but this does not necessarily preclude critical reflexivity and engagement with current debates on history as construct.

REFLECTING ON METHODS IN FIELD RESEARCH ON
DANCE

Part II focuses on the methods and techniques employed in dance
ethnography, including movement notation, film, and recording of
music and language in association with dance and movement practices. Again, the authors do not set out to be directly instructional in
the use of these modes of documentation, but discuss field experiences as a basis for reflection on the potential and shortcomings of
their methodological approaches.

The ephemerality of dancing certainly poses difficulties of textualization in the scholarly enterprise; yet the problems of scholarly analysis of dance experiences cannot be reduced to laments about
inadequate recording techniques. As these essays demonstrate, the
issues are of an epistemological nature which require a more sophisticated approach, taking into account indigenous perceptions and the
changing knowledge of the researcher in the field. At the outset of
field research, Ronström may have sought to fix dance and music as
discrete texts on video and tape ready for later formalist analysis, but
soon realized that, for the people, more significant was appreciation of
the event as a multi-channelled process, framed and constituted as
socially and historically located performance. Hall's tale of the situated rapidity of decision-making, often experienced during fieldwork,
nicely underscores the fiction of the audio recorder as a 'more objective' ethnographic tool than field notes written from memory. Thus,
choices of strategy result from moving through critical dialogues
between self and other in which the technology, be it digital camera or
notebook and pencil, is a third player. Dance and movement ethnographers conduct scholarly inquiry which is fundamentally within the
realm of social hermeneutics and thus ever-shifting; no one method of
documentation can ever be granted pre-eminence.

Whatever choices of recording means are selected, a distinguishing
feature of the dance ethnographer is often the focus upon analytical
documentation of culturally codified movement. Symbol representation through notation systems such as Labanotation (arguably the
dominant mode of enscription[3]) operate as ethnographic devices to
communicate indigenous conceptualizations of time, space and the
body (see chapters by Williams, Van Zile and Farnell). That representation, symbol or otherwise, is achieved not through a dualist
opposition between language and action, but through recognition that
culturally codified movement systems are constituted in discursive

practice. Word and action are thus dynamic communicative knowl-
edges with which the ethnographer continually engages and which, as
Farnell demonstrates, may occur in the field simultaneously.

In preference to notation, Hughes-Freeland employs film to present
sound-images of dance as processual and socially situated action. She
argues that through sensual perception of the dance and its social production, audience reaction to film ethnography may assist in decen-
tring the power of the researcher by incorporating the voices of the
researched into the final product. Johnson Jones addresses this goal
by sharing her specialist knowledge (in Laban movement analysis)
with key individuals in the field to generate collaborative analysis.
Commitment to employing such processes of dialogic and reflexive
ethnography thus travels some way towards renegotiating the hierarchical relationship between the observer and 'observed' in dance
ethnography.

POLITICIZING DANCE AND MOVEMENT ETHNOGRAPHY

Part III invites contributors to share personalized accounts of field
research in the interests of highlighting political and ethical dimensions which are contiguous to the methodology. The passage of time
allows easier identification of the contributory factors and discourses
within which the field was constructed, thus according greater power
to understand and evaluate the results of ethnography. Obviously, the
autobiographical may lead to 'embarrassing self-revelations'
(Williams, 1994, p. 7) rather than to scholarly insights. Yet when exer-
cised with rigour, reflexivity permits the revelation of power relationships, values and ethics in field relations, which in classic ethnographic
texts lay unexcavated – hidden, but now to be judged as incomplete
representation at best, or as deception at worst. Accepting elements of
inadequate recall and self-delusion, autobiography is also a means of
'dismantle[-ing] the positivist machine' (Okely, 1992, p. 3).

The complexities of recognition of self and other in the production
of ethnography (Grau and Gore) have foregrounded a shift in epistemological terms from '*what* do we know?' to the continual question of
'*how* do we come to know what we know?' In answering this, the identity of 'we' is crucial. Ensuring that the 'researcher is grounded as an
actual person in a concrete setting' (Stanley, 1990, p. 12) within the
ethnography makes differentials of economics, society and education
between researcher and researched overt. Knowledge held by the field

researcher and valued by the people under investigation may thus precipitate rupture from any lingering desires towards Cartesian scientism on the part of the fieldworker; he or she is unavoidably constitutive of any ethnographic production. These issues of reciprocity – the gift-exchange of knowledge – is especially acute when the field researcher is hailed as an authority on dance (see Buckland, Koutsouba and Gore).

Evident throughout this collection is a recognition that the field is not a clean space, unsullied by past discourses: the residues of intellectual and political inheritances continue to flow across it. An obvious example is the practice of fieldwork within countries under Soviet influence, both past and present, often reflecting nationalist ideology in practice (Giurchescu, Felföldi and Nahachewsky) and, as a consequence, causing political, moral and intellectual conflict for researchers with access to alternative cultural views. More positively, such juxtapositions of different approaches may result in keener appreciation of the other, particularly when the other may be fellow fieldworkers (Nahachewsky). Practising field research in another culture is a classic anthropological strategy of knowing; through embodied knowledge the researcher may claim greater understanding, although, as Farnell (1994, pp. 936–7) warns, movement participation in another culture should not lead to reductionist and naive assumptions of the universal, essential body. In this respect, ethnography's particular contribution lies in challenging generalist abstractions concerning 'the body' through continuous dialogue between theory and empirical investigation.

Perhaps for many past and potential researchers who adopt an anthropological approach, uncertainties surrounding ethnography are thrown into sharper relief by undertaking fieldwork in one's own country: what then, or who constructs the field and when, if ever, is fieldwork begun or concluded? The fluidity of the ethnographic enterprise, not only in negotiating social but conceptual relations in the constitution of the field (Gore) is not an occasion for jettisoning the endeavour, but an opportunity to travel towards a 'new ethics of authenticity and of theory' (Hastrup, 1995, p. 5).

CONCLUDING REFLECTIONS

This volume is primarily concerned with dance ethnography as fieldwork rather than as textual product, although undoubtedly, as

Gore (p. 209) observes, 'representational practices inform all stages of dance ethnography'. As a text itself, however, this collection is inevitably a partial and initial representation of the practice it both celebrates and interrogates. Through exposure of its richly varied terrain, I hope that these different traditions in dance scholarship will command wider attention, provoke more debate and prompt further lengthy excursions into the field – however how and why that field of dance ethnography is mapped. More immediately, I would like to thank all the authors for their enthusiasm and commitment to this project: for me, it has been an honour and privilege, in particular, to edit contributions from those who continue to pioneer the study of dance in the field.

NOTES

1. Details on the history of dance within the International Council for Traditional Music can be found in Reynolds, 1987, 1988a and 1988b.
2. Witness the repeated printings of her seminal article, 'An Anthropologist Looks at Ballet as a Form of Ethnic Dance' first published in 1969–70.
3. Labanotation, or its European counterpart Kinetography Laban, is employed by most contributors to this volume: Kaeppler, Williams, Giurchescu, Felföldi, Van Zile, Johnson Jones, Farnell, Nahachewsky, Buckland and Koutsouba.

REFERENCES

Barz, G.F. and Cooley, T.J. (eds). 1997. *Shadows in the Field: New Perspectives for Fieldwork in Ethnomusicology.* Oxford: Oxford University Press.
Cooley, T.J. 1997. Casting shadows in the field: an introduction. In Barz, G.F. and Cooley, T.J. (eds), pp. 3–19.
Desmond, J.C. (ed.). 1997. *Meaning in Motion: New Cultural Studies of Dance.* Durham, North Carolina: Duke University Press.
Farnell, B. 1994. Ethno-graphics and the moving body. *Man: Journal of the Royal Anthropological Institute*, 29 [n.s.], 4, pp. 929–74.
Harper, P. 1968. Dance studies. *African Notes*, 4, 3, pp. 5–28.
Hastrup, K. 1995. *A Passage to Anthropology: Between Experience and Theory.* London: Routledge.
Karpeles, M. (ed.). 1958. *The Collection of Folk Music and Other Ethnomusicological Material: a Manual for Field Workers.* London: International Folk Music Council and Royal Anthropological Society of Great Britain and Ireland.

Kealiinohomoku, J. 1974. Field guides. In Comstock, T. (ed.), *New Dimensions in Dance Research: Anthropology and Dance – the American Indian*. New York: Committee on Research in Dance, pp. 245–60 (*CORD Research Annual*, VI).

—— 1997 [1969–1970/1983]. An anthropologist looks at ballet as a form of ethnic dance. In Williams, D. (ed.), *Anthropology and Human Movement, 1*. Lanham, Maryland: Scarecrow Press, pp. 15–36.

Kurath, G.P. 1960. A panorama of dance ethnology. *Current Anthropology*, 1, 3, pp. 233–54.

Lange, R. 1984 [1960]. Guidelines for field work on traditional dance: methods and checklist. *Dance Studies*, 8, pp. 7–48.

Morris, G. (ed.). 1996. *Moving Words: Re-writing Dance*. London: Routledge.

Okely, J. 1992. Anthropology and autobiography: participatory experience and embodied knowledge. In Okely, J. and Callaway, H. (eds), *Anthropology and Autobiography*, ASA monograph 29. London: Routledge, pp. 1–28.

Reynolds, W.C. (ed.). 1987. Dance in the ICTM. *ICTM Dance Newsletter*, 1, 1, n.p.

—— 1988a. History of the study group. *ICTM Dance Newsletter*, 2, n.p.

—— 1988b. Short communications. Czechoslovakia. *ICTM Dance Newsletter*, 3, n.p.

Stanley, L. 1990. Feminist praxis and the academic mode of production: an editorial introduction. In Stanley, L. (ed.), *Feminist Praxis: Research, Theory and Epistemology in Feminist Sociology*. London: Routledge, pp. 3–19.

Williams, D. 1994. Self-reflexivity: a critical overview. *JASHM: Journal for the Anthropological Study of Human Movement*, 8, 1, pp. 1–10.

Part I
Theoretical Dimensions

2 The Mystique of Fieldwork

Adrienne L. Kaeppler

In 1969 Donald MacRae, in a lively article in *New Society*, attempted to find the key that separated sociology from anthropology. He concluded that anthropologists 'have, in principle, all undergone the ordeals of a common *rite de passage*, i.e. they have all undergone at least a year of field work in some exotic area. The field notes of this year are their store of magic potency, their *manna*. It is the magical element in this that makes them spend it so economically; spiritual capital is not lightly to be wasted' (1969, p. 562). Now, some 30 years later – as this book demonstrates – not only anthropologists 'go to the field' to learn about their chosen subject. If one adds that although all anthropologists do fieldwork, all fieldwork is not anthropological, we run the risk of incurring MacRae's further dictum that anthropologists (like other tribes made up of warring moieties) 'unite before any outside threat and are appropriately savage to intruders or threatening groups' (1969, p. 562).

While I would not state these differences quite so strongly, I do believe that there are differences between what anthropologists and others do in the field – both qualitative and conceptual – with reference to the study of dance. To examine these differences, I will explore three questions: (1) What is the aim of an anthropological study of dance? (2) How does an anthropologist do fieldwork? and (3) What is the importance of the audience in the study of dance? As a prelude to these questions, however, it is necessary to ask 'What is dance?' – a distinctly anthropological question.

IS 'DANCE' A CATEGORY OF OURSELVES OR OTHERS?

Cultural forms that result from the creative use of human bodies in time and space are often glossed as 'dance', but this is a word derived from European concepts and carries with it preconceptions that tend to mask the importance and usefulness of analysing the movement dimensions of human action and interaction. Traditionally, in many

13

societies there was no category comparable to the western concept –
although in many languages it has now been introduced. Most anthropologists interested in human movement do not focus on 'dance' but
enlarge their purview to encompass a variety of structured movement
systems, including, but not limited to, movements associated with religious and secular ritual, ceremony, entertainment, martial arts, sign
languages, sports and play. What these systems share is that they
result from creative processes that manipulate (i.e. handle with skill)
human bodies in time and space. Some categories of structured movement may be further marked or elaborated, for example, by being
integrally related to 'music' (a specially marked or elaborated category of 'structured sound') and text.

We usually understand the construction of categories used in our
own culture and language, but often inappropriately apply our categories to 'others'. For example, categorizing the movement dimensions of a religious ritual as 'dance' can easily lead to misunderstanding
across, and even within, cultures. A more appropriate way to classify
and define movement systems is according to indigenous categories –
concepts that can best be discovered through extended fieldwork.

WHY DO HUMANS MOVE IN DISTINCTIVE WAYS AND WHAT TRANSFORMS MOVEMENT INTO 'DANCE'?

The aim of the academic discipline of anthropology is to understand
other sociocultural systems and to understand ourselves better. An
anthropologist traditionally studied everything during a year or more
of fieldwork, especially if he or she was one of the first outsiders to
live in a community. Today, most communities have been scrutinized
by the gaze of outsiders, including anthropologists and other academics, and much has been written about nearly every society.
Nevertheless, most anthropologists still attempt to understand all
aspects of culture in order to understand society in all of its dimensions. Human movement is recognized as one dimension of a variety
of activities and events and an anthropologist studies movement in an
effort to understand the whole.

While observing and participating in activities and events it
becomes evident that people of distinctive groups move in distinctive
ways and categorize their movements accordingly. Anthropologists try
to find the systematic patterns that lead to understanding indigenous
categorization – the emic dimension of movement. To facilitate

description and for cross-cultural comparisons, anthropologists may place specially marked or elaborated, grammatically structured human movement systems into theoretical frames in order to characterize the way the movement systems convey meaning – such as mime, dramatic realism, storytelling, metaphor or with abstract conventions – and may consider them as signs, symbols or signifiers, in any combination depending on their contexts. Movements are cultural artefacts, which, in their specific combinations and uses, belong to a specific culture or subculture and can be activated for specific purposes. Movement sequences may be audience-oriented (Plate 1) to be admired as art or work, they may be participatory to be enjoyed as entertainment, they may make political or social statements, they may bring religious ecstasy or trance, they may be performed as a social duty. Movements given by the gods and ancestors may be perpetuated as cultural artefacts and aesthetic performances even if their meanings have been changed or forgotten as reference points for ethnic or cultural identity.

ANTHROPOLOGISTS AND OTHER DANCE RESEARCHERS

It is instructive to consider how anthropological aims may differ from those of other academics such as folklorists and dance ethnologists, especially as they relate to fieldwork. Generally speaking, anthropologists aim to attain insights into a sociocultural group by studying its movement systems. Although folklorists who study dance and dance ethnologists will speak for themselves elsewhere in this volume, it seems to me that these researchers are more specifically interested in dances and dancing, and take 'a dance' or 'dances' as their primary unit, while anthropologists are more interested in the larger subject of human movement and the abstract concept of 'dance'. Folklorists are often already familiar with the societies they study and they have a different agenda which is community-based and for a long time focused on authenticity (Bendix, 1997). Their aim is often to collect 'dances' as part of this agenda. Dance ethnologists also focus on the content of dances and, if they study the context, it is usually the event context in which the dances take place.

Most anthropologists learn and embrace the four fields of anthropology as taught in many anthropology programmes, especially in the United States (physical anthropology, archaeology, sociocultural anthropology and linguistics) and the theoretical bases that integrate

these four fields. Ethnography is embedded in sociocultural anthropology – which in most universities still requires the fieldwork *rite de
passage*. Thus, anthropologists of human movement are by definition
also dance ethnographers (but not vice versa). Individuals who call
themselves 'dance ethnologists' usually do not have degrees in
anthropology or ethnology and are unlikely to have studied the theoretical background in which anthropology as an academic subject is
embedded. Instead, their degrees are in dance, music, area studies,
cultural studies or some other subject. What is relevant in the present
context is that during fieldwork anthropologists study dance to understand society, whereas dance ethnologists focus on the dances themselves – and those who do study context do so primarily to illuminate
the dances.[1] This influences the amount of time spent in the field –
folklorists and dance ethnologists usually do not spend extended
periods in the field, whereas anthropologists usually stay for at least a
year.

   While anthropologists of dance and movement study meaning,
intention and cultural evaluation, the activities that generate movement systems, how and by whom they are judged, their aim is to
understand how the examination and analysis of movement systems
can illuminate the sociocultural system – data that can be attained
only during fieldwork. My fieldwork has focused on the structure of
the various movement systems used by specific cultures and the
abstract concept of 'dance'. Although I, too, analyse specific dances
(and other movement sequences), I look at them as the surface manifestations of the deep structure and underlying philosophy of a
society. While looking for concepts about movement as part of
systems of knowledge, I do not take for granted that there is such a
concept as 'dance'. Ultimately, my aim is to discover what is involved
in understanding 'communicative competence' with regard to movement: how do individuals combine grammatical knowledge with performance knowledge in order to perform or understand movement in
specific contexts?

   Structured movement systems occur in all known human societies.
They are systems of knowledge – the products of action and interaction as well as processes through which action and interaction take
place. These systems of knowledge are socially and culturally constructed – created, known and agreed upon by a group of people and
primarily preserved in memory. Though transient, movement systems
have structured content, they can be visual manifestations of social
relations and the subjects of elaborate aesthetic systems, and may

assist in understanding cultural values. Thus, an ideal movement study of a society or social group would analyse all activities in which human bodies are manipulated in time and space, the social processes that produce these activities according to the aesthetic precepts of a variety of individuals at a specific point in time and the components that group or separate the various movement dimensions and activities they project into kinesthetic and visual form. Through participant observation our bodies and eyes learn about the distinctive ways in which people move, how these movements are categorized and if there are specially marked movement systems that formalize the non-formal that might generate a concept similar to the western concept of 'dance'. But, more importantly, we also learn about social structure, politics, economics, literature, art, philosophy, aesthetics – that is, the sociocultural system in which movement systems are embedded.

STRANGERS ABROAD LOOKING FOR SYSTEMS

In his 1996 Distinguished Lecture to the American Anthropological Association, Sidney Mintz noted that 'ethnographic fieldwork – our sort of fieldwork – is close enough to the core of our identity as a discipline to be worth preserving at any cost.' What did he mean by 'our sort of fieldwork'? Fieldwork traditions can be traced to our anthropological ancestors, sympathetically explicated in a series of six documentary films entitled 'Strangers Abroad'. Four of these films set the stage and describe anthropological 'strangers' living with 'others', but two are especially important for the study of dance – those that concern Franz Boas and Bronislaw Malinowski.[2]

Boas emphasized cultural relativism which has long been a cornerstone of anthropology. Boas's view was that 'if we choose to apply our [western] classification to alien cultures we may combine forms that do not belong together ... If it is our serious purpose to understand the thoughts of a people, the whole analysis of experience must be based on their concepts, not ours' (1943, p. 314). Likewise, Malinowski felt that our goal should be 'to grasp the native's point of view, his relation to life, to realize *his* vision of *his* world' (1922, p. 25). Added to this was Kenneth Pike's dictum that we should 'attempt to *discover* and to describe the pattern of that particular language or culture in reference to the way in which the various elements of that culture are related to each other in the functioning of the particular pattern' (1954, p. 8). From Pike came the 'etic/emic' distinction: 'emic

criteria savour more of relativity, with the sameness of activity determined in reference to a particular system of activity' (1954, p. 11).

Anthropological interpretations of human movement have evolved
and changed along the same lines as general anthropological theory.
Collecting data, organizing and analysing it according to the basic
tenets of the time, as well as voicing dissatisfaction with past analysts
of the data collected and organized, is as characteristic of studies of
dance as of other fields of anthropology. Our anthropological ancestors seldom focused on human movement systems, especially before
1950, but those who did found that analysis of movement could help
to explicate basic cultural values. Boas, working in North America in
the late nineteenth/early twentieth century, was concerned with data
collection in the empirical tradition and looked at dance as part of
culture rather than using dance data to fit theories and generaliza-
tions. Radcliffe-Brown in his 1922 study of the Andaman Islanders
brings in dance throughout his monograph, describing movements, the
ceremonies in which they are used and their social function. Evans-
Pritchard published an analysis of one Azande dance in 1928, and
noted 'it requires a stereotyped form, a prescribed mode of performance, concerted activities, recognized leadership and elaborate organization and regulation. If these problems are not in the mind of the
observer he will give us an interesting description perhaps, but not
a detailed account of great value to the theoretical worker' (1928,
p. 446). In contrast to the empirical traditions based on fieldwork of
American and British anthropologists, Curt Sachs, deriving his data
primarily from literature, published his *Eine Weltgeschichte des Tanzes*
in 1933 as a theoretical treatise in which dance was used as an
example of the *Kulturkreis* theories of Schmidt and Graebner in which
worldwide diffusion resulted in a form of unilineal evolution. In 1935
Marcel Mauss published 'Les Techniques du Corps' in which he discusses the notion of the body and its movements in cross-cultural perspective. During the 1950s, Gertrude Prokosch Kurath, although not
an anthropologist herself, worked in collaboration with anthropologists to analyse the content of dances so that movement could be
related to its social and cultural background.[3]

It is only since the 1960s that a few anthropologists have focused on
human movement systems in an effort to understand society. Among
them were the ten colleagues invited by Anya Peterson Royce in 1974
to Bloomington, Indiana, to discuss the importance of movement
analysis in the study of anthropology. In 1979, Paul Spencer convinced
a number of his anthropological colleagues to use the movement data

that helped them to understand the societies in which they had carried out fieldwork in a series of lectures at the School of Oriental and African Studies, London. This resulted in the book *Society and the Dance* (Spencer, 1985).

My own fieldwork in Tonga was not intended to focus on dance, but on aesthetics. I was influenced by the empirical traditions of Boas and Malinowski which recognized the importance of insiders' views and ethnoscience. These I intermixed with ideas about competence and performance derived from concepts promulgated by Saussure and Chomsky. My 18 months of fieldwork in the mid-1960s used etic/emic distinctions derived by 'contrastive analysis' and emerged as linguistic analogies, which I then elaborated as ethnoscientific structuralism (1978, 1986). I continued to carry out fieldwork in Tonga during the following 30 years – a period of fieldwork which now totals more than three years. I examined movements and choreographies in order to find the underlying system and I attempted to discover indigenous theories about indigenous movement systems. Systems, of course, cannot be observed, but must be *derived* from the social and cultural construction of specific movement worlds. These systems exist in memory and are recalled as movement motifs, imagery and as system, and are used to create compositions that produce social and cultural meaning in performance. Such analyses involve deconstructing the movements into culturally recognized pieces and learning the rules for constructing compositions according to the system. I also focused on more traditional anthropological subjects – publishing articles on kinship, social structure, funerals, material culture, and what I really went to the field to study, aesthetics. My participant observation in dance and other movement systems was primarily a way to understand society.

Anthropologists are interested in understanding how meaning is derived from movement, how the frame of an event must be understood in order to derive meaning from it, how intention and cultural evaluation can be derived from the framing of the event, the necessity of understanding the activities that generate movement systems and how and by whom the movements are judged.

Although fieldwork is the mainstay of anthropological method and theory, it has seldom been explicitly acknowledged in the anthropological study of dance. How does an anthropologist go about fieldwork when studying movement systems as part of a sociocultural system? There are four aspects of fieldwork which I feel are important: participant observation, language, recording information and preliminary analyses.

1. In participant observation important elements include observing
    movement content and its contexts, taking part by learning the
    movements (if this is permitted) and asking questions about
    the movement and its contexts. Participant observation should lead
    to an understanding of the various structured movement systems,
    how they are indigenously classified, what the relationships are
    between and among movements of ritual, dance, everyday and cer-
    emonial life, and if there even are cultural concepts such as dance.

    While taking part, the structure of the movement systems can
    be derived by using linguistic analogies: that is, what the relevant
    small pieces of movement (kinemes and morphokines – analogous
    to phonemes and morphemes) are, what the characteristic move-
    ment motifs are, and how these movement pieces are put together
    (analogous to phonology and syntax in language). One observes
    surface manifestations and behaviour, making it necessary to ask
    questions about underlying systems and intentions. Behaviour
    plus intention equals action, and it is human action, and inter-
    action in which anthropologists are interested.

2. Learning the spoken language is important not just for communi-
    cation; linguistic emphases also furnish keys to cultural or social
    emphases, and language structure may be the key to movement
    and other structures.

3. Recording information should be done in a variety of ways: taking
    notes, preliminary movement notation, film/video recording of
    performances in their contexts as well as just for the camera eye if
    possible, in your own body by learning the dances or at least the
    important movement motifs, and using fieldguides or question-
    naires if appropriate.

4. Preliminary analyses should be done from your own observation
    and participation as well as through the eyes of performers and
    audience members. One should look for patterns of movement
    and patterns of social action and their meanings and elicit if these
    observed patterns are meaningful to dancers and audience
    members. Video recordings can be used for instant replay for pre-
    liminary analysis, for eliciting information about intentions, for
    clarifying movement motifs and movement sequences and to find
    out about mistakes and if movements (or whole performances)
    can or should be evaluated.

In the field, I watched whole dances to find what body parts moved and
what sorts of movements these were. Next, I tried to watch certain

individuals do the same movements over and over again. Having people teach me dances necessitated that they do the movements repeatedly. While learning, I questioned my teachers if movements should be done one way or another – always asking if the movements were the same or different. If they said it 'didn't matter' or if they did not perceive differences in what I did, I concluded that the differences were not significant. In this way I also learned how much movement varied as done by one person (personal variation). Then I tried to see several people do the same dance or dances of the same genre that used the same kind of movements. From this I learned how much variation there was from individual to individual (interpersonal variation). A combination of these two types of variation gave me a chance to see the same movement performed in several movement contexts (contextual variation). After I learned the movements I performed them in what I considered to be correct and incorrect ways. My teachers would correct versions that were not acceptable. My procedure was to make observations and form hypotheses about what the significant units were. Hypotheses were tested by performing the movements for holders of the movement tradition, thus verifying, modifying or rejecting them.

Most of my anthropological fieldwork, however, was less structured. During my fieldwork in Tonga, I learned about Tongan society, poetry, music, dance, material culture, values and so on. I participated in various aspects of Tongan everyday life and ritual events, accompanying Tongans with whom I resided and attending events with Tongan friends. Besides observing, I asked questions in order to understand Tongan evaluations of performances and how these had changed over time. In the 1960s and 1970s, I had a few special mentors: Queen Sālote, Vaisima Hopoate, Sister Mary Tu'ifua, Kavapele, 'Ahio, Halaevalu Mataele, Nanisi Helu, Kalo Sitani, Tu'ialo Kefu, Baron Vaea, Tu'imala Kaho, Ve'ehala, Queen Mata'aho, Lavinia and Atiu Kalaniuvalu and several others. We were all great friends, and I learned more and more each time I talked to them and attended events with them. I seldom tape-recorded them. Often one of these friends would accompany me to interview Tongan-only speakers if they thought my Tongan was not adequate to understand fully the metaphors and varied meanings of Tongan words (in addition to the cultural prescription that women should not go about alone). After analysing this information with Tongans, and using all available information, I attempted to discover movement and other cultural systems. I wrote about what I had learned and gave my writings to Tongans for their opinions. I found that dance is not something that is 'out there' or movement that can be 'quantified' by 'verifiable facts', but a socially constructed system of knowledge. Anthropologists are 'strangers abroad' trying to find such systems.

WHAT ABOUT THE AUDIENCE?

Finally, I want to emphasize the importance of the audience to fieldwork on human movement systems. Audiences do not have the same role from culture to culture and the audience–performer relationship may be a continuum rather than two distinct categories. Performances require viewers, but who are these viewers and what do viewers see and understand? Viewers may be the gods, engaged audience members, spectators who have little understanding of a performance, or, perhaps, only the performers viewing themselves. Performances range from ritual investitures, the theatre of church services, the marching of brass bands and the presentation of gifts, to dancing as political theatre and dancing as entertainment. Viewing these performances requires knowledge. If an event is to be understood, observers (like performers) should have 'competence' in the movement tradition. Competence in a movement system is acquired in much the same way as competence in a language is acquired. Competence relates to the cognitive learning of the shared rules of a specific movement tradition, as Saussure's concept of *langue* is acquired. Competence enables the viewer to understand a grammatical movement sequence never seen before. 'Performance' refers to an actual rendering of a movement sequence, *parole* of Saussure, which assumes that the performer has a level of competence and the skill to carry it out. Movement sequences are analogous to utterances, and without knowledge of the movement conventions, a viewer will be unable to understand what is being conveyed. In addition to movement meaning, meaning in a larger sense (such as symbolic, narrative and so forth) is not inherent in movement itself, but is attributed to movement by people who are part of the larger activity and depends on knowledge of the cultural systems, such as male and female roles in movement, social status, social structure and access to politics and power.

Ritual has been of special interest to many anthropologists, but the movement element of ritual has seldom been the focus of interest; often people who write about 'ritual dancing' have little idea about what anthropologists mean by the concept. Ritual can be defined as 'the performance of more or less invariant sequences of formal acts and utterances not encoded by the performers' (Rappaport, 1979, p. 175). Such formal acts have a number of features in a more or less fixed relationship to one another, are learned from the ancestors and are not generated by the performer. Performers and viewers may not fully understand the movements, only that it is necessary to do them; the *process* of performing is primary.

Theatre, which in my view includes presentational dances, has roles for performer and audience but these roles vary greatly between cultures and even within a culture depending on context. In theatre the acts are encoded by the performers and rather than the performance itself being the message, the audience is engaged and derives the message from the performance. Performers and audience understand the languages of speech and movement, as well as the stories and cultural values being conveyed – they have communicative competence. A viewer who is not engaged with understanding the performance or knows how to decode what is being conveyed by the movements can be considered a spectator. Nevertheless, performances need not be understood to be appreciated. It is what the beholder brings to the performance that determines how it will be decoded and if he or she will be a ritual supplicant, an engaged audience member or an appreciative spectator. The same movement sequence may be meant to be decoded differently if performed for the gods, if performed for a human audience or if performed as a participant for fun; and it may be decoded differently depending on an individual's background and understanding of a particular performance as well as the individual's mental and emotional state at the time. Choreographers, performers and viewers are socially and historically placed individuals who operate according to sociocultural conventions and aesthetic systems. Dance, like all symbolic systems, creates new meanings by combining old forms in new ways. The product and process interact dialogically, relying on shared understandings among composers, performers and viewers. It is important to record this audience knowledge in the field or this crucial data will be forever lost.

CONCLUSION

Why should anthropologists study human movement? Can human movement studies assist in more general anthropological understand-

24   *Adrienne L. Kaeppler*

ing? Current anthropological concerns include ritual, gender, the body, cognition, identity, the negotiation of tradition, performance, aesthetics and turning the anthropological eye to our own society – concerns often addressed by dance and human movement researchers. Those studying movement systems in the field can contribute to these anthropological concerns, but only if they have the theoretical background and knowledge about fieldwork methods before becoming a stranger abroad looking for systems.

NOTES

1. There are similar conceptual discussions about ethnomusicology: is this field of study primarily about musical content/product or the more anthropological notions that concern processes, events, ethno-aesthetics and cultural constructions about structured sound?
2. 'The Shackles of Tradition' [Boas] and 'Everything is Relative' [Malinowski] (Singer, 1985).
3. See, for example, Kurath, 1956, 1960, 1964.

REFERENCES

Bendix, R. 1997. *In Search of Authenticity: The Formation of Folklore Studies*. Madison: University of Wisconsin Press.
Boas, F. 1943. Recent anthropology. *Science*, 98, pp. 311–14, 334–7.
Evans-Pritchard, E.E. 1928. Dance. *Africa*, 1, 4, pp. 446–62.
Kaeppler, A.L. 1978. Melody, drone, and decoration: underlying structures and surface manifestations in Tongan art and society. In Greenhalgh, M., and Megaw, V., *Art in Society: Studies in Style, Culture and Aesthetics*. London: Duckworth, pp. 261–74.
—— 1986. Cultural analysis, linguistic analogies, and the study of dance in anthropological perspective. In Frisbie, C.J. (ed.), *Explorations in Ethnomusicology: Essays in Honor of David P. McAllester*, Detroit Monographs in Musicology 9. Detroit: Information Coordinators, pp. 25–33.
Kurath, G.P. 1956. Choreology and anthropology. *American Anthropologist*, 58, pp. 177–9.
—— 1960. Panorama of dance ethnology. *Current Anthropology*, 1, 3, pp. 233–54.
—— 1964. Iroquois music and dance: ceremonial arts of two Seneca longhouses. *Bureau of American Ethnology Bulletin*, 187.
MacRae, D. 1969. When is an anthropologist? *New Society*, 9 October, p. 562.
Malinowski, B. 1922. *Argonauts of the Western Pacific*. New York: E.P. Dutton.

Mauss, M. 1935. Les techniques du corps. *Journal de psychologie normale et pathologique*, 32, 3–4, pp. 271–93. Translated by B. Brewster in *Economy and Society*, 2, 1, 1973, pp. 70–88.

Pike, K. 1954. *Language in Relation to a Unified Theory of the Structures of Human Behavior*. Glendale, California: Summer Institute of Linguistics.

Radcliffe-Brown, A.R. 1922. *The Andaman Islanders*. Cambridge: Cambridge University Press.

Rappaport, R.A. 1979. The obvious aspects of ritual. In Rappaport, R.A., *Ecology, Meaning, and Religion*. Richmond, California: North Atlantic Books, pp. 173–221.

Sachs, C. 1933. *Eine Weltgeschichte des Tanzes* (World History of the Dance). New York: W.W. Norton. Reprinted 1963. Translated by B. Schönberg.

Singer, A. (producer and director). 1985–86. *Strangers Abroad*. Film series written and presented by Bruce Dakowski, Central Independent Television, England.

Spencer, P. (ed.). 1985. *Society and the Dance: the Social Anthropology of Process and Performance*. Cambridge: Cambridge University Press.

3 Fieldwork
Drid Williams

Stories about famous figures in social anthropology abound among new graduate students. At the Institute of Social Anthropology (Oxford) in the early 1970s we were no different, but I could verify the anecdotes about E.E. Evans-Pritchard, who (though recently retired in 1970), was available in his rooms at the Institute, or at a nearby pub.

'Is it true that the only advice you give to students about fieldwork is that they make sure they have a folding table, a lamp, and plenty of writing materials with them?' I asked, while sharing a drink at the Gardener's Arms. 'Surely there's more to fieldwork than that!'

He leaned back smiling reminiscently, and said, 'Of course there is, but you can waste a lot of time on your first trip (as I did) if you aren't practical. I did fieldwork among the Nuer and the Azande before you were born. It didn't occur to me to think about whether the southern Sudan had electricity, or that nomads don't carry tables around with them. It's a question of horseshoe nails, isn't it?'

'You mean "for want of a nail the shoe is lost" and all that?'

'No matter what the world may say about social anthropologists', he said, 'they can't accuse us of ivory-towerism! But make no mistake: practicality doesn't replace imagination or keen observation. Both are necessary. Sometimes, all I can remember is how tired I was – writing notes when everyone else was asleep. People forget that fieldwork is just that: field-WORK. Hardest work I ever did!'

Our conversation lasted for two hours. The subjects we covered were locale, theory, observation and reflexivity.

LOCALE

Fieldwork is not an end in itself. The aim of most social anthropological fieldwork is completed doctoral work. At post-doctoral levels, the result of fieldwork is a monograph or book. It is important to connect field research with writing, because, ultimately, that is why one works in the field – wherever 'the field' may be. Ethnographic fact supports writing, which (as I was taught) consists of three parts: 1. description, 2. analysis, 3. interpretation and explanation of the group of people investigated.[1]

When I was a graduate student in the early 1970s, fieldwork in British social anthropology was undergoing a process of change (see Williams, 1982). After World War II, the fieldwork process in the British discipline gradually broadened from preoccupations with so-called 'primitive' societies to include work in the anthropologist's own society or in a parallel culture (see Jackson, 1987). I conducted fieldwork in England – a parallel culture – but this is something that, traditionally, only sociologists undertook:

> Anthropologists and sociologists in Europe have striven hard to distinguish themselves from each other in terms of theory and methodology when examining their own societies; this is a recent phenomenon, however, since most anthropologists still hanker after the more romantic, unexplored parts of the world – if they can get there and stay there … It is possible to say … that the basic difference between sociologists and anthropologists is a love of and a distaste for modern society. Anthropologists try to escape it, along with folkloristic and archaeological colleagues, by going to the remotest parts of the world it is possible to find – in imagination, if not in fact. It is also noticeable that anthropologists are rapidly abandoning their formerly strong interest in social organizations in favour of studying ritual, symbolism, and classification – a complete return to the major interests of the nineteenth century. (Jackson, 1987, pp. 7–8)

Jackson continues, 'The exotic might be only five miles away; it is, indeed, all around one. It is a grave mistake to think that the distant "savage" had more to give to anthropologists' (1987, p. 8). I soon discovered that the Latin Tridentine mass, the ballet *Checkmate* (involving fieldwork with the Royal Ballet) and the Chinese exercise technique T'ai Chi Ch'uan, plus work I had undertaken on Carmelite nuns (Williams, 1975), were more 'exotic' to many Europeans, Canadians, Americans and Australians than are peoples who live in the Pacific Islands, the Amazon Basin, the Arctic or Africa. More to the point, perhaps, is that one's readers often know less about ballet dancers, Catholic priests and nuns and T'ai Chi masters than they do about peoples in faraway places.

THEORY

Field research in sociocultural anthropology always includes participant-observation. 'Participation' means living with (or as close as
possible to) one's chosen people for at least 12 months. 'Participant
field research' means conducting one's investigation in the language
spoken by the community – not the anthropologist's language.[2]
   My teachers and mentors assumed that one's readiness to conduct
field research also meant acquaintance with anthropological (and a
good bit of philosophical) theory and its relation to other modes of
inquiry:

> Without theories and hypotheses anthropological research could
> not be carried out, for one only finds things, or does not find them,
> if one is looking for them. Often one finds something other than
> what one is looking for. *The whole history of scholarship, whether in
> the natural sciences or in the humanities, tells us that the mere collec-
> tion of what are called 'facts' unguided by theory in observation and
> selection is of little value.*
>
>   Nevertheless, one still hears it said of anthropologists that they go
> to study primitive peoples with a theoretical bias and that this dis-
> torts their accounts of [other peoples], whereas the practical man of
> affairs, having no such bias, gives an impartial record of the facts as
> he sees them. The difference between them is really of another
> kind. The student makes his observations to answer questions
> arising out of the generalizations of specialized opinion, and the
> layman makes his to answer questions arising out of the generaliza-
> tion of popular opinion. *Both have theories, the one systematic and
> the other popular.* (Evans-Pritchard, 1969 [1951], p. 64; emphasis
> added)

With the indispensable help of members of their host groups,
modern anthropologists attempt to construct indigenous theories of
culture and events. There is no such thing as simply 'telling it like it
is'. There is no such thing as 'pure description'; thus theoretical
approaches should have pride of place in discussions about field
research.[3]
   Without the kinds of theoretical and philosophical sophistication
that, for instance, Farnell (1994, 1995a and 1995b) brings to studies
of human movement, the field will not grow and improve. It is
systematic theoretical grounding that, literally, *defines* a field of
study.

OBSERVATION

What does an investigator observe in the field? In some ways, it all seems obvious: human beings inhabit (or 'have') moving bodies; yet, western ways of seeing bodies have been 'a serious stumbling-block' with regard to seeing movement. For example, actions are reduced to a position or to a sequence of positions, 'such that a series of photographs, sketches, diagrams, or positions of limbs plotted on a two-dimensional graph are presented as records of movement' (Farnell, 1994, p. 929). In other words, we tend to see *bodily positions*, not movement.

Two books whose titles and content support this contention are *The Anthropology of the Body* (Blacking, 1977) and *Social Aspects of the Human Body: a Reader of Key Texts* (Polhemus, 1978). Polhemus's collection on 'non-verbal behaviour' (a phrase semasiologists abandoned years ago in favour of 'non-vocal behaviour') includes Darwin (1859 and 1872), Efron (1972), Hewes (1955), Birdwhistell (1970) and Hall (1966) – all biologically oriented theories that are rooted in ideas about social evolutionism. With the exception of Hertz (1960) and Mauss (1935) in the Polhemus book and Ellen's work (1977) in the Blacking collection, these books are historically interesting, but of little value to current theoretical interests in the anthropology of human movement studies.

Seeing Actions instead of Movements

Eighteen years later, Farnell produced a collection of essays that are compatible with theoretical interests that emphasize actions instead of movement: *Human Action Signs in Cultural Context: the Visible and the Invisible in Movement and Dance* (Farnell, 1995a). Here, we find approaches that include spoken language among action-sign systems:

> The creation of meaning is above all embedded in human relationships: people enact their selves to each other in words, movements, and other modes of action. All selves are culturally defined, as time and space themselves are culturally defined. Time and space are never simply there; they are continually cut to fit the agenda of the moment.
>
> The property that language shares with all sign systems is its indexical nature: its maintenance and creation of social connections, anchored in experience and the sense of the real. (Urciuoli, 1995, pp. 189–90)

What that means from a practical standpoint was well illustrated by
Dixie Durr (1981, pp. 132–8), who realized that in the participant-
observation method, 'observing' involves much more than ordinary
seeing.

The Movement-Writing Process Can Be Revealing

A trained investigator asks, 'What makes this action-sign system recognizable as itself and no other?' Durr became aware of the differences between 'just seeing' and observation with reference to the
movement-writing process which (for semasiologists) is always connected with fieldwork:

> It was evident from the beginning that pure observation on my part
> was not enough ... Often, it was necessary to ask questions that
> would provide insights into how best to write a movement or a
> phrase of movements.
>
> It became increasingly obvious that Labanotation was the means
> to record the messages (the 's-structures') of movement, but [it] did
> not contain the code (the 'p-structures'). In other words, one can
> record gross physical movements (Figure 1) but this does not mean
> that one has captured the intended movements of native dancers
> (Figure 2).

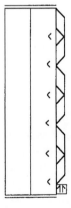

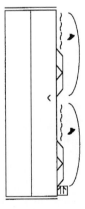

Figure 1   Physical movement of
shoulder-shaking

Figure 2   Shoulder movement from
Karachuonyo score

The two movements are not the same, although they involve the same body parts. Figure 1 is devoid of semantic content. Figure 2 possesses meaning only as it is intended in the context of the Karachuonyo dance .... [T]o rely on a purely observational approach to cross-cultural notation is to record 'behavior' in terms of raw movement as seen through the investigator's own set of mental and kinesic spectacles ....

In the light of my new level of comprehension, it would be difficult to try to justify Labanotation as being more than what [in fact] it is: a script. It can demonstrate the 'how' of a movement, but not the 'why'. This is not meant to be interpreted as any attempt to discredit the system, but merely as an attempt to clarify its usage and importance. Labanotation has the potential to provide credibility to the areas of movement and dance that have long and rightly been criticized for their lack of research and documentation ....

Saussure ... notes that 'the first linguists confused language and writing' (1959: 24); that 'language is a storehouse of sound-images, and writing is the tangible form of those images' (1959: 15), and that 'we generally learn about languages only through writing' (1959: 23). These observations strengthen the need for investigators of body languages to identify Labanotation as a script. (Durr, 1981, pp. 135–36)

The significance of Durr's discoveries regarding the use of movement-writing in field research cannot be overstressed.

She found that writing *movement* and writing *action* are two different things. In addition, she found that writing *actions* means that writers must exercise choice. She had to choose whether to write 'behaviour' ('non-linguified' movements separated from human intentions, context and meaning) or 'actions' (*signifying* acts performed by moving human agents that are simultaneous with and parallel to signifying speech acts).

In any case, *observation is not a kind of 'static visualism'* that

creates objects of vision well removed from the body of the observer .... The participant-observer may participate in a ghostlike manner, wandering through the ethnographic groves, making notes, drawing diagrams, learning to talk and ask questions, but not, for the most part, learning how to dance, how to gesture appropriately, how to make fires or build a hut, make dry meat, pound grain or put a baby to sleep, and all the other myriads of activities that constitute tacit and embodied knowledge in cultural practices. (Farnell, 1994, p. 936)

To my colleagues and me, observation is irrevocably connected with participation in fundamental ways, 'because, in being social, one can direct oneself to respond only insofar as one considers how the other will respond ... to one's own response. The *social being* of the individual is the ... ground of *personal being*' (Varela, 1995, p. 278; emphasis added).

We are not merely complex biological organisms that move. Human beings are the 'indexical site[s] of person[s] [and] human bodies are what they are by virtue of the personhood of the individual' (Varela, 1995, p. 280).

Durr's insights were generated when she discovered the fact that 'shoulder-shaking' is not a move that can be written only one way, then included in that form in any movement text whatsoever. On the contrary,

> The writing of a movement text can be no more 'purely descriptive' than can that of a standard ethnographic text; both are beset with problems of translation and interpretation. As with a standard ethnography, one builds one's interpretations over time and makes choices about descriptions as one's knowledge increases. With a movement text, however, one is aiming at a performable script that encodes indigenous understandings. (Farnell, 1994, p. 964)

One aims for descriptions of people in one's own or another society that 'encodes indigenous understandings'.

THE IDEA OF A PERSONAL ANTHROPOLOGY: REFLEXIVITY

In 'The Native Anthropologist: Constraints and Strategies in Research', Mascarenhas-Keyes (1987, pp. 187–9) produces a lively account of doing field research in her own culture that is flawed only by borrowing 'concepts of transference and countertransference developed by psychoanalysts' when she used herself as an informant. *She did not have to go outside social anthropology to handle self-reflexivity*; however, in spite of that problem, her insights are instructive:

> [T]he native anthropologist ... has to transcend an *a priori* ascribed social position in the society in order, like the Outsider, professionally to relate to the whole spectrum of native social categories. The problem is compounded when the native anthropologist is located in a very complex society such as is found in Goa ... Within this het-

erogeneous society, I was identified by natives in terms of a comple-
ment of immutable characteristics: international Catholic, Brahmin,
female, married, educated, middle-class (but of recent peasant
origins). However, I was extremely reluctant to conform to behavioural patterns and modes of thought culturally expected of my
ascribed position because of my respect for cultural diversity cultiv-
ated through anthropological training, and my intention to operate
as an anthropologist .... I was dismayed to find that I courted considerable criticism and ridicule and it became apparent that, as a
neophyte, I was unprepared 'for the more sophisticated task of
studying [my] own society' (Srinivas 1966: 157). (Mascarenhas-
Keyes, 1987, pp. 180–1)

Whether an anthropologist is an outsider or a native, 'this outside
other becomes an object for my knowledge and understanding *when I
enter into relationship with it*, and what I call my understanding is a
report on that relationship, not on the essential being of that other'
(Pocock, 1994 [1973], para. 13.4; emphasis added).

In a brilliant essay, Pocock describes the ethnographic process using
his idea of a personal anthropology:

It is this making of a report, the offering of my understanding of
the relationship as true, having universal intent, and therefore open
to the acceptance, modification or rejection of my colleagues that
constitutes the difference between *my subjective experience and my
personal anthropology*. (Pocock, 1994 [1973], para. 13.4; emphasis
added)

To semasiologists, one's personal anthropology comprises 'a whole set
of judgments about human nature, authority, sex, money, family,
nation, etc.' (Pocock, 1994 [1973], para. 1.3). Anthropologists go into
the field with these judgements. *They cannot do otherwise, nor can their
perceptions be eliminated*, but they *can* be modified or changed. This is
why we talk about 'homemade models' and 'folk models' with regard
to field research.

Models of Events

A 'homemade model' of the society consists of the judgements, ideas
and perceptions the investigator takes into the field. During the
research process, the 'folk model' of the society emerges. This model
consists of what indigenous members of the society perceive is

happening in any given situation: how *they* classify and categorize from their equally culture-bound viewpoint. Often, these models of events do not agree.

Farnell provides evidence of possible disparities between 'home-made' and 'folk' models in movement:

> Gestures such as those involved in route directions and spatial orientation are usually glossed in English by the word 'pointing,' but little attention has been paid to potential complexities and cross-cultural differences in what seems, on the surface, to be the most simple, direct, and probably universally understood means of denotative reference. ... While it might seem to be the case that pointing to an object with an extended index finger is transparent in its meaning, without contextual information the act is, in fact, entirely ambiguous: how does one distinguish between pointing to the shape rather than to the color, the texture, or the smell for example? Neither is it necessarily the case that pointing is unambiguously interpreted as an intended directional guide for one's gaze. ... [E]ducators from the Crow Reservation in Montana report a school situation in which a non-Indian teacher used a pointer on the blackboard. Non-Indian pupils looked at the end of the pointer. Indian pupils ... looked at the face of the teacher, ignoring the pointer. To these Crow students, who live in a culture where the act of pointing directly is considered rather rude, it was not at all obvious what the pointer was for. (Farnell, 1995b, pp. 158–9)

Farnell could not have written this way if she had not been aware of her own homemade models of events. She had *consciously* to recognize the differences between her interpretations of events and the folk model of her Assiniboine (Nakota) hosts throughout the research process.[4]

Distancing

In my own case, I knew the Latin mass from early childhood, but I knew nothing of what it was like from the viewpoints of the priests who celebrated it.

The awareness of my personal anthropology (the 'distancing') began with a question put to me by a priest: 'I see by your letter of introduction that you were a teacher, choreographer and dancer for many years. Do you consider the Mass, past or present, to be in some sense a drama or a dance?' (Williams, 1994a, p. vii).

My answer was that I *did not* think of the mass as a drama or a dance. Father Preston replied that if I had answered otherwise, the community would not have consented to assist me with the research (Williams, 1994a, p. viii).[5] Like Mascarenhas-Keyes, I had to 'transcend an *a priori* ascribed social position in society' (i.e. being female, a Catholic, a dancer and so on) in order successfully to relate to Dominican categories and classifications.

Reflexivity Defined

Modern students of human performance are fortunate: Pocock's essay on the idea of a personal anthropology is easily available, and, along with it (in a special issue of *JASHM*), a valuable essay on the problem of objectivity (Varela, 1994, pp. 43–64) and a critical overview of self-reflexivity (Williams, 1994b, pp. 1–10; see also Williams, 1976b). However, for the purposes of this essay, I must briefly define 'reflexivity'. To do that, I will examine an excerpt from the field notes for the ballet, *Checkmate*:

> During rehearsals of *Checkmate*, Makarova asked many questions about the sequences of movements she was required to perform as the Black Queen preceding the death of the Red King. 'Do I know that I will stab him, or am I not sure about this?' 'Does the Queen *know* that she is going to win?' (*N.B. the usage of personal pronouns.*)
>
> Depending upon what is the case to the choreographer, the movements Makarova executes subtly change – not in their form, but in character. She is still be carried on by her two black knights. She hovers over the terror-stricken, feeble old Red King, but *her intention regarding the actions* influences *how* the action of stabbing him is performed.
>
> Likewise, Dupreil, as the Red Knight (at the moment when he stands poised with sword drawn over the defenceless Black Queen) knows why he hesitates and turns away. The red knight represents chivalry, thus the dancer's hesitation is connected with a code of honour which ultimately dictates his act: he *cannot* kill a woman.
>
> In a chivalric code of honour, a *coup de grace* requires that opponents are male and armed. The Red Knight's act of restraint makes his subsequent murder by the Queen and her stabbing of the Red King (which completes the ballet), doubly ruthless. They are unmitigated, wanton acts of aggression.

The fact that the kinesemes of action chosen by the choreographer for both Knight and Queen when they raise their swords are virtually the same (as 'raw movement') points to linguistic, ethical and moral differences in the two action signs. Both dancers and choreographer's intentions are primary. (Williams, 1976a (Vol. 1), pp. 187–8)

What is involved here? As I listened to the Royal Ballet dancers, I became acutely conscious of a commonly used linguistic process, although I had not been aware of its importance: the simultaneous existence of (a) the social *persona* of a performer, (b) the controlling self of the performer (so clearly articulated by Makarova), and (c) the 'self' of the theatrical character the performer plays.

This notion of 'multiple selves' is more obvious in theatrical contexts than it is in everyday life; however, when people enact their customary, social roles in ordinary life, they function in the same ways. The idea of multiple selves is built into common expressions.

Example 1

'I have decided that I will tell her that she will be sacked in two weeks time if she can't abide by the rules of conduct appropriate to interpersonal relations in this office.'

Example 2

'I don't know what got into me: suddenly I was beside myself with anger.'

These examples illustrate the use of reflexivity in ordinary life and speech. In Example 1, the 'I' who *decides* to tell the employee she will be sacked and the 'I' who (perhaps) *will tell her* occupy the same physical body, but there are subtle differences in these selves that influence tone of voice, actions and demeanour.

In Example 2, we are confronted with a self ('I') who does not know what motivates another self ('me'), plus an 'I' who is beside another self. Doubtless psychiatrists would have interpretations and explanations of these (and other) common expressions of multiple selves, but for our purposes, they are irrelevant. Suffice to say that reflexive expressions may be so familiar that we fail to see their significance.

Reflexivity is built into English language-use in other ways: consider the (legal) attribution of responsibility involving speech and bodily actions by the phrase *in loco parentis*, where someone acts *not in terms of his or her own social persona, which may not include being a real parent*, but in terms of the social *persona* of another. Self-reflexivity is characteristic of many (although not all) human languages. Suffice to say that reflexivity (and other operations in our thinking) may be so familiar that we may think they are 'natural' – even 'universal'.

As I have tried to illustrate, reflexive styles of anthropology have profound connections with ordinary social *praxis* and 'the recognition of unconscious operations in our communications is no alibi or excuse for irresponsibility; one aims simply to be as conscious as one possibly can recognizing the limitations built into the enterprises' (Pocock, 1994 [1973], para. 13.3).

NOTES

1. A description of fieldwork circa 1951 can be found in Evans-Pritchard, 1969 [1951], pp. 75–85.
2. Although I lived in Ghana for three and a half years before going to Oxford, I did not speak Twi, Ewe or any Chanian language well, which meant that I did not return to Africa to carry out doctoral research.
3. There are, for example, several extant methodologies for the study of human movement, which means that modern students have a range of theoretical choices to make: Kaeppler's 'emic/etic' approach (1972), 'kinesics' (Birdwhistell, 1970), 'proxemics' (Hall, 1966), 'motif-morphology' (Martin and Pesovár, 1961; Kürti, 1980 and European folkloristic styles), Kendon's approach (1995), and semasiology (Williams, 1979, 1981, 1982 and 1995; Farnell, 1994, 1995a and 1995b). In contrast to these are a gaggle of statistical approaches (see Prost, 1995 [1975] and Gell, 1985, for examples). Behavioural approaches are well represented by Argyle (1975) and Peng (1978).
4. In private communications I have heard her say that her first field notebooks were at first full of what she *thought* was going on. It was some time before she could write authoritatively about Nakota ways of thinking and being from their standpoint.
5. Unlike the Dominican community, who did not find it strange that I wanted to study their rite, many members of the Royal Ballet found my efforts mystifying. To them, ballet was not an 'ethnic' form of dancing (Kealiinohomoku, 1997 [1969–70/1983], pp. 15–36), and they seemed unable to imagine what value the arts had to social anthropology.

38   *Drid Williams*

REFERENCES

Argyle, M. 1975. *Bodily Communication*. London: Methuen.

Birdwhistell, R. 1970. *Kinesics and Context: Essays in Body Motion Communication*. Philadelphia: University of Pennsylvania Press.

Blacking, J. (ed.). 1977. *The Anthropology of the Body*, ASA Monograph 15. London: Academic Press.

Darwin, C. 1859. *On the Origin of Species by Means of Natural Selection, or the Preservation of Favoured Races in the Struggle for Life*. London: J. Murray.

—— 1872. *The Expression of the Emotions in Man and Animals*. London: J. Murray.

Durr, D. 1981. Labanotation: language or script? *JASHM: Journal for the Anthropological Study of Human Movement*, 1, 3, pp. 132–8.

Ellen, R. 1977. Anatomical classification and the semiotics of the body. In Blacking, J. (ed.), pp. 343–75.

Efron, D. 1972. *Gesture, Race and Culture*. The Hague: Mouton.

Evans-Pritchard, E.E. 1969 [1951]. *Social Anthropology*. London: Cohen and West.

Farnell, B. 1994. Ethno-graphics and the moving body. *MAN: Journal of the Royal Anthropological Institute*, 29 [n.s.], 4, pp. 929–74.

—— 1995a. Introduction. In Farnell, B. (ed.), *Human Action Signs in Cultural Context: the Visible and the Invisible in Movement and Dance*. Metuchen, New Jersey: Scarecrow Press, pp. 1–28.

—— 1995b. *Do You See What I Mean?: Plains Indian Sign Talk and the Embodiment of Action*. Austin: University of Texas Press (with CD-ROM).

Gell, A. 1985. Style and meaning in Umeda dance. In Spencer, P. (ed.), *Society and the Dance: the Social Anthropology of Process and Performance*. Cambridge: Cambridge University Press, pp. 183–205.

Hall, E.T. 1966. *The Hidden Dimension*. New York. Doubleday.

Hertz, R. 1960. *The Pre-eminence of the Right Hand: a Study in Religious Polarity*. London: Cohen and West. Translated by R. and C. Needham.

Hewes, G. 1955. World distribution of certain postural habits. *American Anthropologist*, 57 [n.s.], pp. 231–44.

Jackson, A. (ed.). 1987. *Anthropology at Home*, ASA Monograph 25. London: Tavistock.

Kaeppler, A. 1972. Method and theory in analyzing dance structure with an analysis of Tongan dance. *Ethnomusicology*, XVI, 2, pp. 173–217.

Kealiinohomoku, J.W. 1997 [1969–70/1983]. An anthropologist looks at ballet as a form of ethnic dance. In Williams, D. (ed.), *Anthropology and Human Movement, 1*. Lanham, Maryland: Scarecrow Press, pp. 15–36.

Kendon, A. 1995. Sociality, social interaction, and sign language in Aboriginal Australia. In Farnell, B. (ed.), pp. 112–23.

Kürti, L. 1980. The structure of Hungarian dance: a linguistic approach. *JASHM: Journal for the Anthropological Study of Human Movement*, 1, 1, pp. 45–72.

Martin, G. and Pesovár, E. 1961. A structural analysis of the Hungarian folk dance: a methodological sketch. *Acta Ethnographica Academiae Scientiarum Hungariae*, 10, pp. 1–40.

Mascarenhas-Keyes, S. 1987. The native anthropologist: constraints and strategies in research. In Jackson (ed.), pp. 180–95.

Mauss, M. 1935. Les techniques du corps. *Journal de psychologie normale et pathologique*, 32, 3–4, pp. 271–93. Translated by B. Brewster in *Economy and Society*, 2, 1, 1973, pp. 70–88.

Peng, F.C.C. 1978. *Sign Language and Sign Language Acquisition in Man and Ape: New Dimensions in Comparative Pedo-linguistics*. Boulder, Colorado: A.A.A.S. with Westview Press.

Pocock, D. 1994 [1973]. The idea of a personal anthropology. *JASHM: Journal for the Anthropological Study of Human Movement*, 8, 1, pp. 11–42. Special Issue on Theory and Analysis: Reflexivity.

Polhemus, T. 1978. *Social Aspects of the Human Body: a Reader of Key Texts*. London: Penguin.

Prost, J.H. 1995 [1975]. Filming body behavior. In Hockings, P. (ed.), *Principles of Visual Anthropology* (2nd edn). The Hague: Mouton, pp. 285–313.

Saussure, F. de. 1959. *Course in General Linguistics*. New York: McGraw-Hill. Translated by W. Baskin; edited by C. Bally, A. Sechehaye and A. Riedlinger.

Srinivas, M.N. 1966. Some thoughts on the study of one's own society (Chapter 5). In *Social Change in Modern India*. Berkeley and Los Angeles: University of California Press, pp. 147–63, 185.

Urciuoli, B. 1995. The indexical structure of visibility. In Farnell, B. (ed.), pp. 189–215.

Varela, C. 1994. Pocock, Williams, Gouldner: initial reactions of three social scientists to the problem of objectivity. *JASHM: Journal for the Anthropological Study of Human Movement*, 8, 1, pp. 43–64. Special Issue on Theory and Analysis: Reflexivity.

—— 1995. Cartesianism revisited: the ghost in the moving machine or the lived body. In Farnell, B. (ed.), pp. 216–93.

Williams, D. 1975. The brides of Christ. In Ardener, S. (ed.), *Perceiving Women*. London: Malaby Press, pp. 105–125.

—— 1976a. The role of movement in selected symbolic systems (3 vols). DPhil thesis, Oxford University.

—— 1976b. An exercise in applied personal anthropology. *Dance Research Journal*, 11, 1, pp. 16–30. Reprinted in 1985 in *JASHM*, 3, 3, pp. 139–67, and as Appendix I in Williams, 1991, pp. 287–321.

—— 1979. The human action sign and semasiology. In Rowe, P.A. and Stodelle, E. (eds), *Dance Research Collage: a Variety of Subjects Embracing the Abstract and the Practical*. New York: Congress on Research in Dance and New York University, pp. 39–64. *CORD Dance Research Annual*, X.

—— 1981. Introduction to special issue on semasiology. *JASHM: Journal for the Anthropological Study of Human Movement*, 1, 4, pp. 207–25.

—— 1982. Semasiology: a semantic anthropological view of human movements and actions. In Parkin, D. (ed.), *Semantic Anthropology*, ASA Monograph 22. London: Academic Press, pp. 161–81.

—— 1991. *Ten Lectures on Theories of the Dance*. Metuchen, New Jersey: Scarecrow Press.

—— 1994a. The Latin high mass: the Dominican Tridentine rite. *JASHM: Journal for the Anthropological Study of Human Movement*, 8, 2, pp. vii–87. *JASHM* Monograph 11, with a foreword by David Pocock.

—— 1994b. Self-reflexivity: a critical overview. *JASHM: Journal for the Anthropological Study of Human Movement*, 8, 1, pp. 1–10.

—— 1995. Space, intersubjectivity and the conceptual imperative: three ethnographic cases. In Farnell, B. (ed.), pp. 44–81.

4 Past and Present in Field Research: a Critical History of Personal Experience

Anca Giurchescu

Field research is a fascinating, yet unpredictable and subjective search for knowledge and understanding of any given socio-cultural reality. The researcher's second-order construct of the perceived reality is necessarily different from the first-order realized by the participants (Schutz and Luckmann, 1973, p. 53). None the less, while aware of the high degree of subjectivity inherent in any attempt to translate an experience into word, sound and image, the researcher aims to draw his or her construct as near to that first-order reality as possible. Paradoxically, then, this subjective activity focuses on the production of 'objective' and 'authentic' documents.

Despite numerous theories, prescriptive texts and technical strategies which can be found on how to conduct fieldwork, the fact remains that the very theory and method of ethnography is dependent upon three factors: socio-cultural and political contexts, the stage in a discipline's development, and the researcher's own scholarly background, ideology and interests. My field experience has been shaped by working in two quite different scientific and ideological contexts; first, in Romania between 1953 and 1979, and then, in Denmark since 1980. This dual background provides a theoretical and empirical foundation for my concern to integrate ethnochoreological and anthropological/ethnological perspectives in field research, despite their intrinsic differences.[1]

FIELDWORK IN ROMANIA: A BRIEF HISTORY

Fieldwork is, of course, but one stage in the research endeavour which comprises: transcription, analysis, systematization and interpretation of the material; theoretical framing through studies dedicated to particular topics; and, in certain cases, pragmatic activity in the sphere of applied or public folklore. Consequently, fieldwork activity is organized in accordance with the immediate and final goals of the whole research process.

Brăiloiu and Approaches to Fieldwork

In 1951, when the Dance Department of the Institute of Ethnography and Folklore in Bucharest was founded, the main task was to create dance-oriented theory and methods of research. Within this framework, field research became one of the most important scientific activities (Bucşan and Balaci, 1966). From an ethnochoreological perspective, dance was conceived of as both an artistic and social process; this determined that the associated fieldwork focused on the context of its social production and its performance situation. The immediate goal of field research was the collection and documentation of dances and dance music, in order to construct a substantial and well-balanced corpus of dance-documents: from such data, the analysis of dance structures and investigation into the processes of diffusion, change and stability could be pursued. Individuals (informants), their beliefs, world view, knowledge and artistic judgements were additional subjects for inquiry. Over 45 years, researchers from the Dance Department conducted approximately 580 field expeditions in 462 localities which resulted in the recording of around 11,000 dances, together with additional sound, and visual and written documents, all of which are catalogued in the dance archives of the Institute of Ethnography and Folklore (Costea, 1994, p. 50).

The Dance Department adapted theory and methods already established by the great musicologist Constantin Brăiloiu (1893–1958) who, with the Hungarian composer Béla Bartók, pioneered modern folk music research. Conceiving of folklore as 'a product of the community, a social fact in its essence', Brăiloiu (1931, p. 3) adopted a sociological view which considered the study of people's musical life and its social determination as the main task, rather than the study of folk music in its formal aspects alone.[2] To limit the researcher's subjectivity, he introduced mechanical recording of music, filming of events and transcription of interviews and questionnaires. Standardized forms were completed in the field as a record of each type of documented information.[3]

Brăiloiu elaborated his sociologically oriented field research methodology during several multidisciplinary monograph research projects carried out under the leadership of Dimitrie Gusti (1880–1955), founder of the sociological school of Bucharest. Conducting research into the life of folk music, Brăiloiu and his team worked with 'sample groups of type informants' (that is, knowledgeable people in a particular folklore genre) who were selected according to social, occupational and gender criteria (Brăiloiu, 1931, p. 8). The folklore event, considered as a synchretic phenomenon, was studied by specialists in music, literature, dance, rituals and film. Team work resulted in a 'direct observation card' which thoroughly recorded the development of an event in time and space (Brăiloiu, 1931, p. 7).

Shifts in Orientation: Communist Ideology and Folklore Research

Under the Communist regime (1945–89), folklore researchers were compelled to harmonize their research goals with dominant political values in accordance with two distinct but sequential ideological and political strategies. In the 'revolutionary' stage (1945–64), the Communist regime sought to suppress pre-revolutionary cultural values – including folklore – and replace them with new ones based on the Soviet-Internationalist model. State cultural management supported and encouraged the selection of folklore products, separated from their original contexts, 'enriched' and 'raised to a superior artistic level'; these then became the transmitters of new political and cultural messages through staged performances. In the 1960s came a period of re-Romanization, which was characterized by rehabilitation of cultural inheritances, reconsideration of Romania's early history and the use of folk traditions (including rituals and ceremonies) as symbols of national identity (Shafir, 1985, p. 227).

Given their roots in nineteenth-century nationalism, folklorists of central and south-eastern Europe already focused on the traditional culture of their own country. Folklore has always been employed in politics to symbolize the nation-state, to awaken and rally people's national consciousness (Martin, 1985). Communist officials have, for over 40 years, tried to direct and control the institutionalized research process and use of folklore in mass culture. This situation resulted in a constant tension between researchers of folklore and 'specialists' in culture management. The works of Gusti and, to a certain degree, those of Brăiloiu were thus discarded. A characteristic trait of research in Romania became the dichotomy between research which focused on the understanding of folklore as a social-cultural activity (the extra-artistic) and that which concentrated on the formal properties (the artistic) of folklore (Pop, 1967, p. 32). The research focus shifted from the social to the art itself, from processes to products, and consequently from a broad interdisciplinary to a specialized choreological approach. The recording and analysis of dance as a folk art form contributed, however, to reveal the dance structure, to reduce variants to conceptual models and to describe the system of Romanian dance culture (Bucşan, 1971; Giurchescu and Bloland, 1995). Fieldwork was carried out primarily in rural settings where around 45 per cent of the population still resides. The urban milieu was little investigated and then only in relation to the immigrant peasants. In spite of political pressure, however, many researchers at the Institute continued to practise Brăiloiu's research methods, making efforts to maintain contacts with the surrounding scientific world.

Personal Directions

Following the accumulation of factual data, a number of questions emerged in the late 1960s to orient my future research direction. These included questions such as: What is dance? What role does it play in society? Who are the people who dance? Why do they dance? I aimed to find a theoretical framework in which ethnochoreological, aesthetic-analytical and anthropological perspectives could be integrated. Consequently, I conceived of dancing as a means of expressive communication which connects dancers, musicians and audience in an intricate network of relationships which takes place in different social contexts (Giurchescu, 1994). This view widens the fieldwork perspective, embracing both the dance and the people who dance within a given social framework.

Such an orientation was at variance with Romanian official cultural policy which, as noted above, aimed to control and manipulate scientific research. In the framework provided by the state organized festival Cîntarea României (Song to Romania), traditional symbols were misappropriated to legitimate political power. Living traditions of folklore which could not be controlled or directed by cultural management and which might express critical political attitudes were marginalized and considered subject to cultural contamination. Conversely, staged performances were officially presented as 'authentic' and artistically 'crystallized' folklore, regarded as primary source materials and hence, appropriate subjects for 'field' research and documentation (Giurchescu, 1987).

On arrival in Denmark, I shifted my fieldwork focus to a Romanian-speaking minority group, the Vlachs (Wallachians) who had arrived in the mid-1960s from north-eastern Serbia (Timok Valley). Between 1986 and 1997, I studied and recorded *hora*, their dance event, and also conducted field research in their home villages in Serbia. Then, after 11 years of settlement in Denmark, I was able to return to Romania to continue fieldwork in my native country.

Three principal topics formed the focus of my research in Romania following the collapse of the Ceausescu regime: the role of dancing in the ritual căluş (Plate 2);[4] the dance symbol as identity marker in the interrelationship between ethnic groups (Hungarians, Roma, Romanians); and people's attitude towards traditions following 45 years of Communist cultural management. From my fieldwork experience spanning over 40 years, I will select aspects for discussion which may provide terms of reference for the reader's own inquiries.

SOME FIELDWORK STRATEGIES AND ISSUES

Working in One's Own Culture

With few exceptions, I have worked in my own culture, a fact which, naturally, has shaped my fieldwork strategies. None the less, I have occupied the position of outsider to the community under investigation, since I possess no kinship relationships with them, am not a member of any of their groups and do not share everyday local life. I learned to be curious, always asking 'why?' and 'for what purpose?', cross-checking doubtful information and never correcting or embellishing their information in order to avoid responses such as 'if you already know better, why ask me?' Thus, working in one's own culture has both advantages and handicaps. On the positive side, I have experience of the socio-political, cultural and economic contexts, more specifically, a perspective on dance systems from neighbouring areas and reference terms to which I can relate when placing collected data in context. I possess critical judgement formulated within my own culture and am thus not easily tempted by 'unexpected' information. A negative point, however, is that important details, considered obvious, can easily be overlooked. During the Communist regime, for example, in order to observe the criteria of 'authenticity' as a basic principle in fieldwork, researchers were tempted to 'select' reality (Bîrlea, 1966, p. 209). Because of this restricted perspective, important aspects or components of the contemporary dance repertoire have been overlooked and lost. People had and still have ambiguous feelings, such as fear and distrust, towards well-known researchers, identifying them with officials. In the tense atmosphere created by the competitive system of staged folklore presentations in Romania, they regarded the researcher as a threat, overtaking or estranging their knowledge, dances and music. It is therefore especially important to gain people's trust from the very beginning.

Field Preparation and Duration

Fieldwork preparation necessitates detailed study of archival material plus wide-ranging reading within a multidisciplinary perspective; this knowledge helps to formulate pertinent questions and to investigate a subject thoroughly, as important information may become lost if it is not brought to people's consciousness through questioning (Bîrlea, 1969, pp. 37–42).[5] Decisions on fieldwork duration relate not only to practical circumstances, but, more fundamentally, to theoretical perspectives; the length of time spent in the field is a major distinction between anthropological and ethnochoreological approaches. Anthropologists and sociologists stay for a longer period, even living in the peasants' houses for at least one month, which enables participation in all aspects of their lives. Only long-term field experience in one locality may lead to both knowledge and understanding of situations, people's world views and their symbols. Indeed, the initial day of my first long-term fieldwork in a village was an unforgettable experience. My task for the first three days was to walk slowly through the village, to greet people, to watch and be watched, to answer but not to question. Consequently, when I finally started working, I was surprised to find how much people already knew about me and how easily I was accepted.

The majority of fieldtrips, however, are short, averaging two or three days in a village. There were occasions when the field team worked for one week in a village or visited two villages in a day. Such time pressures are demanding, requiring strength and dedication. It may frequently be necessary to follow informants to their working places (in the fields, herding animals, cooking, nursing babies and so forth) to gather information without annoying them; to convince a person to give up his or her interests or overcome tiredness to assist in the research (a strategy manipulatory but essential); and to create ad hoc dance occasions, maintaining the participants' spirit and commitment to dance. I frequently find that as a woman conducting fieldwork, I am perceived by the community as a person without a precise gender, an 'honorary male': this positioning affords me more liberty in working with both women and men. I am allowed, for example, to enter male spaces such as pubs and sheepfolds, ask particular questions, observe rituals forbidden to women and climb on roofs and trees to take pictures.

Observing, Experiencing and Recording an Event

According to Gusti, the researcher in the social sciences is of the same essence as the researched object, being an integral part of the social reality. In understanding reality Gusti proposes a 'synthetic method' which combines 'exterior' observation, participatory 'internal' observation, and provoked situations and experiments (1940, pp. 63–4). The material expression of this method is the 'direct observation card', which aims to record an event thoroughly in its full complexity. There are three levels of description: the perceivable reality, information and comments elicited from the participants and personal commentaries.

Adopted and adapted by ethnochoreologists, the 'direct observation card' is generally produced by a small team of specialists in dance, music, literature, ethnography, sound and film, each using his or her own techniques while following a common theoretical perspective. Such a card may reveal the frequency and succession of pieces which structure a local repertoire. It describes such aspects as time and spatial setting, placement of the participants in space (dancers, public, musicians), their patterns of interaction, the timing and succession of the most important activities, dance, music and text notation, drawings and personal notes. Photos and film/video may complete the documentation. Comments and explanations elicited from the audience during the performance address subjects such as the meaning of the event,[6] rules of social and ritual behaviour, style of execution and qualities of a good performer. A basic requirement for realizing an 'observation card' is not to disturb the normal order of the event, especially in the case of the researcher's direct involvement (dancing, playing, acting). Of course, a fieldworker may not have opportunity or licence to take notes or record on the spot; a diary, written up almost immediately, is a good solution here.

On Informants, Interaction and Interviews

Field research constitutes communicative interaction, on intellectual, affective and expressive levels, between the researcher and individual community members; both bring their personalities, life histories, ideologies and knowledge into that exchange. Informants, in my experience, ranged from terrified women who, on being recorded by phonograph (1955), believed that the devil had taken their voice, and others who refused to be photographed (1963) for fear of witchcraft, to those who videotaped their own family celebrations and exhibited interest in the fieldwork results (1993). Today's informants are especially challenging when they maintain old and new world views, a co-existence frequently characterized by a contradictory relationship between thinking, verbalizing and acting.[7] On beginning new field research, the researcher should draw up an initial list of 'type informants', recognized as the best in that genre by the community, always remembering that this emic designation may differ from his or her own expectations. Such type informants play an ambivalent role in the research process. They may indeed be the most competent in their domain, but they may act as 'gatekeepers', imposing their personal scale of values on the rest of the community and guiding the researcher's contacts with new informants. Recognized as local experts, they may filter information through their own representations, correct other informants, arrange situations and reconstruct events. It is important to be aware that specific folk art specialists (the best dancer, musician, etc.), commonly extend their prestige and status into the social sphere, becoming leaders of age, professional or ceremonial groups.

The ability to establish relationships and initiate dialogues with strangers are the most challenging aspects of research. Such communication demands technique and knowledge, but also involves charisma, true interest and the wisdom of accepting that one is not the truth-keeper. Interaction should always be conducted on an equal level, regardless of whether or not the interlocutor is a person of status. All documented interviews may appear to the novice as completely accurate factual records, but in reality the answers received are often ambiguous, incomplete or mistaken. The researcher needs to cross-check the responses, accept rather than correct mistaken statements in interview and avoid formulating questions which suggest the answer. The quality of information is to a great extent dependent upon the informant's origin, competence, education, cultural background, travels and walk of life. Informant cards should now be supplemented by extensive biographies and oral histories; informants who debate politics or any other sensitive, even inflammatory subjects, should be protected by keeping their identity secret.

In a fieldwork relationship both researcher and researched have expectations and aims, which commonly do not coincide. As city people, researchers are supposed to have the knowledge, social contacts and power. Their presence confers prestige to the host family, who, in turn, feel responsible for the way their 'guests' behave. I would advise the fieldworker, even if he or she is anxious to demonstrate sympathy and understanding of the local community, not to imitate the behaviour of informants as this may only result in embarrassment for all concerned; the local people do not expect the researcher, who is of necessity an outsider, to 'go native'. The field visit and behaviour of a researcher may remain long in the local community memory as return field trips undertaken three or four decades since those of Bartók and Brăiloiu have revealed.

Recording Physical and Social Reality

Some examples of the physical and social reality which may be recorded include the geographical milieu, demographic features, the institutional framework and economic status. Documentation on the geographical milieu may include the influence of the environment on the people's sense of space, time and movement style; the way insiders conceptualize natural elements such as beliefs related to hills, trees, forests and clearings; communication between settlements, which is important for delineating areas of homogeneity for dance and music (festivals, markets and fairs may be common); and mutual influence between urban and rural settlements. The way that houses are positioned in a village, according to ethnic and religious criteria, may function as a metonymic symbol for the relationship established among Romanians, Hungarians, Germans and Roma, and may also be expressed in terms of dancing and music making.[8]

In terms of demography, the phenomenon of migration, seasonal work displacement or commuting may also contribute towards the explanation of diffusion and integration of dance types and styles. Institutional frameworks, such as family, gender and age groups, may also support dance practices as in the cases of young men's groups for Christmas ceremonial customs, girls' working bees and children's *hora*. Other examples are sheepfolds, the village pubs, the school and the Culture Home, which during the past 45 years has organized artistic ensembles for stage performances. Identification of economic status can also be discerned from the style of dress and ornaments, in the extravagance of a wedding celebration and in changes of dance and music repertoires.[9]

In certain instances, the representation of reality is deliberately altered due to the insiders' desire to improve their image. Requests from researchers to restore the 'original' context of performance then results in a distortion of a second degree. In 1993, field research carried out in the village of Optaşi in the district of Olt by the International Council for Traditional Music's Sub-Study Group on Field Research Theory and Methods prompted the likelihood of just such a situation. The group expected to experience the ritual căluş in its natural setting, while the leader of the group wanted to show 'something beautiful, not primitive'. To have asked the leader to enact it the 'normal' way would have been in effect a new manipulation.

To retain the significant facts from the transient reality in as many details as possible, technical devices for sound and video recordings are employed. Even if the scientific and practical value of technological devices by which 'information can be collected, encoded, stored, retrieved, and retransmitted' (Stone and Stone, 1981, p. 218) is no longer questioned, recordings cannot be more objective than the person using these devices. Video documents help to improve perception. Watching a filmed subject (a village *hora*, for example), the dance ethnologist can analyse attitudes, gestures, facial expressions, use of space, formalized or spontaneous actions, way of dressing and processes of variation. Only the person who participated in the event is able to complete the recorded images with his/her own feelings, giving the film an 'emotional' dimension.

Experimental Strategies in Fieldwork

Experiment in fieldwork is an important method of research, which is based upon artificially created situations in order to study phenomena and processes. In order to demonstrate changes in dance style and structure between generations such an experiment might involve the documentation of old and young people dancing separately, followed by the contrived situation of recording them attempting to dance together. Other strategies might include returning to a local community many years later to study the processes of change and investigate the local collective memory; the documentation of the same dance performed by different dancers simultaneously and successively to study variation; and, indeed, setting up a fieldwork project which is investigated at the same time by researchers who bring both anthropological and ethnochoreological perspectives to bear on the dance event. This strategy was adopted in 1993 and 1995 (Plate 3) in Romania by the International Council for Traditional Music's Sub-Study Group on Field Research Theory and Methods.

Feedback interviews are yet another means of gaining data which include nonverbal, cognitive and affective behaviour (Stone and Stone, 1981, pp. 221–3). Films and videotapes provide valuable material for the original performers or other members of a community to comment upon. Their observations and emotional reactions are recorded, thus establishing a second level of communication. Images are translated into words, which reveal the meaning and function of marital strategies, proxemics, social behaviour, dress code, and so on. The use of older documentation in feedback interviews may affirm or call into question the accuracy of the original record. Commenting in 1976 on a documentary film on the ritual căluş, made in 1959 in Bârca in the district of Dolj, the surviving members of the original group confessed that they had performed the 'flag burial' purely for the film. As an esoteric action, the flag was in reality buried later, without assistance. The analysis of video recordings undertaken by the informants themselves, combined with feedback interviews, constitutes an experimental strategy whereby insiders may explain their own reality.

The Effects of Field Research on People

Fieldwork affects both those researched and the researcher, who carries a degree of responsibility. The ethical dimensions of research have long been debated and common practices such as preventing the manipulation or misuse of fieldwork results, returning some of the collected material to the community, paying 'copyright' for recordings and quoting the name of informants are basic courtesies. Increasingly, informants are educated people with personal opinions, who request better information about the content and scope of the fieldwork project. The researchers' representation of a social/ethnic group may be quite different from the ideal image the insiders build of themselves. Under certain conditions, such a situation could become explosive as I discovered when representing the Vlachs as displaying paradoxical contrasts and possessing a changeable, ambivalent identity.[10] Such an active response on the part of the informants adds a new dimension to the research process which involves collaboration between the researcher and the researched community (Giurchescu, 1991a, p. 348).

New Domains for Field Research

Instead of deploring the gradual disappearance of 'authentic' folklore, the ethnochoreologist may rejoice in the fact that there are many dance-related phenomena and processes which offer challenging new fields for research. There is the possibility of disclosing traditional models in the structure of urban dance contexts and of investigating dancing among minority groups and in newly emerging sub-cultures. Festivals may prove another focus of research attention in order to understand the mechanism of adapting folklore for the stage, and the large, diverse revival movement certainly requires thorough research to be undertaken. Finally, there is a need to reconsider and experiment with fieldwork theory and method, crossing the borders between anthropological and ethnochoreological perspectives.

NOTES

1. See Kaeppler (1991) and Giurchescu and Torp (1991) for summary views. The classical differences between dance anthropology and ethnochoreology may be viewed oppositionally: cultures world-wide versus national cultures; 'socially constructed movement systems' in order to understand society versus dance systems and their symbolic function for national and ethnic identity; detailed and long-lasting study of a given socio-cultural context versus collection and study of folk dance repertoires in different social contexts and processes of change; and patterned movement systems (the 'language' level of movement) versus formal structural analysis of individual dances (the 'speech' level of movement).
2. 'Where songs are still alive, come to life, change, since they are not separated from the milieu in which they appeared, the musical reality cannot be understood without the knowledge of the social realities' (Brăiloiu, 1931, p. 4).
3. Interest in the role of dance within a community, its social functions, processes of change and the dancers themselves is revealed in the General Questionnaire on dance and in the more restricted Special Questionnaire, which were devised in the first period of the Dance Department's existence (by Veronica Micznik and Vera Proca Ciortea). A similar perspective on dance can be found in the Polish guidelines for traditional dance research compiled in 1960 by Lange (1984).

4. Căluş is a complex ritual carried out over three days around Whitsunday by a group of men compelled by oath to maintain ritual taboos. The ritual functions to cure sick people, protect the community from female demons' evil acts, bring fertility and entertain the public.
5. The practice of dancing around the grave was documented in 1939 by Tiberiu Alexandru. It received no research attention until 1967, by which time the ritual had vanished.
6. For a comprehensive consideration of the event, see Torp, 1989.
7. Examples include driving a Mercedes car yet consulting witches and the response to a question of whether ghosts still exist: 'No, because they are run over by cars when crossing the road from the graveyard' (Giurchescu, 1991b).
8. In Transylvanian villages of mixed population, Germans and Hungarians settle along the main road, while Romanians live at the edges or on the slopes of the surrounding hills. Roma usually live outside the villages in small houses not surrounded by fences, as if in a large family.
9. Display of economic status is symbolized by hiring for weddings famous singers and bands playing a common, up-to-date repertoire.
10. The discussion was brought about by an article published in Danish (Giurchescu, 1988). Some of the Vlachs' opinion leaders commented on the article and the video recordings which I had made, expressing concern at the way I depicted the community and a desire to control and influence my opinion.

REFERENCES

Bîrlea, O. 1966. Principiile cercetarii folclorice (The principles of folklore research). *Revista de Etnografie şi Folclor*, 11, 3, pp. 201–17.
—— 1969. *Metodă de cercetare a folclorului* (The Method of Folklore Research). Bucureşti: Editura pentru literatură.
Brăiloiu, C. 1931. Arhiva de folclor a Societăţii compozitorilor români: schiţă a unei metode de folclor muzical (The folklore archives of the Society of Romanian Composers: sketch of a method for musical folklore). *Boabe de grâu*, 2, 4, pp. 204–19. Also printed as: Esquisse d'une méthode de folklore musical: les Archives de la Société des compositeurs roumains. *Revue de musicologie*, 15, 40, pp. 233–67 (published in Paris by Fischbacher).
Bucşan, A. 1971. *Specificul dansului popular românesc* (Characteristics of Romanian Folk Dance). Bucureşti: Editura Academiei RSR.
Bucşan, A. and Balaci, E. 1966. Metodă de cercetare a dansului popular (A method for folk dance research). *Revista de Etnografie şi Folclor*, 11, 3, pp. 243–50.
Costea, C. 1994. Ethnocoreologie românească (Romanian ethnochoreology). *Revista de Etnografie şi Folclor*, 39, 1–2, pp. 39–50.
Giurchescu, A. 1987. The national festival 'Song to Romania': Manipulation of symbols in the political discourse. In Arvidsson, C. and Blomqvist, L.E. (eds), *Symbols of Power: the Aesthetics of Political Legitimation in the Soviet*

54   *Anca Giurchescu*

Union and Eastern Europe. Sweden: Almqvist and Wiksell International, pp. 163–71.

—— 1988. Dansens dobbelte rolle: om Vlacherne – en folk med hemevé (The double role of dance: about the Vlachs – people with homesickness). *Modspil*, 42, pp. 12–19.

—— 1991a. Methods of research: studying a dance event among the Vlachs living in Denmark. In Buckley, A., Edström, K.-O. and Nixon, P. (eds), *Proceedings of the Second British–Swedish Conference on Musicology: Ethnomusicology*, Cambridge, 5–10 August, 1989 (Skrifter från Musikvetenskapliga institutionen, 26). Göteborgs, Sweden: Department of Musicology, Göteborgs Universitet, pp. 341–56.

—— 1991b. When ghosts are run over: tradition, technique and modern field research. Unpublished paper delivered at the VIII European Seminar in Ethnomusicology, Geneva, 23–28 September.

—— 1994. The dance symbol as a means of communication. *Acta Ethnographica Hungarica*, 39, 1–2, pp. 95–105. Special Issue: Essays on folk music and folk dance of central and eastern Europe; published in Budapest by Akadémia Kiadó.

Giurchescu, A. and Bloland, S. 1995. *Romanian Traditional Dance: a Contextual and Structural Approach*. Mill Valley, California: Wild Flower Press.

Giurchescu, A. and Torp, L. 1991. Theory and methods in dance research: a European approach to the holistic study of dance. *Yearbook for Traditional Music*, XXIII, pp. 1–10.

Gusti, D. 1940. Monografia sociologică: metodă de lucru (Sociological monograph: work methodology); Problema sociologiei: sistem si metodă (The problem of sociology: system and method). *Academia Română, Memoriile secţiunii istorice*, III, XXII, 21, 22, 23, pp. 55–83.

Kaeppler, A.L. 1991. American approaches to the study of dance. *Yearbook for Traditional Music*, XXIII, pp. 11–21.

Lange, R. 1984. Guidelines for field work on traditional dance methods and checklist. *Dance Studies*, 8, pp. 7–47 (and plates 1–15).

Martin, G. 1985. Peasant dance traditions and national dance types in east-central Europe between the 16th–19th centuries. *Ethnologia Europaea*, XV, pp. 117–28.

Pop, M. 1967. *Indreptar pentru culegera folclorului* (Guide for collecting folklore). Bucureşti: Casa Centrală a Creaţiei Populare.

Schutz, A. and Luckmann, T. 1973. *The Structures of the Life World*. Evanston, Illinois: Northwestern University Press.

Shafir, M. 1985. *Rumania, Politics, Economics and Society: Political Stagnation and Simulated Change*. London: Frances Pinter.

Stone, R. and Stone, V. 1981. Event, feedback, and analysis: research media in the study of music events. *Ethnomusicology*, 25, pp. 215–25.

Torp, L. (ed.). 1989. *The Dance Event: a Complex Cultural Phenomenon. Proceedings from the 15th Symposium of the ICTM Study Group on Ethnochoreology, Copenhagen, 1988*. Copenhagen: International Council for Traditional Music Study Group on Ethnochoreology.

5 Folk Dance Research in Hungary: Relations among Theory, Fieldwork and the Archive

László Felföldi

Widespread interest and recognition of folklore, from the late eighteenth century onwards, provided a stimulating atmosphere for the emergence of scientific investigation into folk dance traditions in Hungary. The particular ethos of Hungarian folk dance research, which is shared to a greater or lesser extent with other countries in east and central Europe, has been determined by three specific features: a vigorous and rich traditional dance culture upon which to focus; a well-constructed institutional framework within which to conduct the research; and access to modest technical equipment to support fieldwork and subsequent analysis of the collected materials.

A strict theoretical and methodological model was formulated in Hungary, particularly during the second half of the twentieth century, which focuses mainly upon historical, functional and formal aspects of dance tradition, and which has had a consequential effect upon the concept and conduct of fieldwork. The goal was and is to collect documents of 'authentic folk dance' into an extensive archive and to distribute the knowledge systematically in the form of academic monographs, compendia, type-catalogues and motif-indexes. National cultural policies have aimed to create a homogeneous corpus of new cultural values based on the most genuine, unwritten, vanishing traditions of the folk. Experts from the fields of performance, the arts, education and public life claim to pay strict attention to the most ancient, most national, most adaptable and 'purest' elements of local traditional cultures. These activities of nationalizing, reviving, purifying and rendering the dances archaic have resulted in a specifically shaped, indeed distorted picture of the traditional cultures of eastern and central Europe which, together with international cultural movements and fashions, has gradually reacted upon the dance traditions themselves. Dance research has made efforts from the beginning to grasp this process in its complexity as objectively as possible (Réthei Prikkel, 1924).

THE FOUNDATION OF HUNGARIAN RESEARCH

The present structure of Hungarian folk dance research had its beginnings in the 1930s, when difficulties in the accurate recording of living folk dance and dance music were perceived as a scientific problem. The most important achievements of this period were systematic filming (Plate 5), transcription and publication of folk dances, first by analytical verbal description (Gönyey and Lajtha, 1937; Molnár, 1947) and later by Kinetography Laban (Gönyey and Lugossy, 1947). The theoretical and methodological framework of this period can be traced in its key publications. Sándor Gönyey and László Lajtha in the dance chapter of the large compendium *Ethnography of Hungarians*, first published in 1937, based their hypotheses and propositions on recently made film recordings which were interpreted in the light of the theory of European dance ethnology and dance history. They drew mainly on Curt Sachs's evolutionist and historical comparative approach and the methods of the Finnish geographical-historical school. For the presentation of the 20 or so dances they used verbal descriptions in parallel with a series of photographs and drawings made after the film recordings. Researchers concentrated on dance motifs which they could identify from the short film shots. Generally, they did not record the dance music synchronously with the dance but frequently documented it on other occasions. This recording method and the improvised nature of most Hungarian dances hindered the development of morphological concepts.

István Molnár's collection, published in 1947, can be regarded as a significant move towards establishing a dance morphology. As a professional dancer and choreographer, Molnár approached dance practically and divided the various folk dances into motifs to arrange them in a motif-catalogue according to their characteristic type of movement (steps, jumps, beating, clapping, and so on). At the same time, he gave a full description of the whole dance process by means of code numbers for the motifs. He filmed and transcribed (in verbal form) source material between 1941 and 1947 in nearly 50 Hungarian villages, including some in Transylvania.

Another book published in 1947 is a modest collection of dances with a short presentation of the ethnographic context. Written mainly for practical purposes by Gönyey and Lugossy, it is interesting from a methodological point of view; about 20 dances collected in the 1930s and 1940s are transcribed in both Kinetography Laban and verbal description. Although the dances are only extracts, and the transcriptions stylized and schematic, this book paved the way to the current situation, where Kinetography Laban is widespread in Hungary and used exclusively in our publications.

After World War II, Hungarian folk dance research became an institutionalized long-term scientific programme supported by the state. A new generation of researchers, building on the past in conjunction with fresh field experience, began to develop new research structures. Able to absorb the most modern and relevant theoretical-methodological concepts offered by contemporary folkloristics, linguistics, ethnomusicology, movement theory and music and dance history, they gradually succeeded in making folk dance research academically comparable in its standards to other branches of folklore study, transforming it into a dynamically developing discipline. In the first period after the war, young researchers concentrated on extensive fieldwork and improvement of field techniques. In the second period, the 1960s, emphasis was transferred to analysis and classification. In the third period, the 1970s, Martin and Pesovár's generation began systematic publication of source material, following the example of folk music and folk narrative research. Currently, the new generation's activity involves implementation of the inherited programme, further development of the conceptual bases for research, computer-aided morphological analysis and a special research programme on individual dancers (Pesovár, 1963; Martin, 1982, 1986; Felföldi and Pesovár, 1997; Pálfy, 1997).

THEORIES, METHODS, APPROACHES

The social sciences have similar methods and techniques for acquiring information: observation, interview, questionnaire and different technical aids such as film, video, audio recorder and the like (Pelto and Pelto, 1978). Differences appear when researchers, due to the diversity of social life, necessarily select and limit the object of their research.

Dancing is a complex phenomenon which has to be studied in its social-cultural-ecological contexts and in its historical perspective. It demands study in tandem with other synchronic elements such as music, text and other interactive media such as costume and props. In east and central Europe, folk dance researchers focus on the dancing of one social stratum, that is, the peasantry. The main reference point is the end of the nineteenth and the beginning of the twentieth centuries when dance traditions were relatively vigorous. In our view, the abrupt social and political changes of the later twentieth century caused significant physical and intellectual ruptures which disturbed the manifestation and interpretation of folk dance. These limitations in formulating the object of study derive from the classical concept of folkloristics in which folk dance research is embedded (Martin, 1979b).

The fundamental aim of dance researchers is to depict the most precise picture possible of the 'dancing reality', subject, of course, to the theoretical and methodological paradigm of the period. Hungarian researchers focus on certain basic ethnographic and aesthetic aspects to achieve this aim. We emphasize the social, historical and geographical, which indicates our commitment to the methods of the historical-geographical and comparative-historical schools of research. With regard to the dances themselves, we lay stress on the formal-morphological-structural, the functional-semantic and the musical aspects, which demonstrates our adherence to the morphological schools of European folklore research.

Ethnographic Approaches

Historical perspectives have a long tradition in ethnography and consequently in folk dance research. This tradition stretches from the 'historicism' of Marián Réthei Prikkel (1924), the evolutionist way of thinking and comparative-historical methods of Curt Sachs (1937) followed by Sándor Gönyey and László Lajtha, through the socio-historical approach prescribed by the postwar ethnography, up to the new criticism of historical aspects. Martin and Pesovár's generation conceptualized their historical perspectives in the 1960s in order to create an effective tool to define the historical layers of Hungarian folk dance culture. The core of this concept was the examination of recent folklore in the light of historical sources and vice versa. Within this framework, historical facts provide a wide perspective for the study of change in dance folklore, and contemporaneous folklore practice provides a pattern for the interpretation of fragmentary historical data. In effect, this approach did not generate a new wave of extensive collection of archival materials, but a new type of correlation between historical and folklore facts. This conception is best represented in the type-monographs which contain the conclusions and data relating to a given dance type (Martin, 1979a; Lányi, Martin and Pesovár, 1983; Karsai and Martin, 1989).

Social perspectives, inspired by folkloristics, were introduced into Hungarian dance research in the 1940s to compensate for the single concentration upon the dance form (Kaposi, 1947; Molnár, 1947; Morvay, 1949). Folklore research offered a comparatively wide range of usable concepts concerning the significance of social context, the interrelation of folklore and community, folklore and individuality, the study of folklore events, the process of socialization in folk culture and the distribution of cultural elements. It is a pity that, at the time, dance researchers were unable to translate these concepts completely into practice and were not able to develop them further. Consequently, the study of social function and the significance of dance gradually became superficial; yet it predominated over other aspects of research. The new generation of researchers in the 1960s re-evaluated the role of social context and placed an emphasis on the formal and musical aspects. They created a more balanced model appropriate to their aims and objectives. Instead of the incomprehensibly wide concept of social function, they narrowed their focus to concentrate on the function of dances in the context of a given ritual or dance event (Martin and Pesovár, 1961, 1963). At the same time, they introduced the principle of individuality by which a dance tradition was to be examined intensively through the concrete practice of individual dancers. Such innovations contributed significantly to improving the social-functional approach.

Geographical perspectives have long been pursued in Hungarian research. They were integral to the 'language atlas' and 'ethnographic atlas' programmes throughout Europe and of the Finnish geographical-historical school. They were introduced into folk dance research in 1947 when researchers established a programme to publish a Hungarian dance atlas. The essence of the geographical approach is to collect standard information from a given geographical region, ethnic territory and frequently a language territory of a nation in order to define the geographic distribution of a folk dance culture. This facilitates researchers in determining the regional variance of the elements of a dance tradition synchronically, to investigate the diffusion of elements diachronically and to make predictions about future dissemination. Work on the folk dance atlas was in progress until the end of the 1950s. It resulted in a systematic exploration of numerous ethnic groups and ethnographic regions and villages in Hungary. Another outcome was the publication of the material in the form of regional monographs, village monographs and monographs pertaining to a specific ethnic group (Morvay and Pesovár, 1954; Martin, 1955, 1964; Martin and Pesovár, 1958; Belényesy, 1958). Unfortunately, this work was not integrated with the Hungarian ethnographic atlas with the result that folk dance as a research topic was neglected (in contrast to Slovakia and some other places in Europe) in this comprehensive survey of folk culture. In the 1960s, Martin and Pesovár's generation went on to conduct extensive field research in Transylvania and in all the neighbouring countries, but the nature of the geographical approach gradually changed. The previous programme was transferred into an overview of the Carpathian Basin, revealing the features of a special dance zone in Europe. This proved to be a necessary step for the preparation of solid comparative research (Martin, 1965a, 1968, 1979a, 1985).

Dance Textual Approaches

A focus upon formal, morphological and structural approaches is a particular feature of Hungarian and generally of east European folk dance research. It stems from the fact that in our improvized, individual dance traditions, the dance motif (or figure, as it is known colloquially) is the only unit which can be identified at first sight by the observer. Compositional rules and principles of improvization remain hidden even to an expert. In the nineteenth century this led to the belief that Hungarian folk dances are analytically indecipherable; consequently, it was thought that they could not be mastered and taught by foreigners, that is, by non-native dancers. Generations of researchers have worked to overcome this view, through systematic filming of dances and application of appropriate analytical methods. The main ideas of Hungarian folk dance analysis derive from extensive field experiences, from the different morphological schools of folkloristics (including folk music and folk tales) and linguistic theory (the Prague School). A significant stimulus has been gradually developing research in Hungary into movement theory (Szentpál, 1958; Dienes, 1996).

The principal concerns of folk dance analysis are to identify the various structural units as objectively as possible, to define their relationship to one another, to examine their structural function, and to uncover the rules of their composition into higher structural units.

These factors enable the researcher to delineate the manner and amount of freedom and regulation, that is, the norms of dance creation in the practice of an individual dancer, a local community, a region or a whole dance culture (Martin and Pesovár, 1961, 1963). As the most stable yet basic structural element, the motif has a very important role in folk dance research. The establishment of a repertory of all motifs, arranged in motif indexes according to dance regions, types, individual dancers, and so on, provides an objective basis for large-scale comparison. It should be noted that distinctions between *langue* and *parole*, competence and performance, product and process are not explicit in Hungarian folk dance research, but it does not mean that these concepts are not present in our research (Martin and Pesovár, 1961, 1963; Karsai and Martin, 1989).

Functional and semantic perspectives are derived from study of the social contexts of dances. In the model of Martin and Pesovár's generation, social function and meaning played a subsidiary role, since, as the most rapidly changing aspects of dance, their capacity for formal classification is limited. They are, however, significant in the study of historical changes of dances: Martin and Pesovár selected four factors for attention. First, dance names and folk terminology are extremely useful in ascertaining collective knowledge about dance and may reflect the emotional, moral and mental relation of the community to its practice. Furthermore, such vocabulary may signal the origin and interethnic connection of dances as well as provide a sensitive indicator of changes taking place in such relations. A second social factor is the structure of a dancing community in terms of its participants' number, sex, age, profession, religion, and the like. Investigation of the roles and connections of the community to the individual dancer, for example, of dancer to dancer and of dancer to musician, will reveal a network which can throw light upon how a dancing community operates. Third, the analysis of dance events and dance customs may indicate the temporal, spatial and dynamic features of a community's dance life. The exercise of preferences, prohibition or neglect of particular dances or dance events may reveal explicit or implicit significances. Finally, the approach of Martin and Pesovár's generation to social context included study of the socialization processes within a dance community. These included learning, adoption, transmission, utilization and loss, all processes which may clarify the connection of a dancer or dancing community to a dance tradition or specific dance (Kaposi, 1947; Morvay, 1953; Martin and Pesovár, 1961, 1963).

Martin's focus on the role of music in folk dance analysis and classification owes much in its conceptual formulation to developments in folk music and music history research from the 1960s and comprises independent study of the accompanying music and the relationship between the dance and the music. Behind this approach lies the fundamental principle that the musical factors (metro-rhythmic structure, tempo, affinity to certain schemes of rhythmic accompaniment, the occasional or constant feature of the dance–music connection and the qualitative–quantitative features of connected melodies) are the most stable components of the dance and are very significant in shaping the dance form. Consequently, they cannot be neglected in dance analysis and classification (Martin, 1965b, 1965c, 1979b, 1980; Felföldi, 1995).

Summary

On the basis of the dominant structure of the local dance repertories and the amount of improvization versus fixed form, Martin and Pesovár defined three dialects in Europe. In south-east Europe, they noted that the prevalent forms are the collective, semi-regulated round and chain dances. In east Europe and the eastern part of central Europe, individuality and extensive use of improvisation characterize the dominant folk dance genres of men's solo dances and free couple dances. In western Europe, collective, regulated couple dances such as quadrilles and contra dances are widespread. Martin and Pesovár's thesis is that these geographical differences represent fundamental historical changes in European dance culture over the last centuries. Southeastern European peasantry preserved the characteristic features of the round and chain dance fashion which stretched across Europe during the mediaeval period. Most folk dances of east European peoples date back to the Renaissance when free turning couple dances were widely popular. The quadrilles and contra dances, common to west European peasantry up to the twentieth century, have their origin in the eighteenth century. According to historical sources, these dance fashions were initiated by the social elite and spread by all the social strata (nobility, bourgeoisie and peasantry) through their respective channels of communication. This thesis is predicated on the dominant genres and practice of local dance repertories and excludes from consideration old ritual dances such as the morris dance or căluş. Furthermore, the local reality is actually more diverse in Europe. Nonetheless, the general portrait made by Martin and Pesovár does reflect a general actuality (Martin, 1968, 1974).

THE PRACTICE OF DANCE RESEARCH

Dance is an intimate, rarely verbalized sphere of ceremonial (not everyday) behaviour. The credibility of the documentation in such circumstances is endangered by the use of technical equipment, the intervention of the researcher into the event. This is particularly the case with our individual, improvised dance traditions. Furthermore, the observation of dancing is a culturally determined situation in which participants (researchers and informants) are embedded in different cultures, even if they are from the same nation. Of necessity, they interpret the given dance culture in different ways and this emic–etic differentiation is the result of an inevitable subjectivity on both sides. Finally, in such circumstances, researchers must employ multifaceted procedures and equipment to guard against a one-sided methodology. As a result, theory-building is not a straight route from primary observation to hypothesis and general theories.

Fieldwork

The majority of scientific problems are decided in the field. Most primary data on human action in the social sciences are derived from direct observation and recordings of verbal reactions to and examination of the products and results of behaviour. The objectivity of the documents arising from these sources is dependent on the accuracy of decision-making with regard to the basic questions of documentation: who, what, when, where and how.

In order to illustrate the Hungarian approach I summarize the monographic research undertaken in the Upper-Tisza region (Szabolcs-Szatmár county) in 1954–8 (Pesovár, 1955; Martin and Pesovár, 1958). The programme, initiated by Martin and Pesovár's generation, was based on the comprehensive plan and initial activities of the previous generation. It was conducted by the Work Group for Folk Dance Research (around 20 experts) within the framework of the Ethnographic Department of the Institute of Folk Education in Budapest. The general conception was to undertake monographic research in a region which possessed a vigorous dance life and rich repertory of dances and which would facilitate researchers to test the recently raised modern, theoretical-methodological problems. The plan comprised the whole procedure of research from fieldwork through analysis and classification to publication. The phases of the field research were as follows:

1. Preparation of the work through collection of the widest possible range of existing documents, including historical ones from the state archives and written materials from the local press.
2. Pilot research in around 100 locations from the total 234 settlements of the region, with small-duty film apparatus, by individual collectors.
3. Selection of the places for detailed research based on the outcome of the first two steps. The two main criteria for selection were intensity of the dance tradition and the proportional territorial distribution. In order to pursue the second criterion, in some cases, researchers chose villages with a less thriving tradition.
4. Detailed data-collection through interview techniques, direct observation of dances, dance music and the dance life in and out of social context, and selection of key informants for later filming. The work was assisted by research guides and questionnaires (see the Folk Dance Archives of the Institute of Musicology of the Hungarian Academy of Sciences).
5. Full technical recording of the dance repertory in its traditional order in about 50 places by a team of researchers, which included a film operator (regularly a dance folklorist), sound operator (regularly an ethnomusicologist), photographer (usually a dance folklorist) and a notetaker (usually an ethnographer organizing and recording the whole event).

   In most cases the filming took place at artificial dancing events initiated by the collectors and organized by local helpers. Dance folklorists had to apply this strategy because traditional dance events are rarely suitable for making a document of full value, fit for formal analysis. On full-length recordings the whole body of the dancer is constantly visible without being hidden by anybody else. At the same time, the whole dance has to be recorded from the beginning until the dancer stops, together with a precise indication of the synchronization of musical accompaniment and movements. Although these artificial events bear some resemblance to the actual ones, they are not suitable for classical functional-semantic analysis. The deficiency of this sort of data has to be compensated for by numerous direct observations of actual events. The procedure was aided by film cameras with electric cells, which made it possible to record 30 metres of film without stopping, in contrast to the previous clockwork cameras, which could record only 5–6 metres. Judging from experience in the region, this length is enough for the dancer to perform almost the full motif repertory and to use favourite compositional devices. If we record the dance of the same dancer more times on the same occasion and at some later events, we can gain a good idea of his talent (form-repertory, rules of improvization, creativity). This is important particularly in the case of outstanding individuals (Martin, 1979b).

With regard to research topics, collectors made an effort to record the dances of different generations and social groups. In this region the dances of the gentry and members of the lower nobility, as well as those of shepherds and peasants, are distinctive in the dance tradition. The researchers recorded both outstanding and average dancers, together with the youth, who danced the traditional dances in a rich and dynamic form. They paid attention not only to the traditional dance repertory, but also to the social dances and the impact of the professional and the amateur village dance masters. They recorded the dance compositions of the famous Pearly Bouquet, which had been made for ensembles in the region, in order to study the interrelationship of the local tradition and its stage adaptations. Special attention was paid to the dance traditions of gypsies, who are fairly populous in this region and who shared a similar standard of living with the lower strata of Hungarian peasantry. As a consequence, the interrelationship between their dance traditions appeared to be a promising research topic.

6. Supplementary research was carried out in the villages which formed a focus for detailed collection in order to verify the data and to add new information. This work continues to be undertaken with less intensity by the present research generation but with new techniques, such as life history collection, video documentation in the teaching situation and the recording of verbal comments in response to viewing old films.

7. The programme during the five-year research period resulted in 11,000 metres of film, 4,000 photographs, 12,000 pages of written data and 200 melodies on tape-recorder or in written form from 680 informants of nearly 100 villages. Although a significant amount of the collected data has not yet been published, this monographic programme had great importance in the theoretical-methodological development of Hungarian folk dance research (Martin and Pesovár, 1958).

ARCHIVIZATION, CLASSIFICATION, PUBLICATION

Archivization (collection, registration, systematization, storing and conservation) of dance data is an equally important activity of research. In Hungary 90 per cent of the folk dance documents are stored in the archives of the Institute of Musicology of the Hungarian Academy of Sciences. It was established in 1950 within the framework of the Institute of Folk Art to collect documents of the revival movements. In 1954 it became scientifically based with systematic collection aimed at the documentation of primary forms of dance folklore. In 1965 the whole collection moved to the Academy on Zoltán Kodály's initiative. Since then it has constituted the basis of the work of the Folk Dance Department of the Institute. The archives include film, written pages of interviews, written field record manuscripts, dance and music notations, motif cards and illustrated catalogues of historical sources containing iconographic, musical and text cards.

The aim of classification is to disclose the relationships which exist implicitly or explicitly among the selected phenomena. The validity of the classes (groups, genres, types, and the like) depends on the fundamental aim. In Europe there are some traditional kinds of classification, using various formal, or functional or mixed criteria, which are also applicable in Hungarian folk dance research.

1. Formal classification is based on the most striking and general formal features such as formation, configuration, floor pattern, number of participants in dance, and so on. It results in classes such as round dances, chain dances, line dances, solos, couple dances, small chorus dances and large chorus dances. This method of classification is most useful in dance research on southeast European peoples.

2. Genre as a class is determined through combining the functional and social criteria with the formal. Men's dances, women's dances, children's dances, mixed dances, amusement dances, skill dances, ritual-ceremonial dances and weapon dances are among the most widespread genres in European dance culture.

The categories of genre and form are useful to characterize longer periods of dance history, or larger geographic regions because the popularity and fashion of the dances are closely related to certain periods of dance history, social formations, dance cultures and dance dialects, as indicated in the earlier summary. The polymorphic character of European dances, however, hinders unambiguous classification of dances on the basis of formal-functional criteria. Using such mechanical classification, the different forms of the same dances would fall into different categories. To avoid these problems in part, typological principles may be employed.

3. Type consists of a class of dance variants, which belong to a certain formal, functional-semantic and musical framework of dances. In deciding such categories, a complex group of criteria are used in which formal ones are of primary importance. The most important formal criteria are the motif repertory, the structure of a dance and its connection with the musical accompaniment. In the Hungarian dance tradition, Martin and Pesovár identified eight basic types: women's round dances, shepherds' implement dances, jumping dances, Transylvanian lads' dances, slow lads' dances, old couple dances, csárdás and verbunks.

4. Style as a category of classification is widely used in European folklore research in order to differentiate historical layers. In Martin and Pesovár's practice, folklore dances whose historical parallels can be traced from the eighteenth century back to the Middle Ages belong to the old stylistic layer. Our new style dances date back to the eighteenth and nineteenth centuries. Thus, style constitutes the highest category of classification for our dances, which embraces all the type families, types, subtypes and groups of variants. Other kinds of stylistic categories such as individual style, collective style and motivic style are not accepted in Hungarian folk dance research because of their lack of terminological precision (Pesovár, 1965; Martin, 1970, 1979c, 1983).

CONCLUSION

Fieldwork is an integral part of great significance in the whole procedure of folk dance research; it cannot be conducted in isolation from other elements of the practice of dance research. Its methods and ideas depend on those of the whole discipline. Its aims and objectives are generally in accordance with the aims and objectives of other fields of social interest in traditional dance (art, education, popular culture, and so forth). Following this approach, a new generation of Hungarian folk dance researchers has invested much time in gaining the necessary field experience and theoretical and methodological orientations in order to continue the programme inherited from previous generations. The central tasks determined by current researchers are the further development of conceptual bases for research with computer-aided morphological analysis and a special research programme on individual dancers. This enables them to progress both in the direction of extensive comparative research and in the intensive study of dance creation as a cognitive, psycho-physical process. In this programme, fieldwork remains an important phase of research enriched by new techniques and methods of intensive case studies.

REFERENCES

Belényesy, M. 1958. *Kultúra és tánc a bukovinai székelyeknél* (Culture and Dance of the Bukovinian Széklers). Budapest: Akadémiai Kiadó.
Dienes, V. 1996. *Orkesztika – Mozdulatrendszer* (Orcestics – Movement System). Budapest: Planétás Kiadó. [Edited by Gedeon Dienes.]
Felföldi, L. 1995. The connection of dance and dance music: over or underestimation of their significance. In Dabrowska, G. and Bielawski, L. (eds), *Dance, Ritual and Music: Proceedings of the 18th Symposium of the International Council for Traditional Music Study Group on Ethnochoreology.* Warsaw: Polish Society for Ethnochoreology, Institute of Art, Polish Academy of Sciences, pp. 189–95.
Felföldi, L. and Pesovár, E. (eds). 1997. *A magyar nép és nemzetiségeinek tánchagyománya* (Dance Traditions of Hungarians and Nationalities within Hungary). Budapest: Planétás Kiadó (with CD-ROM).
Gönyey, S. and Lajtha, L. 1937. Tánc (Dance). In Elemér, C. (ed.), *A magyarság néprajza 4: kötet* (Ethnography of Hungarians). Budapest: Királyi Magyar Egyetemi Nyomda, pp. 71–131 (second edition, 1943).
Gönyey, S. and Lugossy, E. 1947. *Magyar népi táncok* (Hungarian Folk Dances). Budapest: Budapest Székesfővárosi Irodaslmi és Müvészeti Intézet.
Kaposi, E. 1947. A néptánckutatás újabb feladatai (New Tasks of Folk Dance Research). *Ethnographia*, LVII, pp. 242–46 (published in Budapest).
Karsai, Z. and Martin, G. 1989. *Lőrincréve táncélete és táncai* [Dance Life and Dances of Lőrincréve Village]. Budapest: MTA Zenetudományi Intézet.
Lányi, Á., Martin, G. and Pesovár, E. 1983. *A körverbunk: története, típusai és rokonsága* (Round Verbunk: its History, Types and Relatives). Budapest: Zeneműkiadó.
Martin, G. 1955. *Bag táncai és táncélete* (Dances and Dance Life of Bag Village). Budapest: Művelt Nép.
—— 1964. *Motívumkutatás, motívumrendszerezés: a Sárközi-Duna metni táncok motívumkincse* (Research and Systematization Motives: the Repertory of Motifs in the Dances of Sárköz and the Region along the Danube). Budapest: Művelődési Intézet.
—— 1965a. East-European relations of Hungarian dance types. In *Europa et Hungaria: Congressus Ethnographicus in Hungaria* (1963). Budapest: Akadémiai Kiadó, pp. 469–515.

—— 1965b. A néptánc és a népi tánczene kapcsolatai (Connections between folk dance and folk dance music). In Dienes, G. (ed.), *Tánctudományi tanulmányok 1965-1966*. Budapest: Magyar Táncművészek Szövetsége, pp. 143–95.

—— 1965c. Considérations sur l'analyse des relations entre danse et la musique de danse populaires. *Studia Musicologica*, VII, pp. 315–38 (published in Budapest).

—— 1968. Performing styles in the dance of the Carpathian Basin. *Journal of the International Folk Music Council*, XX, pp. 59–64.

—— 1970. *Magyar tánctípusok és táncdialektusok* (Hungarian Dance Types and Dance Dialects). Budapest: Népmüvelési Propaganda Iroda.

—— 1974. *Hungarian Folk Dances*. Budapest: Corvina Kiadó.

—— 1979a. *A magyar körtánc és európai rokonsága* (Hungarian Folk Dance and its European Relations). Budapest: Akadémiai Kiadó.

—— 1979b. Tánc (Dancing). In Ortutay, G. (ed.), *A magyar folklór* (Hungarian Folklore). Budapest: Tankönyvkiadó, pp. 477–539.

—— 1979c. Die Kennenzeichen und Entwicklung des neuen ungarischen Tanzstiles. *Acta Ethnographica Academiae Scientiarum Hungariae*, 28, pp. 155–75 (published in Budapest).

—— 1980. The traditional dance cycle – as the largest unit of folk dancing. In Sjöberg, H. (ed.), *Der ältere Paartanz in Europa* (conference report). Stockholm: Arkivet For Folkig dans Dansmuseet, pp. 44–66.

—— 1982. A survey of the Hungarian folk dance research. *Dance Studies*, 6, pp. 9–45.

—— 1983. Gesichtspunkte für die Klassifizierung der ungarischen Riegentänze und ihre Typen. In Dabrowska, G. and Petermann, K. (eds), *Analyse und Klassification von Volkstänzen*. Warsaw: Arbeitstagung der Study Group of Folk Dance Terminology beim International Folk Music Council, pp. 147–59.

—— 1985. Peasant dance traditions and national dance types in east–central Europe between the 16th–19th centuries. *Ethnologia Europaea*, XV, pp. 117–28.

—— 1986. On Hungarian folk dance research. In *International Monographs on Folk Dance*. Budapest: CIOFF and the Methodological Institute of the Hungarian National Centre for Culture, pp. 51–75.

Martin, G. and Pesovár, E. 1958. A Szabolcs-Szatmár megyei monografikus tánckutató munka eredményei és módszertani tapasztalatai (Results and methodological experiences of the monographic dance research in Szabolcs-Szatmár county). *Ethnographia*, 69, pp. 424–36 (published in Budapest).

—— 1961. A structural analysis of the Hungarian folk dance: a methodological sketch. *Acta Ethnographica Academiae Scientiarum Hungariae*, 10, pp. 1–40 (published in Budapest).

—— 1963. Determination of motive types in dance folklore. *Acta Ethnographica Academiae Scientiarum Hungariae*, 12, pp. 295–331 (published in Budapest).

Molnár, I. 1947. *Magyar néptánchagyományok* (Hungarian Folk Dance Tradition). Budapest: Magyar Élet Kiadása.

Morvay, P. 1949. A néptánc-kuntatás két esztendeje (Two years of folk dance research). *Ethnographia*, LX, pp. 387–93 (published in Budapest).

70   *László Felföldi*

—— 1953. *Útmutató népi táncaink gyűjtéséhez* (Guide to Collection of Our Folk Dances). Budapest: Művelt Nép Könyvkiadó.

Morvay, P. and Pesovár, E. (eds). 1954. *Somogyi táncok* (Dances of the Somogy Region). Budapest: Művelt Nép Könyvkiadó.

Pálfy, G. (ed.). 1997. *Néptánc kislexikon* (Small Folk Dance Encyclopaedia). Budapest: Planétás Kiadó.

Pelto, P.J. and Pelto, G.H. 1978. *Anthropological Research: the Structure of Inquiry* (2nd edn). Cambridge: Cambridge University Press.

Pesovár, E. 1955. A néptánckutató munkaközösség módszeréről (About the methods of the Folk Dance Study Group). *Táncművészet*, 2, pp. 312–13.

—— 1963. Der heutige Stand der ungarischen Volkstanzforschung. *Journal of the International Folk Music Council*, 15, pp. 53–7.

—— 1965. Les types de la danse folklorique hongroise. *Studia Musicologica Academiae Scientiarum Hungaricae*, 7, 1–4, pp. 103–8 (Published in Budapest by Akadémiai Kiadó).

Réthei Prikkel, M. 1924. *A magyarság táncai* (Dances of Hungarians). Budapest: Atheneum Nyomda.

Sachs, C. 1937. *World History of the Dance*. New York: W.W. Norton (reprinted in 1963. Translated by B. Schönberg. Originally published in 1933 as *Eine Weltgeschichte des Tanzes*).

Szentpál, O. 1958. Versuch einer Formanalyse der ungarischen Volkstänze. *Acta Ethnographica Academiae Scientiarum Hungariae*, 7, pp. 257–336 (published in Budapest).

6 'Or Shortly They would be Lost Forever': Documenting for Revival and Research
Egil Bakka

'There is nothing to be found any more, at least nothing worthwhile collecting,' my elders in the folk dance revival told me. I was, as I later realized, part of the neo-traditionalist movement[1] of the late 1960s. As an instructor of Norwegian folk dance and student of folklore I sought deeper knowledge of what was then my hobby, recognizing that folk dance was defined as part of folklore, even if my lecturers hardly ever touched upon it. I believed I might be able to redress the balance.

My search resulted in traditional dances which, mainly through filming, I documented to the best of my abilities. I published dances for the folk dance revival, and analysed and researched dances as part of my university education. On graduation, I was immediately employed to establish the Rådet for folkemusikk og folkedans (hereafter Rff-centre), the Centre of the Norwegian Council for Folk Music and Folk Dance. As a centre for documentation and research on folk music and folk dance, its main aim was to act as a service institution for the revival. There, I developed a methodology for collecting, analysing, learning, teaching and publishing traditional dances in cooperation with people from the revival. Then and now, the aim is to restore the dances to the region of collection; many might otherwise have died with their elderly performers.

What follows is an account of the aims, methods and results of my institution with regard to traditional dance in Norway. A variety of potential representations of the past now appear to me: let me begin with my initial position of traditional dance enthusiast.

A FIELDWORK TRIP IN THE MID-1970s

I was picked up with my ten pieces of fieldwork equipment on the small railway station by my local helper and driver, a young folk dance instructor who had never undertaken fieldwork. She told me that I had been correct: nobody, in response to her interview in the regional newspaper, had contacted her with old dances and she was worried about locating informants.

In the small post office, we found our ideal first contact, a friendly lady in her late fifties who knew everybody in the small community. She was able to direct us to good dancers and musicians, now in their seventies and eighties, whom she recalled from her early youth. I recorded all she remembered on an informant's form: details about where people danced and which dances they performed, but she had work to do, so we could not pursue a full interview. None the less, she had no objection to giving us her name, address and date of birth.

We were ready for a long day of knocking on doors in the little community. Some people were not at home, some were working out of doors and, even if they were in their late eighties, felt they could not let the 'young people' down by leaving work. Some were very happy to receive visitors and did their utmost to help us; others were extremely mistrustful and afraid that they would ruin their reputation by talking to strangers on a sinful topic like dance. After about five unsuccessful attempts, we finally came to a 76-year-old man who, we understood, had often been the butt of social ridicule; people admitted, though, that he had been quite a good dancer. He was extremely happy and flattered that strangers were interested in him and his knowledge. As usual, we began by asking what dances he knew: without hesitation, he mentioned some seven or eight, many more than anybody else in the neighbourhood. Some were variants of the very old and rare couple dances, *springar* and *halling*, which differed considerably from one community to another. To our delight, he was willing and able to dance them for us. Following a taped interview, he promised to come to the local community hall to dance for filming whenever we managed to arrange a social gathering. We rushed off to begin recruiting as many dancers as possible for a filming session: even if we had the star, we needed as many other good dancers as possible in their sixties, seventies and eighties. Fortunately, we discovered a fiddler who had played for dancing and were allowed to hire the hall for the next evening.

Having worked late, we continued the next morning as soon as we felt sure that people were awake. Our first priority was to find good dancers, particularly those who knew some of the oldest dances. We also interviewed them on their dance repertoire, requesting perform- ance of the different dances, mapping when and where they had danced in their youth, and registering houses, rooms or locations out of doors where much dancing had taken place before the community hall was built in 1913; we also looked for old photographs. We worked with an intensity strongly inspired by the feeling of struggling fiercely against time.

Eighteen of the 25 people who had promised to come to the filming session arrived. Our star dancer, two other men and two women all in their seventies and eighties knew the *springar*, and only our star dancer, the *halling*. We requested as many performances as possible of dances that we regarded as the most interesting (those with a rich range of improvization) and filmed everything. Additionally we filmed the total repertoire of the generations present, from the *tango* of the people in their sixties, to dances such as the waltz and *reinlender* which everybody knew. We even filmed a couple of singing games which some of the ladies managed to piece together plus some dances known to only a few of the dancers. During the coffee break, we com- pleted the rounds of interviews and even took some photographs. Finally, we filmed a presentation where everybody gave their names in order to facilitate the identification of the people dancing. Gradually, a crowd of rather reserved and sceptical people began to behave as a normal dance party audience. Some young people, looking in out of curiousity, were extremely surprised to see their parents and grand- parents performing dances they had hardly ever seen and acting in ways somewhat removed from their everyday 'old folks' manners. This exceptionally successful evening of documentation started at 7 p.m. and continued until midnight. My helper and I had taken almost two hours in advance to put up lighting, microphones and other equip- ment for 16 mm filming and tape recording, and spent an hour after- wards taking it down.

BACK TO TRADITION – THE NEO-TRADITIONALIST POINT OF DEPARTURE

By the late 1960s, the folk dance revival establishment, represented mainly by national organizations in Norway, Sweden and Denmark (Bakka, 1970, pp. 5ff; Velure, 1972; Sjöberg, 1989; Knudsen, 1981), were under attack from a number of organizations and individuals.[2]

Different situations existed in each of these countries to some degree
of course, but a canonized repertoire of dances recorded in official
manuals was efficiently promoted in all countries. Some of the dances,
like the Norwegian song dances and many of the Swedish group
dances, were choreographies with little basis in traditional dancing.
The selection was not representative of what ordinary people danced,
and constituted a national repertoire that, according to the neo-
traditionalists, threatened and even killed traditional local dances. In
general, the establishment was criticized for having lost all contact
with its roots. The criticism was not new – similar complaints had
already been voiced in the 1920s – but now the debate and criticism of
folklorism brought the question into academic discourse. Some folklorists, through their fierce criticism of folklorism, seemed to deny the
folk dance revival all legitimacy and credibility. In opposition to this
was the neo-traditionalist trend among folk dance enthusiasts who
wished to retain the idea of revival, but saw the need to redefine its
material, its methods and, even to some degree, its aims.

The very basis for these neo-traditionalists was the collection of new
material, which raised a number of questions: are all dances, performed by people in local communities which have not been
influenced by the folk dance revival or dancing masters, of value or
interest? Or, do only dances of a certain age, a certain ethnicity or
with certain qualities represent a heritage worthwhile collecting? A
decision to implement the latter might result in many communities
being deprived of the possibility of presenting their dances as heritage.
No uniform response to such questions emerged from the neo-
traditionalists, as they were not an organized group.

At the Rff-centre all dances learned through unorganized visuo-
kinetic transmission are regarded as traditional dances. Consequently,
ordinary people's versions of twentieth-century dances, including hip
hop and break dance, are considered traditional, even if the label of
folk dance is not used; they are documented together with the very
oldest dances, even if prioritized much lower. There has been vigorous
discussion within the Norwegian revival movement about what kind
of dance material is worthy of attention. The Rff-centre policy has
been criticized, particularly with regard to co-operation with rock-and-
roll enthusiasts to videotape popular versions of this type of dance. It
raises a number of issues: should dances be recorded purely for their
artistic or intrinsic value, for their uniqueness, or should the represen-
tativeness of the collections be taken into consideration? The question of identity is also implicated: it may be of great importance to a

local community that its dances are documented, even if they are relatively insignificant variations of well-known types in a national archive.

As a convinced neo-traditionalist, my main aim was to record the local dance repertoire in as many local communities as possible. In many communities which had earlier been considered lacking in traditions of folk music and folk dance, a strong desire emerged to prove that they did have a heritage to be documented and taken into use. My aims were threefold: to secure traditional dance as heritage; to draw a representative picture of traditional dancing in general, including its most modern forms; and to construct a history for the folk dance revival and, to some degree, a history of other types of social dancing.

The collection is undertaken during intensive fieldwork periods lasting from a couple of days to a couple of weeks. Local people participate as helpers and apprentices, indeed, often prompting the fieldwork. The documentation involves several methods: first, informant forms, one for each person, to note oral information on initial contact; second, taped interviews (formerly by audio recorder, today by video recorder) whenever feasible, and when the interview yields material of substance (Plate 4). An open style of interview is adopted to cover all aspects of dances and dancing. In general, a retrospective approach is employed, prioritizing the youth of people in their fifties upwards. The places and houses where dancing took or takes place is noted, together with relevant objects and photographs. Third, great emphasis is placed on the documentation of dances and dance movement. Notes or even film are taken of on-the-spot demonstrations (Plate 6), particularly if a dance event cannot be arranged. On discovery of dance material of some importance and/or reasonably good dancers, a dance event is organized to document the dances efficiently. Normal dance events are occasionally recorded, but, in our experience, such documentation, for several reasons, is limited in its use and thus receives a lower priority. I confess that this systematic approach results in little deviation from our established path, and an effort is certainly needed to intensify the documentation of the present.

THE PHASE OF ANALYSIS

In the initial years of the Rff-centre, local folk dance instructors who had participated in the fieldwork often became fascinated by the whole concept of collection and reconstruction. Responding to their immediate desire to learn the collected dances, different models of transmission were employed: we loaned them the films, recommending imitation of the older people, and we arranged workshops, where I tried to help the dancers to analyse and imitate the dances directly. It simply did not work: the filmed material was, in general, far too complex to be dealt with in this manner, and it soon became clear that a detailed and careful notation process was indispensable.

The idea of bringing together revivalist folk dancers and elderly traditional dancers to simulate traditional learning processes appeared to be an obvious solution. When, however, traditional learning occurs at normal dance events, the beginners look, absorb and try out the dances over long periods of time. When uniting a few elderly traditional dancers and people from the folk dance revival, the interaction tended to focus on questions and discussions rather than on practical dancing. The folk dancers expected to have the dances explained to them, and the traditional dancers tried as best as they could to accommodate this desire. Their knowledge is, however, silent, unverbalized and even unverbalizable; consequently, answers and explanations tended to be what could satisfy the folk dancers, and revealed more about what the traditional dancers felt their dances ought to be like than the actuality. Our conclusion was that relatively short meetings between the two groups did not help in the transmission of dances, even if it could be valuable in other ways. Either normal dance events were needed or long-standing and close personal contacts on an individual basis.

Our different experiments and attempts finally concluded in a detailed and careful analysis of the film material as a first indispensable step in the process of reconstructing dances.

Transcribing Performances and Describing Local Dance Types

When a few local dancers visit the archive in Trondheim, we begin to analyse the collected material from their region or community, using an editing table where the film can be run with synchronized sound at whatever speed required. A transcription of each dance performance is then made in a standard Norwegian notation system: with complex improvized couple dances, this has to be done in full detail throughout but with simpler dances it might be possible to use shorthand and a summary for some of the material. In tandem with this transcription work, the learning process is begun by trying to master the identified movement elements.

In analysing performances from one small community alone, all performances of a dance type, for example the *springar*, are considered, in order to reconstruct the same dance competence. A dance competence is defined as the sum of motor ability, knowledge and understanding which enables a dancer to carry out a particular dance in accordance with the norms of the group. Dance competence enables the dancers to reproduce, through performance, that which they and others understand to be the same dance, that is to say, the same dance type.

Our aim is not to make dancers reproduce one single performance but to give them a competence on the basis of which they can produce an infinite number of different but acceptable performances. Because of this, comparison of all the transcribed performances is required in order to identify the 'vocabulary' of which they are built up, and to decipher the 'grammar' used to put elements together according to norms. When this analysis is completed, it is written as a description of a local dance type.

When working with material from a larger region, it is necessary to discover whether all performances are so similar that they can be described as belonging to the same local type, or whether the material requires description as two or three different local types belonging to different parts of the region.

REPLANTING THE DANCE AND DEVELOPING DANCE STUDIES

After three or four days of intensive working sessions to transcribe, describe and commence learning one of the old couple dances, the local people return home to work with the dance and its description on their own. They have assimilated a basic understanding of the dance, its vocabulary and grammar, some rudimentary skills in performing elements and even some pedagogical approaches to learning and teaching from our dancing sessions. They continue to practise on their own, perhaps inviting other dancers to join them in order to teach them a little; they even try to work with the older informants if that is possible. During this period they remain in contact with the Rff-centre to ask for advice, and perhaps to attend more work sessions in order to complete a description. After about six months, they feel ready to present the dance to a wider audience, and usually invite me or one of my assistants at the Rff-centre to teach a course for a wider audience. This facilitates the development of a pedagogical approach to the teaching of the dance, the transmission of authority for it to our local cooperators and the opportunity to help their establishment and acceptance as the local instructors. The old dancers are invited to a party on one of the evenings, watch the films, talk to the young people, perhaps dance for and with them and provide us with a further occasion to document them. The dance has now returned, local people have taken responsibility for it and our archive symbolically and practically relinquishes its authority and competence for this particular dance: the process can be compared to the restocking of fish in a river where the species had died out.

At the end of the twentieth century, dance, not least Norwegian traditional dance, has acquired greater weight in the curricula of Norwegian schools. The same trend can also be found within higher education. The Norwegian University of Science and Technology in Trondheim offers dance as a subject based mainly in traditional dance, drawing on the expertise and archives of the Rff-centre, which is housed in the university. The subject has an ethnochoreological profile, taking its departure principally from Norwegian material. In addition to dance analysis, the social and historical contexts of dance (including theatrical dance), dance pedagogy, basic Labanotation and ethnochoreological theory, the programme includes a course in fieldwork where the students undertake field research of their own choosing, employing a video camera and providing a summary report.

PRESERVING CONTINUITY WITH THE PAST AND ACHIEVING CONTINUITY WITH THE FUTURE

Having revealed myself as an involved enthusiast throughout, I will now attempt a more critical distance on this personal history to evaluate and locate the Rff's activities in relation to the discipline of ethnochoreology. Even if the dance activities of the Rff-centre can now be labelled as ethnochoreology, they certainly did not develop from any established basis within this field. The principal contributory academic disciplines were Nordic folklore and ethnology of the 1960s and 1970s, together with particular ideas and aims of the Norwegian revival of folk music and folk dance, which were no doubt influenced by wider, international trends. Today the discipline at the Rff-centre still does not conform to the disciplines of ethnochoreology or dance anthropology as practised in multicultural nations: our style of investigation may reach out towards the field of cultural studies and global perspectives, but the aim is to maintain a firm local core. Given our particular agenda to service the folk dance revival by developing competence in dance as movement and form, based on visual documentation, the Rff-centre's clearly focused horizons inevitably do not coincide entirely with those of more mainstream ethnochoreology.

From being a discipline which asked many questions concerning what and how, ethnochoreology appears to be moving increasingly towards restricting itself only to the question why: the more dominant questions thus avoid direct engagement with the dance product and content. The interdisciplinarity which has undoubtedly brought a rich cross-fertilization into the study (see Kaeppler, 1991, p. 18) has, at the same time, tended to discourage our specialization of dealing with dance as structured movement patterns. Furthermore, the very concepts of folk music and folk dance have been discarded by certain scholars from the international realm of academia as outdated, problematic or Eurocentric notions of little validity. An indicative example of such discourse, which aims to reveal that traditional folk culture is a fiction, is Chapman's conclusion (1994, p. 42) to his article on Celtic music:

'Folk' music now exists, as a genre, recorded, performed, published, sung and listened to in the nearly complete absence of any 'folk' to provide the full social context that once (in whatever arguable or murky sense) might have existed; the social context of 'folk' music today is one of vinyl and magnetic tape, recording studios, published works, media performance and specialist gatherings.

According to this perspective, the phenomenon formerly called folk dance or folk music is an illusion; it no longer exists, even, indeed, if it ever existed. Thus the revival is judged only as wanting to represent a past which obviously cannot be adequately represented in the present. If there is a desire to re-present folk dance as a contemporaneous phenomenon rather than as a museum piece, then it is immediately confronted by the demand to adhere to western aesthetic conditions of continual development and individual, creative originality. In the fields of art and culture these remain a basic precondition for acceptance, even if, in a postmodern age, our faith in endless progress seems to have been crushed.

In discussing the nature of revival, Swedish ethnomusicologist, Ronström (1996, p. 11) proposes a perspective which locates its practice as a fight in a Bourdieu-ian field between orthodoxy (preaching authenticity) and heresy (promulgating development and change). There may indeed be a risk for ethnochoreologists to become involved with orthodoxy when dealing with traditional dance as a text for exact replication; but, it is nevertheless crucial for all kinds of activities concerning traditional dance, that our discipline shoulders the responsibility of constructing well-founded narratives about dances and for maintaining a basis upon which to continue practical expertise and implicit knowledge in the field of dance. Extreme orthodoxy or extreme heresy (or indeed both simultaneously) have caused many a revival of traditional dances to flounder and sink; and all because, in our time of relativism, there are so few relevant new narratives of the past by which to navigate, regardless of our ultimate destination.

At the Rff-centre, however, the symbiotic goals of research and revival locate our practices in the dancing of traditional performers, while searching for an authenticity which transcends notions of illusory and deceptive representation. In our philosophy, the revival of folk dance is of greater scholarly and humanistic value to contemporary culture than postmodern critics of tradition would allow. Contrary to their views, the revival, in our opinion, is neither a mere cipher for the expression of underlying ideologies nor is it a mode of catharsis for ineffectual nostalgia. Navigating such waters of absolute relativity and ultimately empty symbolism denies any possibility of incorporating traditional practices successfully into contemporary life.

In parallel with the position advocated by Kramvig and Eldjarn (1998, pp. 5–6) in their cautionary tale of the reconstruction of Viking ships which sank through lack of knowledge of traditional building techniques, I maintain that the symbolic function of representations of the past is insufficient. Research which aims to achieve a certain kind of authenticity, whether it is to make a ship which can float or to perform folk dances as an integral part of contemporary life, enables a continuity with the past which is both desirable and legitimate. This may be achieved by attending to the study of tradition as a phenomenon which is much more than a historical construct arising in opposition to the processes of modernization. It is instead a form of continuity, a silent knowledge, often acquired through learning bodily techniques and practices from traditional exponents. Thus, through the pursuit of fieldwork which focuses upon dancing as a form of traditional embodied knowledge, we can aim to ensure that our dances are never 'lost forever'.

1. An audience-oriented Samoan dance performed by the Samoan hosts at the
   seventh Pacific Festival of Arts, Apia, Western Samoa, September 1996.

2. Researcher Anca Giurchescu, interviewing a group of căluş dancers in the
   village of Stoicăneşti, Arges, Romania, 1994.

3. Teaching and learning a couple dance *în două lături* during fieldwork conducted by the Sub-study Group on Fieldwork of the International Council for Traditional Music Study Group on Ethnochoreology. Village of Berchies, Cluj district, Romania, 1995.

4. Egil Bakka solicits opinion on the dance tune from one of the local dancers, Birger Nesvold, who has just performed a *pols*, during a field trip to investigate dance/music relationships in Røros, Norway, October 1992.

5. An early example of the detailed photograph documentation of folk dances in Hungary. *Kánásztánc* (shepherd dance). Márcadópuszta (Somogy county), 1932.

6. Andreas Veda performs the *springar* in the farmyard with his daughter-in-law called out to help demonstrate typical motifs. The dance has now been revived for performance, based on subsequent film recordings and Veda's later teaching. Osteroy, near Bergen, Norway, 1966.

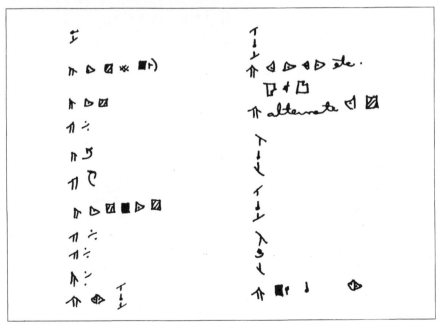

7. Examples of field notes by Judy van Zile using Labanotation (written in real time) of the Korean dance, *ch'oyongonu*.

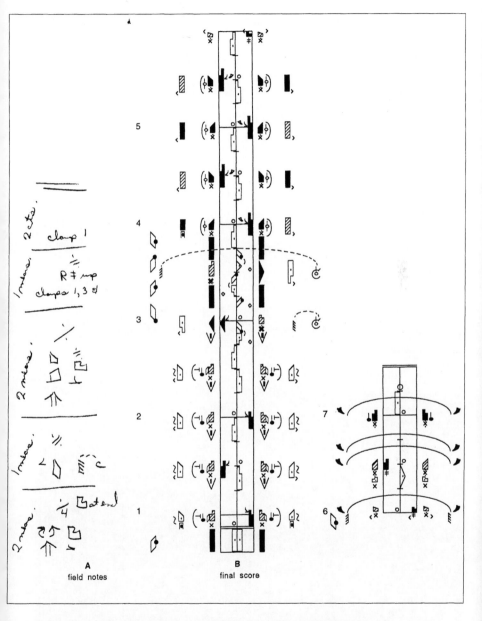

8. Example of Japanese *bon odori* (*Hanagasa Odori*) notated by Judy van Zile in brief as field notes (A) and the final score (B). (Based on van Zile, 1982, pp. 73–74).

9. Susindahati rehearses *Bedhaya*, Yogyakarta, Java, 1987.

10. *Ledheks* perform for the village spirit, Java, 1994.

11. *Milia* dance performed by the dance group Apollon Karyas, at the Alsos Theatre, Athens, Greece, September 1996.

12. Easter celebration of Kostas and Christos Stavrakas's families ending in dancing. Karya, Lefkada, Greece, 1992.

13. Britannia Coco-Nut Dancers, Bacup, Rossendale, Lancashire, England, performing on their annual tour of the town, Easter, 1996.

14. Chief in *pangolin* costume playing the *eben* at Igu'obe, Igue Festival, Benin City, Nigeria, 1985.

NOTES

1. This term was, as far as I know, first used by Henrik Sinding-Larsen (1984, p. 132) about trends mainly within the revival of folk music.
2. This was not a coherent discourse; the participants in the different countries were hardly aware of each other at this stage, and the written material is very scattered, being related more to music than to dance in Denmark.

REFERENCES

Bakka, E. 1970. *Danse, danse lett utpå foten – folkedansar og songdansar* (Dance, Dance, Lightly on Your Feet – Folk Dancer and Song Dancer). Oslo: Noregs Boklag.
Chapman, M. 1994. Thoughts on Celtic music. In Stokes, M. (ed.), *Ethnicity, Identity and Music: the Musical Construction of Place*. Oxford: Berg, pp. 29–44.
Kaeppler, A.L. 1991. American approaches to the study of dance. *Yearbook for Traditional Music*, XXIII, pp. 11–21.
Knudsen, T. 1981. Hvem er folk? (Who are the folk?). *Arbertslund Folkemusikhus Månedsblad for folkekulturen og dens folk*, 5, pp. 24–6 (published in Albertslund, Denmark).
Kramvig, B. and Eldjarn, G. 1998. Tradisjonens hevn over postmodernismen: historien om et forlis. (The revenge of tradition on postmodernism: the history of a shipwreck). *Tidsskrift for etnologi*, 24, 1, pp. 5–23 (published in Oslo by Novus forlag).
Ronström, O. 1996. Revival reconsidered. *The World of Music: Journal of the International Institute for Traditional Music*, 38, 3, pp. 5–20 (published in Berlin by VWB Verlag für Wissenschaft und Bildung).
Sinding-Larsen, H. 1984. Landskappleiken – nasjonalt rituale og lokalkulturell folkefest (Landskappleiken – a national ritual and local popular festival). In Klausen, A.M. (ed.), *Den norske væremåten* (Norwegian Manners). Oslo: J.W. Cappelens forlag, pp. 117–39.
Sjöberg, H. 1989. *Artiklar under 25 år, et urval* (Articles over 25 Years, a Selection). Stockholm: Samarbetsnämnden för folklig dans.
Velure, M. 1972. Levande dansetradisjon eller stagnasjon og kopiering: folkedans som folklorismefenomen (Living dance tradition or stagnation and imitation: folk dance as a phenomenon of folklorism). *Tradisjon*, 2, pp. 3–9 (published in Bergen by Universitetsforlaget).

Part II
Methodological Approaches

7 Capturing the Dancing: Why and How?
Judy Van Zile

A solid grounding in a movement notation system is a necessary component of dance ethnology training. Even if the provision of a full movement score is not the goal, the abilities and understandings concomitant to learning a notation system are mandatory skills. An important ingredient in research is discussion of danc*ing*, the movement dimension of this complex and multifaceted aspect of human behaviour. Whether the focus is on overall cultural context, gender issues, ritual, or some other topic, the movement involved should, at an appropriate juncture, enter the discussion; sophisticated movement analysis may not be necessary, but statements relating to movement are relevant, indeed critical, to a broad array of dance ethnology studies.

The values of notation systems for dance, in themselves and in relation to other forms of documenting movement (such as film), have been discussed in many publications.[1] Most, however, focus on the value of notation for preserving and serving as the basis for reconstructing western concert dance. I will extend some of the points raised in these discussions to dance ethnology applications. Because my own training and work are grounded in Labanotation, I refer frequently to this system and draw examples from it. This should not be construed, however, to mean that Labanotation is the only valid system.[2]

One of the most obvious values of movement notation is its ability to freeze an activity that occurs in time. This is critical for the dance ethnologist for several reasons. Any analysis requires the ability to look at something repeatedly, often from different perspectives. With an easily transportable written score in hand, the researcher can do precisely that. Indeed, it might require hundreds of still photographs to suggest the kinds of motion sequences that can be represented in detail in several pages of a notation score.

Because the score is in written form, one can easily move back and forth in a dance, jump from one part to another, look at only particular features (such as what an individual body part is doing) and lay portions of a dance side by side and examine them simultaneously. Because the researcher is always looking at the same score, the dance remains constant. This is different from seeing multiple performances of the same dance or from asking a dancer to do something again and again. In both of these situations one almost always sees variations in performance.

The constancy of a score as well as its accuracy, however, introduce theoretical issues that must be taken into account. A dance notation system is a script for recording physical activity. It is, therefore, a translation, 'a translated (that is, transcribed-into-another-medium) artifact' of a dance (Van Zile, 1985/1986, p. 42). Most often, the translation is done by someone other than the dancer, which means a score represents an interpretation of movement. It is not 'raw' data in the same way that research information in the sciences is. In order to create a score the researcher must see and understand the movement and make choices about how to describe it. She must determine 'which version' of an often-repeated but almost-always-slightly-different movement to document, how best to describe the movement, and what sort of description/documentation is needed for a particular purpose.[3] When writing the scores, for example, for my monograph on Japanese *bon odori* in Hawai'i (Van Zile, 1982), I was concerned with documenting a generic version of each of the dances. I was not concerned with differentiating movement variations based on age, gender or geographic origin of performers, but rather with the movement ingredients necessary to constitute a particular dance. To do this, I had to see many versions of each dance and identify relevant ingredients. This is explained in the monograph (p. 33) so that individuals reading the scores know that if they see the dances performed, there may be many stylistic variations. Short notation samples are also included to suggest some of the possible variations (see Figure 1A and B). If I were concerned with a stylistic analysis of performance differences between individuals, with determining stylistic variations of the *same* dance, I could use the generic scores as a basis and add details or modifications to capture each variation in a separate score (see Figure 2A, B and C). These scores could then be laid side-by-side to reveal *the dance* clearly as well as its *variants*.

Notation scores can provide data for explaining things. In a 1992 study, an examination of selected aspects of a Labanotation score revealed what contributed to certain impressions I had of a dance. As I watched performances and teaching sessions of the Korean dance *Ch'ŏyongmu*, I had a sense of great solidity and stability. As I notated

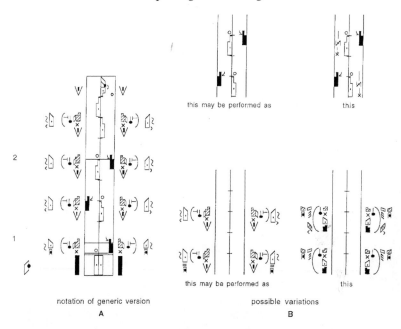

this may be performed as   this

notation of generic version   possible variations
A   B

this may be performed as   this

Figure 1   Notation of *Hanagasa Odori* (from Van Zile, 1982, pp. 34, 35, 73).

the dance, I became aware of a great number of repeated movement phrases. But as I watched the dance in performance, for some reason the repetition was not boring. The length and complexity of the dance made it difficult to see, during a performance, why it was not boring. By freezing the dance in time through a notated score and focusing on only one movement component (use of space), I was able to determine specific ways in which space was used, and to hypothesize that this usage contributed to the qualities I perceived as a viewer (see Van Zile, 1992).

In analysing a different dance, *Chinju kômmu*, I discovered a similar use of space (Van Zile, 1996). Together, these two studies suggest a recurring characteristic of Korean dance. A corpus of two items is insufficient for drawing significant conclusions, but it does suggest a possibility of pursuing through analysis other dances to provide a sufficient database for articulating a common aesthetic principle of Korean dance. Focusing on other movement components (such as the use of time and body parts) or kinds of actions (such as rotary

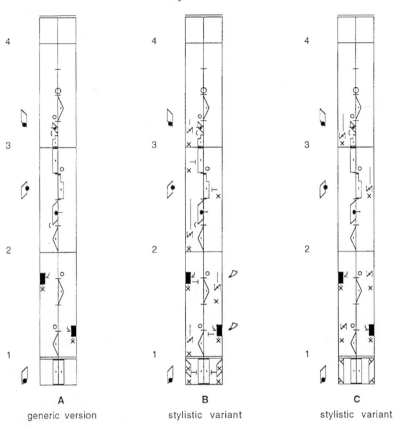

A	B	C
generic version	stylistic variant	stylistic variant

Figure 2   Notation of Footwork of *Soma Bon Uta*: Generic Version and Two Stylistic Variants (based on Van Zile, 1982, p. 66).

movements and contraction-extension) could then contribute to a complete picture of movement characteristics.

Capturing a dance in a notated script allows for an unlimited number of kinds of analyses. In 1977, for example, Kwok used the analysis of Labanotation scores to determine regional dance characteristics among the Paiwan ethnic group of Taiwan. She then compared these 'dance zones' to linguistic areas and concluded that dance 'dialects' paralleled linguistic dialects. The delineation of dance regions, together with tracing the migration of dances, is a common theme among Hungarian dance researchers, and Labanotation is a key ingredient in almost all their analyses (see, for example, Martin, 1979; Martin and Pesovár, 1961; Dömötör et al., 1990). In 1994 Reynolds based an examination of improvisation in Hungarian dance on Labanotation scores. In 1983 I analysed the score of an item from the *bharata natyam* repertoire of India to determine characteristics of the item as well as how it was choreographically structured. Aided by Labanotation scores, Gellerman in 1978 examined cultural attitudes evidenced in Hasidic dance.

Analyses based on Labanotation are useful in movement contexts. In 1981 Ohtani placed a musical score alongside a Labanotation score of Okinawan *kumi-udui*, a dance-drama genre related to Japanese *noh*, and analysed the relationship between movement and music. Requisite movements for drumming in classical Okinawan music were documented in Labanotation and analysed in a 1980 study by Sutton (assisted by a notator). Farnell's 1991 discussion of Native American storytelling was facilitated by Labanotation, and in 1988 I proposed a theoretical model, rooted in Labanotation concepts, for examining movement used in the music-making process.

In addition to freezing movement in time and supplying data for analysis, movement notation also provides a means for furnishing data to readers and communicating clearly about movement. In her analysis of Hawaiian *ha'a* and *hula pahu*, Kaeppler compares two versions of a dance in the repertoire of two different lineages that have perpetuated these traditions. She states that the execution in one version 'is much stronger' than in the other, and that the text is 'performed in a much more declamatory style. The movements, too, could be characterized as declamatory' (1993, p. 215). The volume containing Kaeppler's analysis includes Labanotation scores, and Kaeppler refers readers to a notated example demonstrating what she considers to represent a 'declamatory style' in movement (1993, pp. 99 and 248). Because not all of her intended readership are likely to know Labanotation, she also provides a verbal description informed by concepts embedded in the system (1993, p. 215). Although this verbal description accurately suggests the movement that substantiates Kaeppler's claim to a declamatory movement style, the Labanotation score contains more detail and 'states' those particulars more succinctly than the quantity of words needed to make a similar statement. Kaeppler's simple verbal assertion identifying a stronger, more declamatory style, together with reference to relevant portions of the Labanotation scores, convey, in a concise way, all the information necessary for the knowledgeable reader.[4]

Because notation is a non-word-based script, it allows for the communication of movement information without having to deal with language differences. Thus, dancers and researchers who do not share a common language can communicate a great deal about movement through notation.[5]

Notation may freeze a dance for analytical purposes, communicate complex information efficiently and allow the crossing of linguistic barriers; the principles underlying the system can prove invaluable for truly understanding movement, a prerequisite for producing a good movement score. In fact, some notation systems, based on writing decisions made by the notator, can represent the way movement is conceptualized from the perspective of the performer. For the researcher dealing with movement, eye training, the ability to perceive precisely what is happening, is critical and developing this ability is part of learning movement notation systems. Equally crucial, however, is the ability to understand how movement is conceptualized. For example, when notating a common sitting position in Labanotation, a Javanese dancer included signs stating that the pelvis was tilted forward-high and that the chest and head were each, also, tilted forward-high (see Figure 3A). The dancer's notation teacher, who was not familiar with Javanese dance, 'corrected' the notation by saying that a simple indication for the whole torso being forward-high was all that was necessary (see Figure 3B). Such a statement automatically means the pelvis, chest and head are included in the forward-high tilt; writing more symbols would be redundant. The teacher connected what she saw with some basic assumptions that can be made in Labanotation. The dancer, on the other hand, focused on how the movement is conceptualized within the tradition – an indigenous point of view. If the point of the notated score was to communicate the movement in the most economical way, the teacher's version of the notation could suffice. If trying to capture the way the dancer, and in this case the tradition, thinks about the movement, writing

A   B
Javanese dancer's version   non-Javanese teacher's version

Figure 3   Seated Javanese Dance Position.

more symbols would be more appropriate as well as invaluable for research.[6]

Other considerations surrounding the use of notation concern ethics and field research. Because a notation score creates a tangible artefact of an ephemeral event, it creates a lasting record. The same record which contributes to one of the major values of using notation may also result in a significant concern. For some performers (particularly in certain contexts), notating dance is much like capturing their soul in a photograph. Notation translates something from one medium into another, is most often created by someone other than the individual who created the original, and is an interpretation of the original. (If the job is done well, the interpretation will be accurate.) It therefore becomes critical to determine the appropriateness of ever creating a notation document. A former graduate student at the University of Hawai'i was sufficiently accepted by a group of Australian aboriginal women that she was allowed to witness secret events that included dance on the condition that she not make details of the event public. Despite her fluency in two movement notation systems, and her solid understanding of the activities, she could not make her research available to other scholars. She was, however, able to complete work on non-secret activities (see Morais, 1984). The first question that must be asked, therefore, is whether or not it is appropriate to notate a dance and, if so, whether the notation must serve simply as a form of field notes for the researcher or can become a part of the 'public record'.

Another question relates to how a dance will be learned by the notator. The researcher may notate the dance primarily from observation or learn the dance in order to utilize kinesthetic knowledge as the basis for the notation. She or he may prefer the advantages of a conspicuous location during an event and ask questions whenever she or he desires. Or indeed, the researcher may opt for a less obvious position on the sidelines and rely on more discrete procedures. Each method has advantages and disadvantages. If one notates from observation, either in performance or as a dance is being taught, it is easy to assume one is being objective; the researcher can see subtle differences in the performance execution of others and can listen to comments of audience members or teachers. By learning the dance, it becomes possible to know the dance kinesthetically. At the same time, however, it is easy to become so engrossed in one's own effort to master the movement that important cues (such as comments from a teacher to another student) may be overlooked. It is also possible that since one is an outsider to the tradition being studied (whether by virtue of being an outsider of the particular group involved or by virtue simply of being a researcher), inaccurate performance of the movements will be accepted, while they would not be if performed by insiders. The researcher then assumes accuracy when errors are present and the errors are incorporated into the notation. All of these issues must be considered in making choices (if they are available) regarding the context in which to notate, and effort must be made to counteract any negative impact. I have experienced these issues when notating in both contexts. By consciously shifting back and forth between both modes of learning, and by having others read and 'perform' the resulting scores, it is possible to work successfully in each context.

Whether one uses notation signs or words based on the meanings of such signs, it is possible to use a notation system as a shorthand during field research. While doing research on the Korean dance *Ch'ŏyongmu*, I wanted to determine how the dance was modified in various contexts. I was not concerned with differences in execution of specific movement phrases, but in seeing what was included or excluded from various versions. I had already created a full score of one version and then had the opportunity to view videotapes of other versions. The creation of a full score of the other versions was not necessary for my goal. While I was watching the videotapes I was able, without stopping them or playing them in slow motion, to jot down sufficient information to capture the entire choreographic flow of the dance (see Plate 7). I was then able to use these notes in conjunction with the full score to determine quickly, for example, which phrases repeated in the original version were executed only once in the alternate versions, which were left out and so on. The analysis necessary to produce the original score of the dance gave me a thorough understanding of its structure and performance details, and the notation signs provided me with an additional tool for taking 'movement notes' in real time (that is, as the movement was happening).

Likewise, after notating a large number of *bon odori* I realized that certain phrases formed a basic vocabulary from which movements were drawn in constructing dances. Since, within the tradition, a dance is comprised of a relatively short movement sequence which is repeated for approximately three to five minutes, when I observed a new dance for the first time, I was able to draw on my knowledge of the basic vocabulary and use notation signs to suggest complete phrases, which I could then fill out the next day at my leisure (see Plate 8A and B).

A common criticism levelled against notational systems is that they take too long to learn. The basic principles of most notation systems can be learned quite quickly; the ability to use them accurately, to produce meaningful scores, and to use scores as analytical tools, however, takes considerably more time. Learning to use notation fluently is somewhat analogous to learning to speak a language fluently. Learning fundamentals to facilitate the beginnings of solid movement description and analysis can be relatively speedy; many people can gain notation survival skills quickly. Becoming a proficient movement notator and analyst, however, demands mastering the skills of a specialist, which requires time and practice. But what dance ethnologist would consider going into the field without the requisite linguistic skills? Should she or he consider doing the same without requisite movement notation/analysis skills?

Another common criticism is that it takes a great deal of time to actually do notation. As described previously, notation can be used as a shorthand for notetaking in the field – a process that can, if desired, be combined with line drawings, sketches and verbal notes. Using a combination of these skills can be much quicker and more thorough than verbal notes alone. Additionally, complete, or highly complex, detailed scores may not be necessary for a particular research focus; the complexity needed in a score must be considered in relation to the use to which the score will be put.

Writing a complete score, however, does take time – just like any other kind of analysis or the writing of research notes and research presentations. Computer software such as LabanWriter for Labanotation now takes a considerable amount of work out of the mechanical production of the written score (that is, of drawing the symbols). Once decisions have been made on how to notate something, LabanWriter functions much like a word processing program and allows for the production of meticulously clear camera-ready copy and for easy editing of the copy. Computer tools are also being developed to assist in research analysis. Hungarian researchers are developing a program to facilitate the identification of phrases of movement repeated identically or in modified forms, a program that examines Labanotation scores (see Fügedi, 1995). While this has potential for speeding the research process by examining a large data source quickly, skilled notation specialists are still required to provide the data and to instruct the computer on its searches.

A significant concern that must be considered continually is the potential for an existing notation system to control one's movement perception and conceptualization. Linguists discuss how languages develop to express the particular concerns and ideas of a people. Despite the fact that movement notation systems are scripts and not languages (see Durr, 1981), and that at least some have developed to document movement of the human body apart from how it is used in any particular dance style, the frameworks on which they are built are based on certain ideas about movement. It is important, therefore, continually to see beyond the system in which one has been trained. The example of the Javanese dancer and the notation teacher is an important one to remember in this regard.

Rather than provide definitive explanations of the reasons for capturing dancing in a notation system or a comprehensive listing of all of the ways in which notation has been used or could be used by dance ethnologists, my intent has been to point out a number of key issues, and to propose that whether one ever produces a complete notation score or simply uses notation as the basis for various facets of research, movement notation skills are critical for the dance ethnologist. If one chooses to document dance or some other form of structured movement, notation can serve as an end in itself. If analysis is the desired goal, notation can provide a tool to achieve this end. One of the most important reasons for notating, however, is the contribution the notation process makes to understanding movement. The analysis required to notate movement provides ways to separate movement components and to conceptualize them; the process of notating automatically becomes a way to understand movement. This does not obviate the validity of dance-related studies by individuals from other disciplines; there is much to be gained from approaches such as anthropological, literary and religious studies of dance. The point is that *dance* ethnologists require dancing-related, that is, movement, documentation and analysis skills.

ACKNOWLEDGEMENT

I wish to express appreciation to Dixie Durr, Sheila Marion and Barbara B. Smith for helpful comments on an early draft of this chapter, and to Megan Morais for assistance with Benesh Movement Notation references.

NOTES

1.   See, for example, Blum, 1986; Chan, 1982; Guest, 1984 (especially
      chapters 1 and 2); Herbison-Evans, 1988; Reynolds, 1990; and Williams,
      1996. For a history of notation systems see Guest, 1989. For a discus-
      sion of using notation as a tool to identify individual dances, see Van
      Camp, 1981, chapter 4.
2.   Two other systems used today are Benesh Movement Notation (see
      Benesh and Benesh, 1969) and Eshkol-Wachmann Notation (see Eshkol
      and Wachmann, 1958). Labananalysis, often referred to today as LMA
      (Laban Movement Analysis) but originally known as Effort-Shape, is an
      analytical tool for describing and notating qualitative aspects of movement
      (see Dell, 1970). Although LMA and Labanotation (see Hutchinson, 1977
      for the major text on Labanotation) both originated from theories of
      Rudolf von Laban, Labanotation deals with structural aspects of move-
      ment. Labanotation practitioners often notate entire dances; some quali-
      tative features are inherent in the structural description. LMA
      practitioners seldom notate an entire dance. Instead, they notate repre-
      sentative qualitative phrases, or add qualitative indications to a
      Labanotation score. (For examples of ethnographic dance studies based
      on LMA see Ness, 1992 and Wenzl, 1997.)
3.   Kaeppler (see, for example, 1972) discusses whether a movement is dif-
      ferent or not based on how it is conceptualized by the performer. She
      argues that even though viewers may see what they consider to be a
      physical difference, if the performer considers the variations to be 'the
      same movement', there is no difference. Williams (in Williams and
      Farnell, 1990) discusses the importance of understanding the per-
      former's conceptual intent.
4.   Although Kaeppler's description of a 'declamatory' style may suggest
      qualitative aspects that might be described in LMA terms (see note 2),
      structural features obvious in the Labanotation score support this
      description.
5.   For discussions of the values of notational systems versus film/video-
      tape for documenting dance see, for example, Barnes, 1997; Guest,
      1984, chapter 2; and Williams and Farnell, 1990, p. ii.
6.   For additional examples of works using Labanotation, see Bartenieff
      et al., 1984; Foley, 1988; Iyer, 1994; Lange, 1988; Nor, 1986; Puri and
      Hart-Johnson, 1995; Shennan, 1991; Torp, 1990; Wolz, 1971; and Yoo,
      1995. For works using Benesh Movement Notation, see Grau, 1979,
      1983 and 1993; Marett and Page, 1995; Mirano et al., 1989; and Morais,
      1984, 1992 (which includes Labanotation) and 1995. For a work using
      Eshkol-Wachmann Notation, see Eshkol, 1988. Examples referred to
      here are not intended to be comprehensive nor to involve evaluative
      judgment of quality; they are included to suggest the varied nature of
      studies that employ notation.

96   *Judy Van Zile*

REFERENCES

Barnes, C. 1997. Dance in 2-D. *Dance Magazine*, LXXI, 5, May, p. 122.
Bartenieff, I., Hackney, P., Jones, B.T., Van Zile, J., and Wolz, C. 1984. The potential of movement analysis as a research tool: a preliminary analysis. *Dance Research Journal*, 16, 1, pp. 3–26.
Barwick, L., Marett, A., and Tunstill, G. (eds) 1995. *The Essence of Singing and the Substance of Song: Recent Responses to the Aboriginal Performing Arts and Other Essays in Honour of Catherine Ellis*, Oceania Monograph 46. Sydney, Australia: University of Sydney.
Benesh, R. and Benesh, J. 1969. *An Introduction to Benesh Movement Notation* (revised, extended edn). Brooklyn, New York: Dance Horizons.
Blum, O. 1986. The value of recording dance. In *Dance: the Study of Dance and the Place of Dance in Society. Proceedings of the VIII Commonwealth and International Conference on Sport, Physical Education, Dance, Recreation and Health*. London: E. & E.F. Spon, pp. 37–43.
Chan, L. 1982. The importance of notation to the development of dance. In *Singapore Festival of Dance '82* (festival programme). Singapore: National Trust Theatre, pp. 24-8.
Dell, C. 1970. *A Primer for Movement Description Using Effort-Shape and Supplementary Concepts*. New York: Dance Notation Bureau.
Dömötör, T., Hoppál, M., Niedermüller, P., and Tátrai, Z. (eds). 1990. *Magyar néprajz vi: népzene, néptánc, népi játék* (Hungarian Ethnography: Folk Music, Folk Dance, Folk Games). Budapest: Akadémiai Kiadó.
Durr, D. 1981. Labanotation: language or script? *JASHM: Journal for the Anthropological Study of Human Movement*, 1, 3, Spring, pp. 132–8.
Eshkol, N. 1988. *The Quest for T'ai Chi Chuan*. Israel: Research Centre for Movement Notation at the Faculty for Visual and Performing Arts, Tel Aviv University.
Eshkol, N. and Wachmann, A. 1958. *Movement Notation*. London: Weidenfeld & Nicolson.
Farnell, B. 1991. Nak'ota mak'oc'e: An American Indian storytelling performance. *Yearbook for Traditional Music*, XXIII, pp. 80–99.
Foley, C. 1988. Irish traditional step-dance in Cork. *Traditional Dance*, 5–6, pp. 159–74.
Fügedi, J. 1995. Analyzing dance structure and motive collections by computer – DanceStruct 1.0. In *International Council of Kinetography Laban: Proceedings of the Nineteenth Biennial Conference, 23–30 July, 1995*. Ohio: Ohio State University, pp. 71–82.
Gellerman, J. 1978. The mayim pattern as an indicator of cultural attitudes in three American Hasidic communities: a comparative approach based on Labananalysis. In Woodruff, D.L. (ed.), *Essays in Dance Research from the Fifth CORD Conference*. New York: Congress on Research in Dance, pp. 111–44 (*CORD Dance Research Annual, IX*).
Grau, A. 1979. Some problems in the analysis of dance style with special reference to South Africa. Unpublished MA thesis, Queen's University, Belfast.
—— 1983. Dreaming, dancing, kinship: the study of *yoi*, the dance of the Tiwi of Melville and Bathurst Islands, North Australia. Unpublished PhD thesis (Social Anthropology), The Queen's University, Belfast.

—— 1993. Gender interchangeability among the Tiwi. In Thomas, H. (ed.), *Dance, Gender and Culture*. New York: St. Martin's Press, pp. 94–111.

Guest, A.H. 1984. *Dance Notation, the Process of Recording Movement on Paper*. New York: Dance Horizons.

—— 1989. *Choreo-graphics: a Comparison of Dance Notation Systems from the Fifteenth Century to the Present*. New York: Gordon and Breach.

Herbison-Evans, D. 1988. Dance, video, notation and computers. *Leonardo*, 21, 1, pp. 45–50.

Hutchinson, A. 1977. *Labanotation or Kinetography Laban: the System of Analyzing and Recording Movement* (3rd edn). New York: Theatre Arts Books (originally published in 1954).

Iyer, A. 1994. Hand gesture in Indian dance. *Dance Studies*, 18, pp. 51–111.

Kaeppler, A. 1972. Method and theory in analyzing dance structure with an analysis of Tongan dance. *Ethnomusicology*, XVI, 2, pp. 173–217.

—— 1993. *Hula Pahu: Hawaiian Drum Dances. Volume I: Ha'a and Hula Pahu: Sacred Movements*. Honolulu, Hawai'i: Bishop Museum Press.

Kwok, M. 1977. Dance of the Paiwan aboriginal people of Pingtung County, Taiwan with implications of dance for tribal classification. Unpublished MA thesis (Music/dance ethnology), University of Hawai'i.

Lange, R. 1988. The dance folklore from Cuiavia. *Dance Studies*, 12, pp. 7–223.

Marett, A. and Page, J. 1995. Interrelationships between music and dance in a wangga from Northwest Australia. In Barwick, L., Marett, A., and Tunstill, G. (eds), pp. 27–38.

Martin, G. 1979. *A magyar körtánc és európai rokonsága* (Hungarian Folk Dance and its European Relations). Budapest: Akadémiai Kiadó.

Martin, G. and Pesovár, E. 1961. A structural analysis of the Hungarian folk dance: a methodological sketch. *Acta Ethnographica Academiae Scientiarum Hungariae*, 10, pp. 1–40.

Mirano, E.R. (researcher), Oshima, N.M. (photographer), Mirano, E.R., Roces, M.P., and Aquino, G. (concept), Villaruz, B.E. (dance notator), and Mirano, E.R. (music transcriber). 1989. *Subli: isang sayaw sa apat na tinig. One Dance in Four Voices*. Philippines: Museo ng Kalilnangang Pilipino.

Morais, M. 1984. A culture in motion: a study of the interrelationship of dancing, sorrowing, hunting, and fighting as performed by the Warlpiri women of Central Australia. Unpublished MA thesis (Music/dance ethnology), University of Hawai'i.

—— 1992. Documenting dance: Benesh movement notation and the Warlpiri of Central Australia. In Moyle, A. (ed.), *Music and Dance of Aboriginal Australia and the South Pacific: the Effects of Documentation on the Living Tradition*, Oceania Monograph 41. Sydney, Australia: University of Sydney, pp. 130–44.

—— 1995. Antikirinya women's ceremonial dance structures: manifestations of the dreaming. In Barwick, L., Marett, A., and Tunstill, G. (eds), pp. 75–93.

Ness, S.A. 1992. *Body, Movement, and Culture: Kinesthetic and Visual Symbolism in a Philippine Community*. Philadelphia: University of Pennsylvania Press.

Nor, M.A.M. 1986. *Randai Dance of Minangkabau Sumatra with Labanotation Scores*. Kuala Lumpur: Department of Publications, University of Malaya.

98   *Judy Van Zile*

Ohtani, K. 1981. The Okinawan *Kumiodori*: an analysis of relationships of text, music and movement in selections from *Nido Tekiuchi*. Unpublished MA thesis (Music/dance ethnology), University of Hawai'i.

Puri, R. and Hart-Johnson, D. 1995. Thinking with movement: improvising versus composing? In Farnell, B. (ed.), *Human Action Signs in Cultural Context: the Visible and the Invisible in Movement and Dance*. New Jersey: Scarecrow Press, pp. 158–86.

Reynolds, W.C. 1990. Film versus notation for dance: basic perceptual and epistemological differences. In *The 5th Hong Kong International Dance Conference – the Second International Congress on Movement Notation: Notation Papers*. Hong Kong: Hong Kong Academy for Performing Arts, pp. 151–64.

—— 1994. Improvisation in Hungarian folk dance: towards a generative grammar of European traditional dance. *Acta Ethnographica Academiae Scientiarum Hungariae*, 39, 1–2, pp. 67–94.

Shennan, J. 1991. Maori dance terminology. *Dance Studies*, 15, pp. 68–99.

Sutton, R.A. 1980. Drumming in Okinawan classical music: a catalogue of gestures. *Dance Research Journal*, 13, 1, pp. 17–27.

Torp, L. 1990. *Chain and Round Dance Patterns: a Method for Structural Analysis and its Application to European Material*. Denmark: University of Copenhagen, Museum Tusculanem Press.

Van Camp, J.C. 1981. Philosophical problems of dance criticism. Ph.D. dissertation, Temple University. (Available at <http://www.csulb.edu/~jvacamp/diss.html>).

Van Zile, J. 1982. *The Japanese Bon Dance in Hawai'i*. Kailua, Hawai'i: Press Pacifica.

—— 1983. Balasaraswati's 'Tisram Alarippu': a choreographic analysis. In Wade, B.C. (ed.), *Performing Arts in India: Essays of Music, Dance, and Drama*, Monograph Series No. 21 (Center for South and Southeast Asia Studies, University of California, Berkeley). Maryland: University Press of America, pp. 47–104 (reprinted in *Asian Music*, XVIII, 2, Spring/Summer, 1987, pp. 45-102).

—— 1985/1986. What is the dance? implications for dance notation. *Dance Research Journal*, 17, 2 and 18, 1, pp. 41–47.

—— 1988. Examining movement in the context of the music event: a working model. *Yearbook of Traditional Music*, XX, pp. 125–33.

—— 1992. The use of space in *Ch'ŏyongmu*. In *International Council of Kinetography Laban: Proceedings of the Seventeenth Biennial Conference*, 1-12 August, 1991. Ohio: International Council of Kinetography Laban, pp. 55–66.

—— 1996. The use of space in *Chinju kômmu*. In *International Council of Kinetography Laban: Proceedings of the Nineteenth Biennial Conference*, 23-30 July, 1995. Ohio: Ohio State University, pp. 39–51.

Wenzl, Z. 1997. Dancing for the Gods: a Movement Analysis of the Balinese *Topeng Tua* and *Pendet* Dances via Kinesthetic Description, Laban Movement Analysis, and Labanotation. Unpublished MFA thesis, University of California at Irvine.

Williams, D. 1996. The credibility of movement-writing. *JASHM: Journal for the Anthropological Study of Human Movement*, 9, 2, Autumn, pp. 73–89.

Williams, D. and Farnell, B. 1990. *The Laban Script: a Beginning Text on Movement-writing for Non-dancers*. Canberra: Australian Institute of Aboriginal and Torres Strait Islander Studies.

Wolz, C. 1971. *Bugaku: Japanese Court Dance, with the Notation of Basic Movements and of Nasori*. Providence: Asian Music Publications.

Yoo, S. 1995. Young-Sook Han's *Salp'uri chum*: Labanotation and stylistic analysis of a traditional Korean dance. Unpublished MA thesis, Ohio State University.

8 The *Choreographic Notebook*: a Dynamic Documentation of the Choreographic Process of Kokuma Dance Theatre, an African-Caribbean Dance Company

E. Jean Johnson Jones

AFRICAN PEOPLES' DANCE IN BRITAIN

In Britain, the performance of African peoples' dance is principally visible within a theatrical setting. Many of the dances seen on stage were formerly part of community-defining participatory rituals and have become dance events in which the traditional dances are standardized representations for an audience with little firsthand knowledge of African or African-related cultures. The term 'African peoples' dance' aims to reflect the complex diversity of dance and movement practices of both the African continent and the African diasporic cultures which can be witnessed in Britain. Introduced by dancer and choreographer, Peter Badejo (1993, p. 11), the term avoids the monolithicism of 'African dance' (see Kealiinohomoku, 1997 [1969–70/1983], p. 18) and has become common usage among people fighting for greater appreciation and promotion of African-derived dance, particularly as a theatre-dance artform.

From a dance anthropologist's point of view, the fact that these dances are staged makes them neither less interesting nor less amenable to ethnographic analysis. Undoubtedly, removal from their former contexts alters their meaning; but the movements of the staged dances maintain a cultural validity which can act as a window through which more understanding can be gained of the people who perform them. While Lomax's choreometrics project of the 1960s has rightly been criticized (see, for example, Williams, 1974) for its fundamentally flawed methodology and reductive evolutionist interpretation, his use of Birdwhistell's concept of a 'movement community' remains potentially fruitful for the movement analyst who wishes to study a theatrical dance company through the lens of dance anthropology:

> As Birdwhistell put it, 'Humans move and belong to movement communities just as they speak and belong to speech communities'.... There are kinesic 'languages' and 'dialects' which are learned by culture members just as speech is learned, and which have a matching distribution with speech, languages, and dialects. (Lomax, Bartenieff and Paulay, 1968, p. 229)

Of further potential use for the movement ethnographer of a dance company is Kaeppler's notion of 'structured movement systems' which she defines as 'systems of knowledge which are socially constructed...created by, known, and agreed upon by a group of people and primarily preserved in memory' (1992, p. 151). Dancing is thus a structured movement system which, if documented and approached anthropologically, may reveal aspects of the world view and values of a community that are otherwise difficult to access. This chapter discusses how ethnographic methods of a dialectical nature can be employed to create better comprehension and appreciation of a dance culture transposed into the aesthetics of the western proscenium arch.[1]

THE *CHOREOGRAPHIC NOTEBOOK* OF KOKUMA DANCE THEATRE

Historically, practitioners of African peoples' dance and their British audiences have not understood one another: a chasm of cultural difference has prevented the development of a common language through which the performer could communicate the character and intention of his or her work to the observer.[2] From 1996 to 1998, Kokuma Dance Theatre, one of Britain's major African-Caribbean dance companies, worked with the Labanotation Institute, based at the University of Surrey, Guildford, England, to develop a strategy to remedy this problem.

Founded in 1978, Kokuma Dance Theatre is one of the oldest African peoples' dance companies in Britain; its vision is 'to enhance enjoyment, appreciation and understanding of African and Caribbean culture and history through dance and music'.[3] The *Choreographic Notebook* project constituted the first attempt to document the work of a British company which specializes in dance of African and/or Caribbean origin, using Laban movement analysis. This system of movement analysis and documentation is more commonly associated with western dance forms. It was hoped that the particular project would lead to the evolution of a means by which the repertoire and choreographic intentions of any company specializing in African peoples' dance might be documented for posterity and better understood. The title, *Choreographic Notebook,* identifies the research project which first investigated the concept of a Labanotated score based upon the choreographic process, the methodology which developed from the project and also the final product itself: the name is derived from the methods by which a notebook is completed.[4]

Starting from the premise that it is the responsibility of the artist to make art accessible to the audience, it immediately became evident that practitioners of African peoples' dance in Britain need to be able to express their methods and intentions clearly in western discourse to people with entirely different perspectives from their own. Consequently, the methodology employed was dynamic, inclusive and process-oriented in order that the final product might reflect the combined effort of all the dance company members. This included the artistic director, choreographer, musicians and other staff who related directly to the Laban movement analysis. The objectives were to enable company members to benefit from an understanding of this particular system, to provide participants with an additional means of understanding and communicating their work, and to bridge the distance between movement analyst and artistic personnel.

A key individual in the formulation of the *Notebook* was the artistic director, Jackie Guy, who, born and educated in Jamaica, was instrumental in developing the distinctive repertoire and movement vocabulary of the company. A former member of the National Dance Theatre of Jamaica, where he gained his understanding of African and Caribbean dance forms, he was artistic director of Kokuma Dance Theatre from 1988 until 1995. During the course of the *Choreographic Notebook* project, it became necessary for Jackie Guy to grasp the fundamentals of Labananalysis – motif writing, Labanotation and effort/shape.

Introduced by Rudolf Laban in the 1920s as a symbol notation system which records movements of the human body, Labanotation has the capacity, when used by a trained movement analyst, to depict precisely the direction, duration and intensity of human motion through three dimensions of space. It is most commonly used in the world of dance, although the system can be applied to sport, physical therapy or any other area of life where there is a need for precise documentation and analysis of movement. The method has distinct advantages over the notoriously unreliable human memory, the cumbersome and subjective written word and even (though the two are often used together) the videotape which is two dimensional and often misleading.[5] In Laban's system of notation, symbols are standardized to represent parts of the body and the motions that they are capable of making. By combining symbols representing arms, legs, head and feet with those representing bending, stepping, folding, jumping or twisting, the Labanotator is able to record all the movements that a dancer's body executes during the performance of a dance.

While Labanotators are interested in the mechanics of movement – *what* part of the body moves through space – Laban movement analysts concern themselves with *how* the body moves through space. The Laban movement analyst breaks movement down into the elements of which it is composed: body, effort, shape and space. He or she examines the manner in which the body changes in response to internal and external stimulation, the energy flow which is caused by the movement and the qualitative dimensions of time, space and weight. The term Labananalysis is used in this discussion to include both Labanotation and Laban movement analysis.

LABANANALYSIS AS A TOOL FOR THE DOCUMENTATION OF AFRICAN PEOPLES' DANCE

The dance heritage transcribed in the Laban system of movement analysis and notation has been inventoried in *Laban Notation Scores: An International Bibliography* compiled by Mary Jane and Frederick Warner (1984). The text, along with its addendum, consists of more than 3,000 entries of which only 15 make specific reference to African peoples' dance. In addition, I have transcribed a further five dances which are archived at the Labanotation Institute. While the usefulness of Labanotation for the documentation of western theatre art dance has been acknowledged, its application to the documentation of African and Caribbean-derived dance forms has been questioned. The merits of documenting dance as part of both artistic and anthropological endeavours are well established, but with the exception of the University of Ghana, no national institution in Africa has considered any form of western movement notation to be appropriate for the systematic analysis and documentation of African peoples' dance. It is a view shared by most practitioners of African peoples' dance working in the west.[6] Obviously, great care must be exercized in utilizing intellectual strategies developed in other cultures, as Bohannan (1995, p. 78) cautions:

> One of the major flaws in social science occurs when a scientist allows a culture-bound story – or, more often, a theory developed in his own society or his own discipline – to become the basis for comparison.

There have always been questions about the flexibility of not only Labanotation but any system of notation to document this form, and whether or not the notator has the ability to shed his or her cultural biases in order to view objectively what is happening in a dance. A further challenge to this method has been made by dancers and scholars working with indigenous dance throughout Africa. Layiwola (1997, p. 1) acknowledges the merits of western methods of notation in having 'conquered three dimensions of space'; but he calls attention to what he describes as the fourth and fifth dimensions of African dance. These include non-material phenomena, empathy and story line which Layiwola claims are inaccessible to western documenters. Indeed, 'how will a simple notation which is sophisticated in the interpretation of form account for the empirical content of ... a dance?' (1997, p. 7). Harper, working in Africa in the 1960s, expressed general concerns about the appropriateness of dance notation:

> Dance notations, forms of symbolic transcription, are extensively used in Europe and America to record dance. However, these transcriptions are too reliant upon personal and cultural factors to be trusted as a recording technique in Africa where a vast amount [of] material of great variety needs to be recorded in field conditions. (Harper, 1968, p. 12)

Her notion of documentation in the field, however, suggests an older ethnological model of collection and transcription rather than the participant-observer, dialectical strategy which formed the guiding philosophy of the *Choreographic Notebook* project. The latter approach is more in sympathy with an ethnography which treats dance as social action rather than as artefacts to be collected.

The absence of a documented dance history which records the 'movement systems' and reflects the experience of practitioners of African peoples' dance as practised in the west needs to be addressed, whatever the shortcomings of notation systems. Of course, argument over the cultural relevance of western notation systems is not peculiar to dance study nor is it totally insurmountable: western music notation is used as a tool of communication, analysis and documentation among musicians throughout the world and, in this regard, shares many of the attributes of a lingua franca.[7] It may, after all, be possible for Labananalysis to fulfil a similar function, as Layiwola (1997, p. 5) comments:

> If indigenous music can be scored into notes, there is no reason why indigenous dances cannot be so reduced to script.

WORKING WITH KOKUMA DANCE THEATRE AND THE ROLE OF THE ARTISTIC DIRECTOR

From an academic perspective, the objectives of the project were to gather data towards consideration of dance in its cultural context; to present a structural analysis of one dance; to collect and archive published reviews of Guy's work; to analyse and evaluate textual descriptions; and to identify European influence on Guy's choreography. From the perspective of Kokuma, the undertaking proposed to analyse and preserve the artistic product and singular technique of the company; to facilitate the teaching and learning of the Kokuma approach to African-Caribbean dance; to add to the company's inventory of exportable material; to protect the company's exclusivity through the production of copyrighted material; and to expand the use and capability of the system of Labananalysis. The overall aim was to work towards mutually fulfilling these objectives.

The Kokuma project, then, consisted of the documentation in Labananalysis of the dance company's technique class, one dance from the company's repertoire and one work in progress. Over six months a system for the recording of dance emerged which was to have a major influence on the analysis and documentation of the dancing. Procedures for the gathering of data and the role of the artistic director in the process of documentation both represented significant departures from customary approaches, but were influential factors in the overall success of the project. It is usual for movement analysts to notate dance principally from observation at a

distance, assisted by videotape recordings of the choreographic
process. The Kokuma project, however, extended these strategies for
recording as its methods allowed for direct interchange between
notator and artistic personnel – choreographer, dancers and musicians. Following an ethnographic directive to achieve movement competence in the community under investigation, the notator became
part of the choreographic process. This necessitated physical engagement in the movement as well as interaction and collaboration with
artistic personnel during the course of movement sessions.

This method of work, however, is not without its problems; the level
of subjectivity implied may be perceived as threatening the validity of
the results.[8]

> As a consequence, observation of movement behavior made by the
> actual participants in the event itself may be less elaborate and
> detailed than the leisurely impressions cultivated by a spectator.
> Participant observers tend to see only as much as they need to see in
> order to be able to act or react in the on-going stream of interactions
> in which they are being immersed ... The participant must perceive
> movement behavior, interpret it, and properly intervene in the on-
> going movement event which is in flux ... However, the rewards are
> worth the effort. (Moore and Yamamoto, 1988, pp. 216–17)

Through the activity of physical engagement in the movement, not
only was a knowledge of the nature of the dance behaviour acquired,
but the foundation for kinesthetic empathy was laid. Moore and
Yamamoto explain,

> while the perception of movement of other human beings is primarily
> a visual experience, it can be heightened by what is often called *kines-
> thetic empathy*. Kinesthetic empathy involves physical identification
> with the movements one observes being executed. (1988, p. 53)

Layiwola (1997, p. 7) points to the notion of 'empathy' as one issue
surrounding the inquiry of the documentation of African dance:

> It is true that in Western dance forms, notes and story lines do
> accompany dance notation; but where empathy is necessary for the
> dancer's accomplishment, we are faced with a limitation.

Information gained from the 'doing' of the movement provided the
movement analyst with a means of communicating with the artistic personnel in the field situation; the analyst was able to pose questions and
to make comments about the dancing in 'their' (choreographer's,

dancers') terms. Participatory observation was a cornerstone that facilitated the integrity of the project. Through the process of 'physical engagement' the analyst was able to lay a base for kinesthetic empathy; a tool to be utilized for distance observation. Significantly, this procedure established a professional bond with artistic personnel; artistic staff felt certain that the analyst understood the work from 'their' point of view. The building of such a relationship provided the adhesive that would stabilise the final documentation of the movement. Such participatory observation may usefully become 'standard practice' when recording not only African peoples' dances in the west but also indigenous African dances, in an attempt to form part of a formula to provide the notation score with the 'empathy' called for by Layiwola.

When examining staged rather than ritual dances, there exists a level of communication between choreographer and notator which allows a dance to be recorded to the satisfaction of its creator. Rarely, however, does the author of a dance composition possess the knowledge of movement analysis that would enable him or her to document his or her choreography in Labananalysis; the designer of a dance relies upon a movement analyst to record his or her work.

If the project was to fulfil its purpose(s) an objective approach to movement analysis would need to be established. With the agreement of Guy, questions were posed and clarification sought during the course of rehearsal; this process was then elaborated upon at regularly scheduled 'analysis' sessions. The interaction which occurred within the rehearsal period proved invaluable. These sessions (which included both participatory and distance observation) enabled the analyst to understand how Guy conceived of, analysed and transmitted his work. This insight into his personal system of analysis formed a substructure on which to build a knowledge and appreciation of Laban movement analysis and Labanotation. An understanding of this system empowered Guy to make decisions on how his work was to be encoded and to record some of it for himself. As a member of the culture from which the dances that inspired his work had come, and having gained a tool of analysis through which to examine his choreography, Guy was in a prime position to record the contextual descriptions of his work. His approach was akin to that of a dance ethnologist for whom the focus is

> often on the dance content, and the study of the cultural context of the dance aims to help illuminate the dance ... The dance itself and changes over time are foregrounded. (Kaeppler, 1991, pp. 16, 17)

His role thus extended far beyond that of choreographer. Though not able to take full responsibility for the analysis and documentation of his work, he was in an extraordinary position, becoming proficient enough in his knowledge of the system of Labananalysis to discuss, clarify and, most importantly, to choose how his work was to be finalised. Rarely, does a choreographer develop (or care to develop) such a facility with this system. The understanding of Labananalysis, according to Guy, has had a fundamental impact on his teaching, choreography and viewing of dance in general. In his estimation, the experience has enabled him to look more objectively at his choreographic process and output, providing him with a valuable tool for critical evaluation. Through making decisions on how his choreographed movements were to be notated, Guy gained greater control of how his work will be interpreted and reconstructed in the future.

CONCLUSION

Through focusing on the repertoire of Kokuma Dance Theatre, the *Choreographic Notebook* was designed not only to analyse and preserve the artistic product of Kokuma Dance Theatre, but also to investigate the suitability of Labananalysis as a tool for the documentation of African peoples' dance. The dialectical strategy employed to collect data and the role of the artistic director in the recording process have both made a large impact on the final product of the dance score. Through such approaches, which necessarily integrate the ethnographer's experiences of participating in the movement, the Laban analyst can gain a closer, more intimate look at dancing and the culture from which it derives than previously. Participant-observation in this context demands the acquisition of movement competence and sharing of skills in which not only are both parties enriched, but a solid base is laid for the development of an archive of African peoples' dance and more widespread appreciation of its aesthetics and myriad forms.

NOTES

1.   Compare Glasser (1996) for an anthropologically informed process of transferring south African ritual dance onto the stage.
2.   See Gore (1994) for consideration of the perceptions of past documenters of traditional dance in West Africa from where many of the theatricalized performances of African peoples' dance in Britain are

derived. Oyortey (1993) is a useful discussion of reviews in the English press; for a wider discussion of African-derived cultures and the arts in general in Britain see Gilroy (1987).

3. Kokuma Dance Theatre publicised itself as an 'Afro-Caribbean dance company' in its 1990–1 season programme; the vision statement appears in its 1995 touring season programme.

4. The *Choreographic Notebook* of Kokuma Dance Theatre is to be produced as a three-part collection, beginning with *The Dance Technique*.

5. For a more detailed consideration of the relative merits of alternative means of recording movement in an ethnographic context see Farnell, 1994, pp. 937–54.

6. For texts on evaluating the appropriateness of Labanotation to record western theatre art dance see bibliography of Van Zile in this volume. The question of the system's relevance to African peoples' dance was raised by Peter Badejo during a public seminar entitled 'Modernity – What is Black Dance?' held at Ballroom Blitz on 14 August, 1993 (see Semple, 1993).

7. See, for example, Ellingson (1992a; 1992b) on transcription and notation in ethnomusicology.

8. For discussion of this problem in the context of dance anthropology, see Williams (1994).

REFERENCES

Badejo, P. 1993. What is black dance in Britain? *Dance Theatre Journal,* 10, 4, pp. 10–13, 47.

Bohannan, P. 1995. *How Culture Works*. New York: Free Press.

Ellingson, T. 1992a. Transcription. In Myers, H. (ed.), pp. 110–52.

—— 1992b. Notation. In Myers, H. (ed.), pp. 153–64.

Farnell, B. 1994. Ethno-graphics and the moving body. *Man: Journal of the Royal Anthropological Institute*, 29 [n.s.], 4, pp. 929–74.

Gilroy, P. 1987. *There Ain't No Black in the Union Jack: the Cultural Politics of Race and Nation*. London: Hutchinson.

Glasser, S. 1996. Transcultural transformations. *Visual Anthropology,* 8, pp. 287–309.

Gore, G. 1994. Traditional dance in West Africa. In Adshead-Lansdale, J. and Layson, J. (eds), *Dance History: an Introduction* (2nd edn). London: Routledge, pp. 59–80.

Harper, P. 1968. Dance studies. *African Notes*, 4, 3, pp. 5–28.

Kaeppler, A.L. 1991. American approaches to the study of dance. *Yearbook for Traditional Music*, XXIII, pp. 11–21.

—— 1992. Theoretical and methodological considerations for anthropological studies of dance and human movement systems. *Ethnographica*, 8, pp. 25, 151–7.

Kealiinohomoku, J.W. 1997 [1969–70/1983]. An anthropologist looks at ballet as a form of ethnic dance. In Williams, D. (ed.), *Anthropology and Human Movement, 1*. Lanham, Maryland: Scarecrow Press, pp. 15–36.

110   *E. Jean Johnson Jones*

Layiwola, D. 1997. The problem of literal documentation in African dance studies. Unpublished conference paper presented at Confluences: International Conference on Dance and Music, University of Cape Town, South Africa, 16–19 July 1997.
Lomax, A., Bartenieff, I. and Paulay, F. 1968. Dance style and culture. In Lomax, A. (ed.), *Folk Song Style and Culture*. Washington, D.C.: American Association for the Advancement of Science, pp. 222–47.
Moore, C-L. and Yamamoto, K. 1988. *Beyond Words*. New York: Gordon and Breach.
Myers, H. (ed.). 1992. *Ethnomusicology: an Introduction*. London: Macmillan.
Oyortey, Z. 1993. Still dancing downwards and talking back. In Thomas, H. (ed.), *Dance, gender and culture*. London: Macmillan, pp. 184–99.
Semple, M. (compiler). 1993. *Black to the Future I: a Report*. London: M. Semple. Papers from a seminar entitled 'Modernity – What is Black Dance?' held at Ballroom Blitz on 14 August, 1993.
Warner, M.J. with Warner, F.E. 1984. *Laban Notation Scores: an International Bibliography*. Michigan: International Council of Kinetography Laban. Distributed by the Dance Notation Bureau in New York.
Williams, D. 1974. Review number two: choreometrics ... discussion in Lomax, Alan, *Folk Song Style and Culture* (a staff report). *CORD News,* VI, 2, pp. 25–9.
—— 1994. Self-reflexivity: a critical overview. *JASHM: Journal for the Anthropological Study of Human Movement*, 8, 1, pp. 1–10.

9 Dance on Film: Strategy and Serendipity
Felicia Hughes-Freeland

As soon as moving cameras were invented, film-makers began to capture dance on film. And yet, 100 years on, the use of visual methods in dance research continues to be neglected in favour of representational systems such as dance notation. Against a background of debates about the contribution of visual methodologies to the development of cross-cultural understanding in social anthropology, this chapter argues for the value of film as a research tool in dance studies. Visual anthropology has a dual aspect. It is both 'the use of visual material in anthropological research' and 'the study of visual systems and visible culture' (Morphy and Banks, 1997, p. 1). The most lucid writer on anthropology and film is the film-maker David MacDougall who, as far back as 1973, suggested that we think of a film as 'an arena of inquiry', rather than as an aesthetic or scientific performance (1995, p. 128). MacDougall's arguments have contributed to my two film projects on Javanese dance, which have been part of ongoing research over nearly 20 years and which provide the focus of this chapter.[1]

THE ANTHROPOLOGY OF DANCE

Ritual and performance inevitably strike the outsider as significant because of their exotic appearance only. Dance analysis has tended to go behind physical appearances to seek out the meaning of embodied practices. There are two basic options for analysing dance: as 'patterned movement performed as an end in itself' or as it is 'shaped by cultural standards and values' (Royce, 1977, pp. 8, 216). An example of the first 'closed' approach is to analyse dance as a grammatical structure.[2] The second 'open' approach rejects the grammatical foreclosure in favour of what Hanna called a 'dynamic communication model' (Hanna, 1979) which distinguished three analytical domains of meaningfulness of dance: pragmatics (the relation of signs to interpreters); semantics (the relation of signs to contexts, and so to signification); and syntactics (how signs may be characterized, ordered

111

and inter-related). Anthropologists have tended to follow the 'open' approach, and have variously analysed dance as part of social situations: as a safety valve (catharsis theory), an organ of social control (functionalist theories), a cumulative process (theory of self-generation), an element of competition (theories of boundary display) and ritual process (Victor Turner's theory of communitas and anti-structure) (Spencer, 1985). Both approaches have been criticized by Best (1978) for their reductiveness. He also identifies a confusion between action and metaphor in the 'open' approach, and argues that dance should not be treated as a symbol of something; it *is* action in itself. So these models tended to regularize the dance event to a pattern by failing to account for unique factors which enter into a specific situation, and omitted disruption and contestation as extraneous factors bearing on meaningfulness. Ultimately, the two broad approaches either do not explain the variations in how audiences experience performances within the culture, or ignore them. They treat dance as text, rather than as action or practice. Even Ness's recent attempt to represent the iconicity of specific Filipino performances (Ness, 1992) slips into a textual account based on pragmatics which produces an homogenizing and essentialized account of 'culture' (Day, 1995, p. 130).

Currently there is a reaction against the 'textual' model of society and the dramaturgical metaphors of action-as-performance which refer to everything except dance and performance (Hughes-Freeland, 1997b). After developing his processual analysis of ritual, the anthropologist Victor Turner (1982) started to examine dance and theatre as performance, rather than as a part of ritual activity. Since his death, anthropologists have (belatedly) started to pay serious attention to performance as a phenomenological object, rather than solely to its metaphorization into meaning and text (Jackson, 1996). None the less, however much we return to what Foster has called 'the corporeal play that is vital to cultural production and to theoretical formulation of cultural process' (1996, p. ix), the dialectical relationship between the body and the imagination should not be overlooked (Johnson, 1987).

DANCE RESEARCH IN JAVA

The dancing body is here conceptualized not as universal and biological, but contingent on historical and social factors and constructions which are themselves transformed by the innovations and actions of individuals, deliberately or accidentally (Hughes-Freeland, 1997a). My research on dance has been shaped by Kaeppler's crucial arguments that dance cannot be separated from the stuff of social events and action; instead it is one of a number of 'movement dimensions' (Kaeppler, 1978, p. 47). What we might call 'dance' needs to be understood and constituted by the contexts of practice and understanding in which it occurs and is understood and discussed.[3] Dancing for me is not interesting as 'patterned movement' in itself, but as the physical dimension of human existence which is at once embodied and imagined, and I have researched dancing to examine how social values, real and ideal, are embodied. In other words, dancing is an activity situated in the body which cannot be understood sociologically without reference to notions of order, measure and proportion (Turner, 1984).

I have not used film or video in the first stage of research. In my first stage I used my own body to understand Javanese dance in the court of the sultan of Yogyakarta. I learnt Javanese systems of mnemonics for representing and remembering choreographies which I documented by means of still photographs. My approach differed from existing anthropological approaches to dance in both method and theory. Instead of looking at dance-as-language, dance-as-symbol, or even dance-as-dance (the existing alternatives in the late 1970s), I turned instead to local categories and connections about what movement is and what it measures under particular circumstances. There is no single word for dance in Javanese (Hughes-Freeland, 1997a); specific forms had specific associations with court ceremonial and ritual. These events had belonged to courtly life during the colonial period of Java which ended when the Japanese invaded in 1942. When Java became part of the struggle to establish the Indonesian Republic in 1945, there were new events and new words which turned these movement styles into something called 'dance'. So in this research, dance was analysed not simply as movement, but as movement as appraised and interpreted by its practitioners and connoisseurs.

BĚDHAYA ON FILM

In 1987 I spent three months in Yogyakarta shooting *The Dancer and the Dance* as part of a training in documentary film-making.[4] I was given a budget of £10,000, a three-month visa, and for two months the help of a fellow-student, Amy Hardie, who was in charge of the camera.[5] My roles were producer, translator, fixer, transcriber, sound recordist and, subsequently, editor. The objective was to produce a

visual counterpart to the verbal account of dancing presented in my
PhD thesis. But here was a challenge: how was I to extrapolate an
aspect of the research and convert it into a cinematic narrative of not
longer than 50 minutes? How was I to manage the transformation, a
shift from what MacDougall has described as a 'word-and-sentence-
base' to 'image-and-sequence-based anthropological thought' (1997,
p. 292)?

My documentary tutor, Herb DiGioia, had taught me that the most
important thing in documentary film-making is to 'bring it back alive'.
He showed us the classic example, a hunting scene from Robert
Flaherty's film, *Nanook of the North* (1922). Flaherty keeps his camera
low with the hunters, and he allows the shots to unfold, so that we see
the hunters pulling on the rope until the object of their efforts is
revealed: the walrus. Flaherty managed to keep the moment alive by
his use of timing and restraint, thus maintaining suspense. All the documentary students were encouraged to use developing shots, rather
than Hollywood style 'reverse angle' editing, to tell a story by following the action. To this end, where Flaherty had filmed on a tripod
without sound, we were trained in the spirit of the 'direct cinema' of
the 1960s to shoot from the shoulder in a choreographic collaboration
with the sound recordist. Equipped with these basics, then, my task
was to return to Java, and, somehow, to bring back alive on film the
dancing which had been on my mind since I had first seen it, ten years
earlier.

After much thought, I decided to concentrate on the most beautiful
and elaborate court form, the *Bĕdhaya* (Hughes-Freeland, 1991,
1997a), and present my research findings on this dance in the guise of
a portrait film. I intended to select a dance association preparing a
Bedhăya dance for a concert – ideally to be given in the court itself –
and to 'cast' a dancer who would provide a focus for the film's story,
which would follow her through the process of rehearsal and preparation, and conclude with her participating in the final performance.

Research always occurs within a time frame, and so did the filming,
which was scheduled to last two months. It was extremely fortunate
that the Siswa Among Bĕksa association was planning a *Bĕdhaya* as
part of a concert which would take place just before the film visas
expired. It was less straightforward to cast the dancer who would 'star'
in the film. It became clear that my first choice had transferred her
enthusiasms from dance to drum bands; an interesting story, but not
the one in production. Meanwhile, more drastically, during one of
many observation sessions in which I explained the dancing to my

camera woman and planned with her how to look at it through the lens, I discovered that the concert we had been hoping to film had been cancelled, indefinitely. We were half way through our shooting schedule, and had not shot a single roll. The film suddenly seemed very fragile, if not at death's door. What was I to do?

The following day the dance organization was giving a concert – but not with a *Bĕdhaya* dance – at a wedding. If we wanted to film a young woman being transformed into a dancer, we would have to do it there. The next day we shot eight out of 30 rolls of our precious stock:[6] the preparations for the wedding, the dancers' make-up, and, although we had not expected to be given access, part of the performance in the wedding itself, a love duet, *Langĕn Nawung Asmara*. By chance we had filmed Susindahati, who performed in the duet, while she was being made up. With the crucial transformation scene in the can *and* the subsequent performance, we had found our star. We later spent a day with her, from one evening to the next (scenes 3–5 in the film; see appendix).

After this we started to film *Bĕdhaya Gandakusuma* in rehearsal at Siswa Among Bĕksa (Plate 9). As this choreography lasted 90 minutes there was no possibility that it could all be filmed with one camera with our five hours of film stock. During observational sessions I had timed various sections of the dance in order to be able to fit them into ten-minute rolls of film. We had decided that our framing of the dance would start from the idea of Amy's camera participating in the dance formations, like a tenth dancer. We filmed over four rehearsals, and I subsequently selected sections in the order they appeared in the dance, and cut a ten-minute sequence. This would have been very difficult had my camerawoman not shot close-ups of the musicians. In the editing room I was able to use these close-ups to cut from one sample of the dance to the next to build up the correct choreographic sequence, although the different elements had not been filmed in that order. Before the dance starts, I used the sound from the sequences of my own dance teacher and choreographer of *Bĕdhaya Gandakusuma*, B.R. Ay. Yudanĕgara, against shots of Susindahati practising before the dance, so that the sound-image describes simultaneously how practical dance movement and dance theory produce the aesthetic of 'flowing water' (scene 7).

Meanwhile, another character had entered the film by chance. Pak Sena, a friend from my first period of research, asked me to film him singing Javanese didactic poetry. I agreed, though I was uncertain how the sequence would fit my imagined script. As the camera rolled and the lighting – hurricane lamps – exploded in flames, I put a question to him about how the moral verse related to dance. Initially annoyed at being interrupted, he soon warmed to his subject and explained a crucial theory of dance on camera (scene 6). This unplanned sequence yielded my missing link: Susindahati had discussed the physical problems of dance; now Pak Sena explained the theory. In order to bring the story and dancing back alive, I contrived for Pak Sena, who did not normally attend dance rehearsals, to come to one session to talk about learning dance and how he understood the *Bĕdhaya* we were filming.

This sequence was crucial in the editing. As my original idea for a closing scene had been destroyed with the cancellation of the concert, I reversed the film narrative. It would move *from* the fully costumed performance of the love duet about which the film's audience would know nothing, on to a portrait of the dancer's life and interest in the dance, then to an older expert's understanding, expressed in relation to the *Bĕdhaya* dance, a collective form in which we lose our individual dancer. Instead of a portrait culminating in a performance, the film's story moved from an external view of the *appearance* of the performance to a gradual revelation of its significance.

The slow pace of the film communicated the tempo of Javanese life when lived according to the conventions for polite interaction of which dancing forms a part.[7] This progress of the narrative, based on chronological events as filmed, also represented an important ethnographic fact: that the individual dancer in Javanese court dance has been subsumed into the collective form: the audience watches the dance, not the dancer. However, I closed the film with a shot of Susindahati riding off into her future on the pillion of her boyfriend's motorbike: into a future where the dance we had seen would no doubt become something different.

TAYUBAN ON HI-8 VIDEO

The role of women's court dancing defines Javanese ideas of polite femininity (Hughes-Freeland, 1995). This ideal is defined in contrast to the performance of professional dancers who are called *ledhek* or *ronggeng* (Hughes-Freeland, 1993). In 1989 I spent a year in Java researching cultural politics. In particular, I looked into different forms of patronage of performance, concentrating on court dance in an urban setting and the dancing of the *ledhek* at village events called *tayuban* at rituals held once a year and which form part of a sort of harvest festival. After a distribution of food, men dance with professional female dancers. Their allegedly sexual ethos makes these *tayuban* unacceptable as national culture, but the dancing is a gift to the protective spirit in exchange for well-being, and represents community identity.

I lacked the resources to take a video camera with me to Java in 1989, but when I returned in 1994 to review changes in the different venues surveyed five years earlier, I took a hi-8 video camera with me. The objective was to document a *tayuban*, if possible in the highland village where I had first witnessed the event, because it involved a daytime *tayuban* which was an offering to the protective spirit (Plate 10). I would also contextualize this dancing through interviews with dancers. Whereas luck had been against me in 1987, in 1994 when I arrived for a two-month visit in Yogyakarta, my research assistant in Yogya informed me that the *tayuban* I had hoped to film would indeed be taking place during my visit. There was a small matter of funding the event, as the sponsor had used up his resources on another ritual obligation, so I lent him £30 as a deposit to hire the dancers. The *tayuban* was on, and so was the film.

Unlike my previous film project, this filming was done during a period of intensive research into dance patronage, without a special shooting budget. I filmed on only three occasions: during the 24-hour activities at the village; on a short visit to the dancer's home village; and in a short interview with my assistant. I had hoped to follow the procedure of the 1987 film, and focus on a dancer I already knew, but unfortunately, the sponsor of the event hired dancers from another village whom I had not met before. This is evident in the rather awkward interview with the youngest dancer (scene 5). I only included the interview because it is revealing of Javanese gender relationships. The young dancer is muted and hardly gets a word in edgeways, as the (male) troupe leader and her mother hijack each question and provide answers which are sometimes contradictory.

While I was filming the event, I had already thought what 'story' the edited video would tell so that it would be useful for courses about dance or Southeast Asia instead of joining the piles of dance rushes I shot in Java and Bali without any thought for their purpose. I had planned to introduce the video with a sequence of photographs taken in 1989 to explain the event and the research context. I had hoped to close the story with a strong statement by a dancer about the pressures to modernize and refine the dancing, but this hope was not realized. I decided to close the film with an interview with my research assistant about the research. This made sense because the film had a reflexive dimension in the way I imagined (and produced) the opening, and had acknowledged his role in previous research. As he was a trained actor, he could be relied on to 'deliver' to the camera spontaneously. Most significantly, we had 'danced the village spirit' by paying money and making a vow so that Harjanto's eldest son would recover from a continuing cold.

This interaction between the research team and the event under examination seemed a highly appropriate element to identify in the film and to use as a conclusion. It identified the way in which current research methodologies and anthropological practice in general are attending to power relations in the construction of the research object, and to the role of dialogue and interaction. The broader 'context' for the event is summed up in a closing section of commentary, which describes how these dancers, who traditionally learnt by becoming apprenticed to an established *ledhek,* are disappearing. Governmental repression of *tayuban* is giving way to a revival as part of the heritage preservation programme which is also linked to the development of the tourist industry. When state-sanctioned *tayuban* take place, the performers are graduates of dance schools and academies. These dancers have been through various 'upgrading' programmes to learn movements inspired by court dance, but it is uncertain how much longer they will be able to earn a living from the dance. Their courtly counterparts dance for honour not cash in the refined circles of concerts and dinner dances for tourists, and earn much less than their village sisters. However, these village women are losing their professional status, as dancing is converted into polite culture which fits in an honorarium economy, rather than a viable system of material exchange.

CONCLUSION

Both films give a sense of the tempo of dancing in their different contexts of social interaction which is impossible to achieve in writing. There are longueurs in both films, which have long developing shots and a minimal use of interventionist commentary: the idea is to let the audience be exposed to an event as a sound-image construct, not pictures with explanatory words relentlessly superimposed. The ten-minute sequence of the *Bĕdhaya* feels much longer, and is a deliberate challenge to a western audience's conventional expectations of cinematic pacing. In the *tayuban* film, I used captions sparingly to clarify actions that are otherwise obscure.

Watching the two films together also gives a sense of the difference and similarity of the two kinds of dancing. First, we can see that the village dancing is of a different order from the high art of the court. After dancing until 4 a.m., the dancers are weary when they start dancing again at 10 a.m., and their movements are so minimal and unenthusiastic as barely to constitute performance. The energy-expending performers are the villagers who pay money to the local religious expert, who stands as the invisible spirit dances with the dancers and enjoys the music and singing, and the young men who use the occasion for a bit of social display and sexual bravado.

The films also provide striking images of femininity. Whereas in the court *Bĕdhaya* the women perform in a withdrawn, desexualized but highly focused and concentrated state, in *tayuban* the women are overtly sexual but performatively unfocused and unconcentrated. Their attention is dispersed around the event; they are not centred in their performance. This is why it is not always appropriate to use 'performance' as a category: the *ledheks* are present, but their dancing is almost a form of inaction. In contrast, the highly trained and rehearsed court dancers work hard to produce the effect of inaction, the easy fluid grace which conforms to the aesthetic of 'flowing water'; the village *ledheks*, whom Javanese people perceive as a total contrast to *Bĕdhaya* dancers, achieve a similar look of inaction because they have run out of steam. What is a deliberate aesthetic effect in one case, in the other is the result of too much work. Also, what appears to be rather formal and restrained dancing to us in the *tayuban* film, for the Javanese is wild and overly demonstrative and sexual.

These findings emerged from the making of the films, and from audience responses to them. Just as the making of the films resulted from a combination of strategy and serendipity, so too the research implications emerge interactively.[8] It is not only the film in the making which is an arena of inquiry. The showing of the film also reveals insights hitherto not observed because too familiar. My own films have elicited audience responses which make my familiar research become strange, and make manifest new understandings.

Methodologically, the two films give some – if not all – of the context whereby certain forms of human behaviour and skill become identified as dance, as art, as performance (Hughes-Freeland, 1997b). The contrast between the rhythms of the different contexts, and the field of interaction which prevails both during and around the events in which embodied performance occurs, can both be documented directly: the audience can get a sense of what it was like. More generally, I try in my work to let others speak – the dancers, the experts, the observers – in order to give students of anthropology or dance the chance to acknowledge that objects of study are not constructed out of purely theoretical projects, defined clearly (and scientifically) in advance. Rather, they emerge in the research, which may or may not enable certain situations to be observed and responded to. The filming, like traditional participant-observation, is determined by a process of planning and intention, which is disrupted by accidents and enhanced by serendipity. The editing of the film or video, like the writing of books and articles from field notes, is a matter of skill, training, and integrity. In both cases, bringing it back alive describes the objective of ethnography as a process and as a product, itself alive because unpredictable and interactive.

APPENDIX

The Dancer and the Dance

1. Preparing for a performance.
2. The love dance at a wedding.
3. Susindahati at home.
4. Susindahati at school.
5. Susindahati explains the difficulties of dance.
6. Pak Sena sings and talks about dance philosophy.
7. Dance training at Siswa Among Běksa.
8. Pak Sena explains learning to dance.
9. *Bědhaya* sample in rehearsal.
10. Pak Sena interprets *Bědhaya*.
11. Susindahati rides a motorcycle.

Tayuban: Dancing the Spirit in Java

1. Reflexive introduction with photographs.
2. Afternoon: food distribution; interview with the religious official.
3. Night-time *tayuban*.
4. Daytime *tayuban*.
5. Visit to the home of the youngest dancer for an interview.
6. Harjanto tells the anthropologist about his experiences at the *tayuban*, and the gift the spirit gave him.
7. Comment on the transformation of these village practices.

NOTES

1. *The Dancer and the Dance* (Hughes-Freeland, 1988) is 44 minutes long and is available on VHS or 16mm. *Tayuban: Dancing the Spirit in Java* (Hughes-Freeland, 1996) is 30 minutes long and is available on VHS. Both films are distributed by the Royal Anthropological Institute (50 Fitzroy Street, London W1P 5HS) and may also be rented from its film library.
2. Woodward (1976) analysed the Javanese *golek* dance using Javanese categories learnt during her dance training in Java but not in the way Javanese choreographers use them.
3. This approach is the opposite of Lomax's massive comparative choreometrics project (1995) or Williams's 'semasiology' (1982).
4. This opportunity was made possible by a Royal Anthropological Institute Leverhulme Film Training Fellowship at the National Film and Television School, Beaconsfield, England.
5. I had decided not to shoot the film myself as I anticipated, correctly, that being the person in the know in charge of the production would leave me too exhausted to muster the concentration to look and focus precisely, especially taxing when working with 16mm film.
6. At that time a ten-minute roll of film plus processing cost £40.
7. The 44-minute film had only about 60 shots – as many cuts as I counted in a 1-minute-long television advertisement. My editing was so economical that I was given a discount when the negative was cut in preparation for printing.
8. This fashionable emphasis on interaction in research was first emphasized by Scholte (1972).

REFERENCES

Best, D. 1978. *Philosophy and Human Movement*. London: Allen and Unwin.
Day, A. 1995. In search of Southeast Asian performance. *Review of Malaysian and Indonesian Affairs*, 29, 1–2, pp. 125–40.
Foster, S.L. (ed.). 1996. *Corporealities: Dancing Knowledge, Culture and Power*. London: Routledge.
Hanna, J.L. 1979. Movements towards understanding humans through the anthropological study of dance. *Current Anthropology*, 20, 2, pp. 313–38.
Hockings, P. (ed.). 1995. *Principles of Visual Anthropology* (2nd edn). Berlin: Mouton de Gruyter.
Hughes-Freeland, F. 1988. *The Dancer and the Dance*. London: Royal Anthropological Institute. 16mm/VHS, 44 mins; © National Film and Television School/Royal Anthropological Institute.
—— 1991. Classification and communication in palace performance. *Visual Anthropology*, 4, 3–4, pp. 345–66.
—— 1993. *Golek menak* and *tayuban*: patronage and professionalism in two spheres of central Javanese culture. In Arps, B. (ed.), *Performance in Java*

and Bali: Studies of Narrative, Theatre, Music, and Dance. London: School of Oriental and African Studies, pp. 88–120.

—— 1995. Performance and gender in a Javanese palace tradition. In Karim, W. J. (ed.), *'Male' and 'Female' in Developing Southeast Asia*. Oxford: Berg, pp. 181–206.

—— 1996. *Tayuban: Dancing the Spirit in Java*. London: Royal Anthropological Institute. VHS, 30 mins; © F. Hughes-Freeland and University of Wales, Swansea.

—— 1997a. Art and politics: from Javanese court dance to Indonesian art. *Man: Journal of the Royal Anthropological Institute*, 3, 3, pp. 473–95.

—— 1997b. Introduction. In Hughes-Freeland, F. (ed.), *Ritual, Performance, Media*. London: Routledge, pp. 1–28.

Jackson, M. (ed.). 1996. *Things as They Are: New Directions in Phenomenological Anthropology*. Bloomington: Indiana University Press.

Johnson, M. 1987. *The Body in the Mind: the Bodily Basis of Imagination*. Chicago: University of Chicago Press.

Kaeppler, A.L. 1978. Dance in anthropological perspective. *Annual Review of Anthropology*, 7, pp. 31–49.

Lomax, A. 1995. Audiovisual tools for the analysis of cultural style. In Hockings, P. (ed.), pp. 315–34.

MacDougall, D. 1995. Beyond observational cinema. In Hockings, P. (ed.), pp. 115–32.

—— 1997. The visual in anthropology. In Morphy, H. and Banks, M. (eds), pp. 276–95.

Morphy, H. and Banks, M. 1997. Introduction. In Morphy, H. and Banks, M. (eds), *Rethinking Visual Anthropology*. New Haven and London: Yale University Press, pp. 1–35.

Ness, S.A. 1992. *Body, Movement and Culture: Kinesthetic and Visual Symbolism in a Philippine Community*. Philadelphia: University of Pennsylvania Press.

Royce, A.P. 1977. *The Anthropology of Dance*. Bloomington: Indiana University Press.

Scholte, B. 1972. Towards a reflexive and critical anthropology. In Hymes, D. (ed.), *Reinventing Anthropology*. New York: Pantheon Books, pp. 430–57.

Spencer, P. (ed.). 1985. *Society and the Dance: the Social Anthropology of Process and Performance*. Cambridge: Cambridge University Press.

Turner, B. 1984. *The Body and Society*. Oxford: Blackwell.

Turner, V.W. 1982. *From Ritual to Theatre: the Human Seriousness of Play*. New York: PAJ Publications.

Woodward, S. 1976. Evidence for a grammatical structure in Javanese dance: examination of a passage from *Golek Lambangsari*. *Dance Research Journal*, 8, 2, pp. 10–17.

Williams, D. 1982. Semasiology: a semantic anthropological view of human movements and actions. In Parkin, D. (ed.), *Semantic Anthropology*, ASA Monograph 22. London: Academic Press, pp. 161–81.

10 Madness and Recall: Storied Data on Irish Dancing
Frank Hall

Back at [a teacher's home] after the world championships we sit around and have tea and people tell stories about competitions. One of the main themes is the tension involved. The theme also implies the judgement that people take it too seriously. The comment may be heard, 'All the fun has gone out of it'. One person mentioned that some competitors vomit after their performances because of the tension.

Mary told a very funny story about a woman, a teacher, who became ill because one of her students didn't get a 'recall'.[1] Mary and others abandoned what they were doing to take care of this lady. One of the people in attendance, however, kept giving out about the judging, fairness, etc., constantly raising the patient's blood pressure. A doctor was sent for and saw the patient but the madwoman wouldn't leave the room. The doctor finally came out and told the others that the patient wouldn't die unless the madwoman killed her with her bother. [laughter] ... The doctor said he had just one question, What is a 'recall'? [peals of laughter] When they explained, he said he had thought it had something to do with a seance. 'The sick woman kept muttering about a recall'. The doctor said whatever else happened that night he had learned that he would never send his children to Irish dancing. [more laughter] (Field notes, 26 March 1991)

The above notes were taken by the author in Limerick City in 1991. My interpretation is that the storytellers laugh at themselves, the seriousness with which they take this business of dancing: 'Sure, we're all mad, Frank.' In this story a woman becomes physically ill at the disappointment of defeat. This causation is understood by the other teachers. They go to her side; they even call a doctor. The 'madwoman', probably another teacher in attendance, brings up an always present and dangerous suspicion, that the competition is not fair, not objective, that social relationships influence the outcome of what is supposed to be a contest of pure cultural competence. It is ambiguous in the story whether her madness is only a matter of her timing and her 'bother' – the sick woman does not need this commentary at this time – or is she mad to dwell, at all, on the faults in the model of aesthetic competitions? The doctor, the objective outsider, recognizes the madness of both the haranguer and Irish dancing itself, which together are the occasion of the present drama and merriment.

I see the stories themselves as an enjoyment, full of humour, and delivered with style, in the rhythm and reciprocity of live performance and appreciation. They also accomplish important work for participants by organizing conflicting values and passions into moments of lucid perspective including, in this case, a critical appreciation of competition, its social and cultural effects, and the proper way to handle those effects. The stories reveal important dimensions of the activity to the teachers themselves; in this case, a glimpse from the doctor's perspective.

On this night when the theme of dealing with competitions emerged at tea, I did not recognize the significance of the stories being told, although I did recognize that they were somehow important. I wondered at the time whether I should get out my tape recorder. As it happened, one of my consultants suggested the same. I did not tape record, but later made field notes about events of the evening. These events include the story above, as well as the situated decision on the use of recording techniques and implied issues of objectivity and personal relations.

In deploying recording technology such as a video recorder, audiotape recorder, or camera, the dance researcher simultaneously confronts issues of objectivity and personal relations.

> Several times during the evening Cathleen says to me, 'You should be tape-recording this'. I joke and make light of it, saying all the while 'I should'. But my feelings are that a tape recorder would intrude into the 'crack' [fun] of the evening and give us all more pause before we speak. I resolve not to try to tape this kind of event, but rather raise questions and references to stories and such when talking to people in an interview setting. This is a choice that has to do partly with how I want to be seen and regarded among these (and really any) people. (Field notes, 26 March 1991)

This note records a negotiation between consultant and researcher. A young teacher recognizes the stories as data and says I *should* be taping. This is more than an invitation, it is a moral exhortation to enact my profession in a certain way. As it happens, I did not conform to her notion of what I should do. The note reveals a concern with my identity as a person as well as researcher. Although my reason for being there was manifestly to do research, I could not accept that as my sole identity. I also wanted to be a friend, someone who can enjoy a party. I wanted human relations beyond that of observer. In addition to this issue of personhood/social role, the note records that I felt the tape recorder would have an inhibiting effect on the activity. Thus, there are two dimensions to this very small crisis: a practical judgement about the appropriateness of a particular recording method, and personal judgement about how I could and should wear the mantle of dance researcher. These dimensions, now available to me through the note written later, were fused at the time in one decision.

I might have pulled out a tape recorder and had fine results. One question is whether I did the right thing from some putative standard of research methodology. I still wonder about the road not taken. A more germane point, however, is that, in the course of carrying out research, every investigator must confront his or her morals, identity, sense of mission, desire for multidimensional relations with consultants, and personal limits of various kinds, at the same time as making critical evaluations regarding how to register data. These are unavoidable requirements of participant-observation research.

These issues are to some extent personal, but they are not merely subjective. Personhood is not only a matter of individual opinion and psychological states, but a social accomplishment, a negotiation, a dialectical process of definition and redefinition between mutually interested actors.[2] The distinction between personal and subjective aspects of research is key because it implies important issues of knowing and theories of objectivity, which must be considered central issues in all research. There are subjective aspects to the note above. These include my feelings 'that a tape recorder would intrude' (opinion), and my desire to stress the participant side of my dual role (psychological state). But these feelings and desires enter the inter-subjective realm of personhood and social role through my interactions with the teacher in question. My identity and role are dependent to a certain degree on her reactions and those of the other people present. My consultants allow me to participate, or they do things to remind me of my observer status. Here, one teacher says to me, in an aside, that I should tape record. She does not insist and my judgement prevails, for better or worse.

In actuality, consultants treat me both ways, and I play both roles. This is the schizophrenic, if also productive, nature of cross-cultural participant-observation. An outsider can never participate as an insider. However, in participating to the extent possible, allowed by intersubjective negotiation, one gains knowledge unavailable to mere observers.[3] One year of fieldwork research on competitive Irish step-dancing revealed that understanding competition itself, as a model of human interaction, is one preoccupation of dancers, teachers, and participants of all sorts. Coming to this realization was a slow process of recognition, which included familiarization with the form and structure of the movement itself, the activity of dancing in a contest, the people involved, their relationships, the way they talked, their manners of joking and being serious, and so on.

The impossibility of making the study of dancing – the semantic aspects in which I am interested – a laboratory procedure may make it seem more like art than science. Here, in the management of social relations with consultants, there is a certain artfulness. However, the data produced, the methods of analysis, and the fit between results and reality are open to critical review and judged for relevance, validity and accuracy as they are in any science, and as they are not (or not necessarily) in art (Bruner, 1986); hence the concern for objectivity.

THE OBJECTIVITY PROBLEM

Scientific notions of objectivity have shifted dramatically since the mid-twentieth century. Connectedness appears where separation was assumed. Connectedness between observer and event, culture and science have emerged from scientific discovery itself, notably in particle physics and applied mathematics (see, for example, Kline, 1962). The shift from a Newtonian to an Einsteinian paradigm has brought out the participant nature of observational methods in experiment. In addition, the socio-political as well as metaphysical (ontological and epistemological) dimensions of research, so long denied by positivist science, have been shown to affect, even permeate, scientific practice and results.[4]

The problem of objectivity is apparently insolvable by procedural methods, because the facts of human knowing are tied to personal dimensions, further implicated in social and cultural forces.[5] Methodological Dualism, as sociologist Alvin Gouldner (1970, 1974) called the positivist paradigm, believed in the possibility of a value-free mind for the researcher, but not the layman. It held to a subject–object dichotomy which entailed a detachment of the researcher from the socially determined world in which the objects of his or her study lived. This inconsistency had to be maintained by various means, including 'self-obscuring' methodologies.

> That is, they obscure the sociologist from himself. The more presti-gious and 'high science' these methodologies are, the less likely it is that the sociologist will recognize himself as implicated in his research or will see his findings as having implications about himself.... Even if one were to assume that this serves to fortify objectivity and reduce bias, it seems likely that it would be bought at the price of dimming the sociologist's self awareness...the more rig-orous the methodology, the more dimwitted the sociologist: the more reliable his information about the social world, the less insightful his knowledge about himself. (Gouldner, 1970, p. 55)

It is no longer tenable to deny that researcher and subjects share the same world, a moral world where social and cultural forces and influences affect all occupants. If the positivist belief in a value-free mind has been exposed as acritical, amoral, anti-intellectual, alienat-ing and servile (Varela, 1984, p. 68), it has not been replaced by a new conception of objectivity, fully formed. Rather, it is a dialogue now ('one of *the* dialogues of our time' [ibid., p. 71]), which assumes a certain familiarity with the problems of what Varela called object-ivism, and Gouldner called Methodological Dualism. Objectivist notions of method have not simply disappeared. They play a mythic role in scientific practice, in part, because they hold some important truths and values. One of these is the value of objectivity itself. To reject the value of objectivity is to land oneself in the same acritical, amoral trap.

> Idealized notions of accountability, objectivity, and truth are prag-matic presuppositions of communicative interaction in everyday and scientific settings. They form the basis of our shared world and are the motor force behind expanding its horizons through learning, criticism, and self-criticism. In the encounter with other worlds they represent a major alternative to resolving differences through coer-cion, the alternative of reasonable dialogue. (McCarthy, 1991, p. 34)

If objectivity is to be embraced as an ideal and recognized as a problem, insolvable by procedural means, then how are we to proceed? Gouldner's answer is, with critical self-awareness. As Varela points out, for Gouldner, 'the recovery of the knower in the knowing process is the recovery of the knower as critic' (1984, p. 56).[6] Among other things this means a certain openness to 'bad news'.

> 'Objectivity', then, is not neutrality; it is realism concerning our own situation, desires, and interests. Here 'realism' means being aware of the continual vulnerability of reason to interest and desire, of the limits that interest and desire impose on rational discourse. (Gouldner, 1974, p. 10)

Gouldner's treatment of the objectivity problem is more intricate than is possible to summarize here. The relevant point, however, is that objectivity is not a matter of procedure in the sense of mechanically guaranteed neutrality of information. Rather, it is a critical self-awareness of our own situation, desires and interests, and their likely effects on our reasoning.

Critical awareness of the researcher is brought to bear on the whole process of research, from the formulation and reformulation of questions to the analysis and re-analysis of data in light of changing contexts of consideration. The very process of data registration is a matter of analysis requiring the critical application of recording technologies. Thus, one does not necessarily obtain more objective data by employing a tape recorder in a given situation.

TECHNOLOGY AS TOOL AND SIGN

To consider a tape recorder as a tool and a sign is to see one thing from two simultaneously extant perspectives or sets of concerns.[7] In fact, it is the relation between the functional and signifying aspects of the tape recorder that is of interest here. It is also instructive, however, to consider these aspects separately.

As a tool, a tape recorder registers real-time aural information as magnetic information and mechanically retranslates this information to sound on playback. The sound emanating from the speaker is very different from the phenomenal sound in the location of its recording (which itself varies depending upon the position of the listener/microphone). We have become familiar with the various kinds of distortion involved in this double, mechanical translation process. Distortion is something for which we can correct, or in spite of which we can preserve great amounts of information. We may be adept at interpreting the sounds coming out of the speaker and hearing 'what was said', for example. Even here we must recognize that 'what was said' refers only to that part of 'the what' that has been encoded in sound. As specialists in human movement know, there is more to language-in-use than the aural channel. The tape recorder is thus a selective device, as all recording devices are and must be, in that it records only sound. Tape recorders also deliver ambiguous audio information, as anyone who has transcribed a tape knows. Thus, interpretive skills at various levels of sound recognition (for example, phonetic, phonemic, environmental, electronic) are required, not to mention the many levels of content and context.

There is no technology that can avoid all or even most of these problems. Yet, because audio tape is able to record in 'real' time (as the sounds occur), it is a powerful tool. Information which was not recognized or not understood at the time can be rediscovered if preserved mechanically on tape. Also, it can be played back to consultants for their reactions, clarifications, translations, and so forth. This is a power of information storage which is not to be denied. It is also a power, however, that emerges only in combination with the memory and knowledge of participant(s) who can provide the many levels of context required to make the information understandable, that is, transform it into data. Information must be evaluated, selected, contextualized and indexed (in the widest sense of the term) to become data. All of this is a matter of connecting raw information to theory, that is, to knowledge.

Confronted with the power of the tape recorder, the question may arise: Why not always tape record? Several problems present themselves. First, the output of real-time recording requires a factor of processing time anywhere between one (to listen to what was recorded) and four (to transcribe clear conversation or monologue) times the recording length, or more. The fact is that a small amount of recording produces an enormous amount of information. If the process of registering data (connecting raw information with theoretical context) is left until after the participation phase, the researcher is then burdened with the nearly impossible task of processing mountains of audio tape. The alternative is to limit one's participant-observation research time or tape recording.

A second problem with always recording is that a tape recorder is not only a tool but also a sign. The researcher defines oneself in the process as an extension of that technology. The observer status of the participant-observer is continuously foregrounded. The participant status is at least qualified, if not contradicted in some deep sense by the consistency with which one's human capacities are subordinated to the observational occupation, like the cameraman who must be constantly looking for the photographic moment. This may produce a problem in social relations, matching the expectations and tolerances of consultants with the single-minded strategic actions of the researcher.

As a sign, the recorder affects the meaning of the event in which it is used, as it does the person using it. The fact that a tape recorder unselectively records audible sound is its power (for the researcher) and its danger (for the people being recorded). In order to have a minimum effect on the unfolding of the event, social relationships of mutual responsibility, trust, and reciprocal obligations must bind the people in whose presence the recorder is used. Even with felicitous relations, the tape recorder may shape the event by encouraging participants to monitor their speech, thus heightening the performance nature of the event.

This is not a problem to be avoided, so much as understood in the critical application of recording technologies. There is no possibility of being a 'fly on the wall'.[8] Each choice of means for recording data requires the critical evaluation of relative advantages and disadvantages. Trade-offs are built into the decisions. Mechanical means thus do not ensure objectivity and, in fact, introduce as many problems as they solve. All means of recording have their limitations. Field notes are highly selective in terms of what they record, but they reveal much of the context, especially personal aspects regarding perspective, assumptions, interests, and the like. For this they gain a certain authority, that of authorship. Audio recordings lack this situational and contextual information, but in their unselective real-time recording of sound allow for more exact rendering of acoustic information, in this case, stories.

STORIED DATA

The need for exact rendering of information ultimately depends on the research question and its relation to the particular phenomenon being observed and documented. Had I been researching storytelling as an art-form, the need for exact rendering, hence recording, would have been more acute. For research in dance, video recording and, especially, movement scripts are key for recording the movement. Talk, however, often informs the movement itself, the situations in which dancing takes place, the relationships of participants, even the model of the dance event, which in the case of Irish dancing is competition. In the realm of spoken language, stories often stand out as good data, because as a verbal art they are nicely packaged and highly expressive.

Often I did not understand at the time the full significance of the story I had heard. Such is the case with the story of 'madness and recall'. My original notes put the story in the context of dealing with tension. This aspect turned out to be fairly insignificant. It was rather assumed: of course competition makes people tense. The story weaves together more themes and perspectives than I could appreciate at the time. But I still managed to record the story, preserve the plot, and remember the laughter: all of which preserved its significance for later recognition. Who knows what stories I missed by not tape recording as advised by one of my consultants? Who knows what effect the recording machine would have had on the storytelling?

In one sense, it does not matter exactly which choices one makes in these 'on the ground' research methods. What matters much more is the sense of critical self-awareness one manages to keep in the process. In this sense we are much like the Irish dancers who howl with laughter at their own predicament, that in taking ourselves very seriously, we set ourselves up for jokes at our own expense, and recognize ourselves in earnest.

NOTES

1. A recall is the invitation from the judges to participate in the final round of the competition. Everyone who enters a competition performs two dances in a preliminary round, a light shoe dance (slip jig or reel) and a hard shoe dance with audible rhythm (hornpipe or double jig). Performers who are placed above a determined score get a recall, meaning they qualify to dance in the final round where they may perform one or two 'set dances' (hard shoe dance composed to a particular musical piece).

2. I rely on the notion of person as a fundamental concept found in the work of Strawson (1959 [1963], pp. 81–133), Grene (1966, pp. 152–6ff) and others, and as explicated by Varela: 'The fundamental importance of achieving a metaphysically rigorous conception of the person is that it enables him to demonstrate that the concept is a major solution to the problem of Cartesian dualism ... Strawson has shown that the person is lost in Cartesian dualism, and its restoration is realized by understanding that Cartesianism, against itself, in fact presupposes the person, and thus our primordial social being (1959: 101–3)' (1995, p. 254 *et passim*).

132 Frank Hall

3. Knowledge, here, means more than information. It includes the perspective and context which make information sensible.
4. The literature in the history and philosophy of science, dealing with this epistemic shift, may be regarded as beginning with Kuhn's *The Structure of Scientific Revolutions* (1962) and Polanyi's *Personal Knowledge* (1958), as Varela (1984) has argued. The point of this discussion will not be understood if considered in a postmodernist stance as a rejection of objectivity or the deconstruction of science as metanarrative. It is, rather, a more objective reckoning with human ways of knowing, a calibration of scientific method, so to speak. The work of Heisenberg (1959) and Mandelbrot (1982), for example, is decidedly within the metanarrative of science, a continually rewritten story of discovery in a knowable universe, including aspects of human knowing itself.
5. I am indebted to Charles Varela's article, 'Pocock, Williams, Gouldner: Initial Reactions of Three Social Scientists to the Problem of Objectivity' (1984). This discussion led to a rereading of Gouldner's *The Coming Crisis of Western Sociology* (1970) and *The Dark Side of the Dialectic: Toward a New Objectivity* (1974), and has greatly influenced this discussion.
6. The lesson that knowledge is personally located has taken all too well in some quarters, where ethnography has come to focus as much on the ethnographer as on the ethnos ostensibly being described. This may have its uses as a genre of anthropological writing. However, it is interesting to note that Gouldner argues it is the knower *as critic* that is essential to a new conception of objectivity, not necessarily the knower as a personality, history, psychology, and more. While these aspects of the person undoubtedly come into play in criticism, they are not necessarily required as focal information in ethnographic description.
7. All of these observations and issues apply, *mutatis mutandis*, to video as well.
8. The idea of a concealed tape recorder may present itself as a solution; however, even as a hidden sign, the tool and its use both signify and shape the event in a wider sense. For a start, the spy model invokes the subject-object split of the positivist paradigm and denies the role of the consultants as interpreters of their own actions. Again, the objectivity problem does not succumb to procedural solutions.

REFERENCES

Bruner, J. 1986. *Actual Minds, Possible Worlds*. Cambridge, Massachusetts: Harvard University Press.
Gouldner, A. 1970. *The Coming Crisis of Western Sociology*. New York: Basic Books.
—— 1974. *The Dark Side of the Dialectic: Toward a New Objectivity*. Dublin: The Economic and Social Research Institute.
Grene, M. 1966. *The Knower and the Known*. Berkeley: University of California Press.

Heisenberg, W.C. 1959. *Physics and Philosophy: the Revolution in Modern Science*. London: George Allen and Unwin.

Kline, M. 1962. *Mathematics: a Cultural Approach*. Reading, Massachusetts: Addison-Wesley.

Kuhn, T.S. 1962. *The Structure of Scientific Revolutions*. Chicago: University of Chicago Press.

Mandelbrot, B.B. 1982. *The Fractal Geometry of Nature*. Oxford: Freeman.

McCarthy, T. 1991. *Ideals and Illusions: On Reconstruction and Deconstruction in Contemporary Critical Theory*. Cambridge, Massachusetts: The MIT Press.

Polanyi, M. 1958. *Personal Knowledge: Towards a Post-critical Philosophy*. London: Routledge and Kegan Paul.

Strawson, P. 1959 [1963]. *Individuals: an Essay in Descriptive Metaphysics*. London: Methuen. Reprinted by Doubleday.

Varela, C.R. 1984. Pocock, Williams, Gouldner: initial reactions of three social scientists to the problem of objectivity. *JASHM: Journal for the Anthropological Study of Human Movement*, 3, 2, pp. 53–73.

—— 1995. Cartesianism revisited: the ghost in the moving machine or the lived body. In Farnell, B. (ed.), *Human Action Signs in Cultural Context: the Visible and Invisible in Movement and Dance*. Metuchen, New Jersey: Scarecrow Press, pp. 216–93.

11 It Takes Two – or More – to Tango: Researching Traditional Music/Dance Interrelations
Owe Ronström

INTRODUCTION

Within the second half of the twentieth century, music has moved from the realms of the special occasion to the everyday: from belonging to the 'Sunday sphere' of life, when work is over and all other duties are taken care of, music has become a major component of everyday life's soundscape. At the same time, from being an activity for the few, those especially inclined, gifted or wealthy, music has become a pursuit in reach of almost everyone. To a lesser extent the same is true for dance: take Sweden as an example. Here, well into the twentieth century, dance was seen as an activity merely for the young. It was customary to stop dancing after marriage or at least after the arrival of the first child. Today, dance is a favourite activity not only among the young, but also among the middle-aged and the elderly. 'Senior dance', a genre of specially designed 'folk dances' for the elderly invented in Germany in the mid-1980s, has become a popular dance genre in Sweden since the early 1990s, and continues to spread fast (Ronström, 1994).

To meet this development, the music industry has made an almost infinite number of dance and music styles, genres and so forth globally available. These constitute an enormous palette of expressive forms through which people can express and communicate the most detailed and nuanced messages about themselves: who they are, what they stand for, their wishes, dreams and hopes. In the past, literature was regarded as a sound indicator of personal interests, affiliations and values: today, it is more likely to be the record collection.

Such radical changes have made music and dance newly central to the formation of individual and collective identities, local, regional, national and international; to ways of socializing and networking; to the world economy, as the music industry has become one of the largest capitalist concerns in the world, and to the allocation of cultural and economic capital and power; and much more. Two major consequences are, first, that any attempt to understand contemporary human life, culture and society that ignores the serious consideration of music and dance will be inadequate and misrepresentative. Second, instead of dwelling on the peripheries of academia, ethnomusicologists and ethnochoreologists have now taken on a new and crucial role in research on human life, culture and society.

FIELDWORK

Greater insight into the complexities of contemporary human life may be gained through the method of 'thick description' advocated by anthropologist Clifford Geertz (1975).

Such descriptions can only be produced through meticulously performed fieldwork. Initially at least, music and dance researchers often possess an advantage over fieldworking colleagues from other disciplines. Much of what is important to people is performed backstage, in the private sphere, well covered, sometimes even hidden. Access to these areas of life is often restricted for outsiders. In contrast, it is not usually difficult to gain access to the arenas where music and dance are performed. As entertainment and pleasure, these pursuits are happily shared, even with ethnomusicologists and ethnochoreologists; yet, they may carry intense meaning and significance for the participants.

If access is easy, the rest is not. For many reasons, research in music and dance is a notoriously difficult task. One problem lies in the discrepancies between insiders' and outsiders' perspectives: the 'emic' and the 'etic'. The cognizance of the community being investigated is seldom the same as that of the newcomer from the outside. A second difficulty is the disjunction between the feelings and experiences of those involved in the music- and dance-making and the aural and visual perception of the more removed onlooker.

Most music and dance research has been restricted to observation from the outsiders' perspective, leading to interpretation from a distanced position. A third and perhaps most important problem is the necessary verbalization of observations in the research process. Many individuals in western societies have some knowledge and competence in music and dance, but often this extends only to *doing*. Few are able to provide verbal accounts of their engagement in music or dance, and here I refer not only to a lack of specialized, technical and analytical language. Indeed, most people appear not to talk much about music and dance at all; rather, they do it. Even when they do talk, their words may seem disassociated from their actual practice. Relatively trivial statements such as 'It is our tradition, you know', 'We have always done it like this' or 'Because I like it' frequently belie the complexity and significance of the activity. This may well result in isolating the music and dance researchers with their own observations and interpretations, trapped with their own words.

It is essential to remember that music and dance are about *doing*, and that whatever research is about, it concerns, first of all, *words*; the acquisition of at least some competence in performing the dance and music being investigated may go some way towards bridging the distance between the experiences of researcher and researched.

ONE UNIT OR TWO INDEPENDENT PRACTICES?

Music and dance, so tightly knitted together, are often perceived of and treated as separate phenomena. While is true that, in certain parts of the world, music and dance are two entirely different practices, this is certainly not the rule. On the contrary, in most parts of the world, music and dance are considered as one unit. The separation into two different practices has led to a number of questions concerning the interface between music and dance: what are the relations between music and dance? how do musicians relate to dancers, and dancers to musicians? which comes first, the music or the dance? what aspects of the music are important for dancers? Such questions have been regularly, if not frequently, addressed in ethnomusicological and ethnochoreological research over the years (see, for example, Dabrowska and Bielawski, 1995).

The interrelations between music and dance are both obvious and obscure: obvious in that people do dance to music and musicians play for dancing; obscure since, as already noted, there are problems of perception, description and analysis. A productive way to address some of the difficulties is to approach the study of music and dance, not as two independent expressive forms, but as parts of a larger and more important analytical level: the *event*.

In academic discourse, it has long been customary to treat music and dance as abstract 'texts' that can be laid out and analysed as concrete items of art. This practice has resulted in a distinction between the main object of analysis, that is, the text, and the time and place where the music and dance are performed, that is, the context. The latter has frequently been treated as a secondary source of additional and less important information, but this is to turn things upside down.

Music and dance are, in fact, situated performances; therefore, the situation, the time and the place of performance cannot be over-looked, or ruled out as less important or, indeed, less interesting. An event is not a mere context, but *the* text itself, the primary unit of observation and analysis.

Such an approach to music and dance as situated performance and event may run contrary to some established academic research prac-tices, but in fact accords more closely with the perspective that musi-cians and dancers tend to take; that is, the *performance* perspective. In the 1970s, this perspective was developed, mainly by American folk-lorists such as Dell Hymes (1972), Roger Abrahams (1977, 1981), Dan Ben-Amos (1971) and Richard Bauman (1975, 1986) into a theory of expressive forms and aesthetically marked behaviour of different kinds. They insisted that to start from a story, a piece of music or a dance before consideration of the situation or context was to proceed backwards, because oral poetry, music and dance are communicative processes which are primary forms of existence. Dell Hymes drew a distinction between *behaviour*, which is anything people do, *conduct*, which is behaviour according to social norms and cultural rules, and *performance*, which is when one or more persons take on a special responsibility for how some behaviour is performed (Hymes, 1972). Performance is a mode of communication that binds actors and audi-ence together by producing a mutual focus not only on what is com-municated, but on *how*. More could be said about performance theory, but my intention here is not further examination of this per-spective on music and dance, but presentation of some examples of what this approach achieves.

In 1984, I started what became an eight-year research project among Yugoslavs in Stockholm and in Yugoslavia (Ronström, 1992). My idea was, through detailed ethnographic fieldwork, to investigate the role of music and dance in culture-building among migrants. With tape recorder and video camera, I set out to record all the music and dance I encountered and soon found that music and dance, as sepa-rate, independent activities, had little relevance to the people being studied. What mattered were the weekly dance evenings, the organ-ised folk music and dance rehearsals and the Yugoslav 'cultural events' where such *folklor* (a staged folklore presentation) was displayed to an audience. Changing my perspective from that of music and dance as objects and products to that of events, processes and performances, I soon realized further dimensions to record than simply the tunes and steps.

To begin with, at a *zabava* (pl. *zabave*) or *igranka,* that is, a dance evening, there were of course the musicians, young professional or semi-professional singers and instrumentalists of Yugoslav origin, hired to play for dancing: and so they did, for 4–6 hours, with only a few short breaks. Then there was the paying audience, Yugoslav families from all over Stockholm, coming to dance, sing, drink and eat. And so they did, partly because there actually was little else they could do: the music was normally so loud that talking had to be reduced to occasional screaming remarks, except in the short breaks. The focus was on the dancing of round dances, such as *kolo, vlasko kolo,* a slow dance in 7/8 known in Stockholm as *makedonija,* and a few others.

In addition to musicians and dancers, there were others who, without actively participating in the dancing or music-making, played a more invisible, but nevertheless very important role. These included the people responsible for setting up the room, collecting entrance fees, serving food and drink, and so on; often they were board members of the arranging associations, or their families and friends. Organization of a *zabava* was not always easy, and it soon became clear that there was no reason to exclude such personnel from my studies, since the success of the event hinged as much upon their efforts as those of the musicians and dancers.

Another perhaps even more important part of the audience that seldom took an active part in the dancing or music-making was the elderly. Among the Yugoslavs, dancing was perceived as a collective phenomenon, which concerned not only the musicians and dancers, but the whole community. The role of the elderly was to represent this community, by carefully watching the dance, listening to the music, commenting upon who dances with whom, who is behaving properly and who is not. Therefore the dancing could not happen in the dark, as a restricted concern of dancing individuals, as in most other dance events in Sweden. Instead the dancing was for all to see, in full electric light. Only when the band occasionally shifted to 'modern western dance music' were the rooms darkened, so as to mark the beginning of something of less interest to others than the dancers themselves.

A TANGO FOR TWO, OR A ROUND DANCE FOR FOUR
OR MORE

By transferring my focus from 'music and dance' to 'events', it became evident that an important reason for arranging dance evenings was actively to socialize the young generation, mostly born and brought up in Sweden, into the Yugo-Swedish community in Stockholm. Important to the older generations were not only that the young could talk their parents' language, but also that they could sing their songs, dance their dances and enjoy their traditional food. Through the *zabave,* the young were introduced to all kinds of behaviour and conduct important to their parents: from how to eat, talk, and dress, to how to stand, walk, and move. Among the older Yugoslavs, young Swedes were often regarded as ignorant and sloppy, often because of a somewhat more indistinct movement style. To the older generations, 'being Yugoslav' in Sweden included an upright carriage of the body and the use of distinct, controlled movements. One of the very few sources where such behaviour, marking the important border between 'us' and 'them', could be learnt and internalized was the dancing.

Thus the *zabave* were not only a tango for two, musicians and dancers, but more akin to a round dance for at least four; the personnel and the elderly being equally important as the other two. At some events there was another influence on the dancing and music-making that proved a little more difficult to apprehend: this concerned judgements on the contemporary performance of the music and dance which stressed the 'here and now'. This form of evaluation is concrete and specific, prioritizing communication between the people present and thereby reinforcing social relations: a successful ('authentic') performance thus produces 'a good atmosphere' and brings people closer together. But among the Yugoslavs there was often another competing criterion against which the performances could be valued and judged. Rather than emphasis upon the contemporaneous, this measure of success concerned the 'there and then', 'history', 'tradition' or simply 'the way we always have done it', thus appealing to the general, abstract and absent while stressing the formal and the individual.

By this yardstick, a good, authentic performance is one that carefully reproduces old, highly formalised and legitimized patterns of behaviour, irrespective of how they are received in the present. Evocation of this criterion allows for the invitation of all the musicians and dancers of long ago, who together created and passed on the music and dance, to take their place alongside the present performers, thus influencing and shaping their performances.[1]

Both the 'here and now' and the 'there and then' horizons were always available to the Yugoslavs. At the *zabave* the 'here and now' horizon was the norm, but at any time the 'there and then' could also be introduced, consequently changing the focus, mode of interaction, and meaning of the event. At the *folklor* both performers and audience usually filtered their communication through a 'there and then' horizon, outside their direct control, which they called 'down there', 'our old traditions' or 'the Yugoslav way'. There were also instances when the musicians and dancers started to invest such energy, intensity and competence into their performances that this horizon shifted into the background and the 'here and now' became more relevant for the interpretation and evaluation of the dancing and music-making.

As my main unit of observation and analysis, the event became a prism, in which my searchlight could split in several directions: the microlevel of steps and tunes; the intermediate level of human relations, interaction patterns; and the macrolevel of tradition, history, culture and society. All these levels were enacted simultaneously at the events. Now my understanding could approach that of my informants. It was exactly in this way that most musicians and dancers apprehended what they were doing: not as tunes or steps, nor as 'culture' or 'tradition', but as interaction, communication through certain expressive forms, of which steps and tunes, as well as culture and tradition, are constitutive parts.

WHO FOLLOWS WHOM?

The question of who is leader and follower in a dance and music performance is one sometimes discussed among ethnomusicologists and ethnochoreologists. In theory, there are limited possibilities: the dancers follow the musicians; the musicians follow the dancers; both parties in some way or another follow each other; or the musicians and dancers do not interrelate at all.

A quick glance at music and dance traditions throughout the world reveals that all these theoretical possibilities have their empirical counterparts. In most parts of Europe the rule is for the dancers to follow the musicians, as for example in Serbia, where there is a traditional saying: 'start to dance when you wish, finish when you may' (Mladenović, 1973). In Central Asia and India, there are highly developed genres in which the musicians carefully follow the dancers. Filming over the tabla player's shoulder, in an Indian *kathak* performance, revealed how the dancer controlled the performance through small and intricate signals to the musicians.

According to Elliott, the ideal in English morris dancing is a complete sympathy between the music and the dance. When this happens, 'it may be impossible to sort out who is leading and who is following, although both are occurring constantly' (Elliott, 1995, p. 187). The same ideal is also common among fans of the traditional Swedish *polska*. Some fiddlers believe that it is impossible to be a good dance musician without being an experienced dancer. In practice, though, many traditional fiddlers do not dance very well, preferring the freedom to play their favourite tunes rather than selecting the particular dance repertoire. My own experience is that a common attitude among Swedish folk musicians is: 'I don't care if and what they dance as long as I can play what I want'. Many Swedish folk dancers claim that dance and music have to follow each other closely, but in reality it is usually enough if the musicians can provide a steady beat and good rhythm.

There exist some performances in which a totally disjunctive relationship between dance and music appears to be the only other plausible explanation. The Swedish ethnochoreologist Mats Nilsson, in his research into dance life in Gothenburg from 1930 to 1990, found among some elderly workers a type of dancing called 'sailing'. This is a kind of waltz, often performed to medium tempo foxtrot music; the fun of it seems to lie in *not* relating to the beat, rhythm or tempo of the music (Nilsson, 1991). Even then such an 'anti-relation' is of course a relation, although somewhat unusual.

If the relationship between dance and music in any genre seems obvious enough at a general and abstract level, a closer look will reveal a much greater complexity. Again, performance theory can be helpful, because of its focus on the event as a whole and on communication between the performers. The interaction between musicians and dancers depends on the type of event, arena, style or genre, level of formality and competence; a change in any one of these factors can completely transform the overall communication. As already noted, in Western Europe the rule is for the dancers to follow the music, but when performing informally, the musicians and dancers may interact so closely that it is hard to tell who is following whom. If the level of formality rises, both parties can start to interact with a real or imagined audience, outside the event itself. When folk dances are performed on stage, both the dancers and the musicians can start to reproduce the music and dance as if it were existing objectively, and as if they themselves were part of a script everybody had to follow. In such cases the role of the musicians is often reduced to a secondary, merely accompanying role, even if the script prescribes the musicians to take a leading role. This gap between what is supposed to be and what is actually performed is sometimes so great that unintentionally a comic effect is produced.

The dance–music relation can also change, of course, within one and the same event. Much is dependent upon who is in focus, who is performing and 'where the action is' (to paraphrase Goffman, 1967). During a fieldtrip to Transylvania, Romania, I and some colleagues more or less stumbled into a gypsy wedding in a small village not far from Cluj. After the prescribed ceremonial and ritual music, the band continued with dance music. The tunes were combined into long sets, up to 20 minutes or more, beginning with a slow couple dance, the *purtata,* passing through a number of couple dances in a constantly rising tempo, and finishing off with a *hrtag,* a couple dance in a wild, breathtaking tempo. To begin with, the musicians took the lead; the violinist and the singer alternated as primary focus of attention. The wedding guests were obviously stimulated by the interest from the unexpected extra guests, but even though some of the attention was directed towards the dancers by our video camera, it was clear that the musicians were in charge. After some time, when the dance couples were warmed up, they began to increase their intensity; their jumps became higher, their leaps and turns more complicated. Towards the end, the focus of the performance had moved from the musicians to the space in between the musicians and the dancers, and at the very end, when approaching the absolute maximum tempo, the two performing parts finally merged into one closely interacting unit. After a short break the musicians moved on to the next set of dances, repeating the same scheme. A little later the musicians were asked to play the *fecioresc rar,* a solo dance for men. One by one a number of young men jumped up to dance, directly in front of and facing the musicians. Now it was the dancers who were in charge. The musicians followed the many intricate leaps and jumps very carefully, slightly changing tempo when needed, emphasising accents with beats on the drum and so on. After some five or six men (and one woman) had danced, the band shifted back to the couple dances, thereby again taking the lead.

Much of the answer regarding who is following whom concerns the level of competence and intensity of the performance. An increase of competence and intensity can change the flow of interaction even in one and the same dance. In Stockholm in the mid-1980s a Yugoslavian association had invited a gypsy brass band from southern Serbia to perform during a three-day *zabava*, in memory of the legendary Vuk Karadzic. Many people attended and the band willingly played whatever traditional and modern dances were requested: *kolo, cacak, cocek*, and many more. They took little, if any, notice of the dancing going on around them, owing to, I later understood, their discontent with the dancers' level of competence, most of whom were young 'Yugo-Swedes'. Late on one of the evenings, however, a young talented male dancer arrived and at once took the lead of the *kolo* round dance. His exquisite dancing prompted the musicians to turn their instruments towards him, following his footwork as closely as possible. The increased competence and intensity of the dance performance almost immediately moved the focus from the musicians to the dancers.

CONCLUSION

Music and dance are meaningful expressive forms which communicate important messages about people, culture and society. Detailed ethnographic study of dance and music, therefore, facilitates a better understanding of people's lives but only in conjunction with a perspective that leaves room for more than just the tunes and steps, which for so long have occupied music and dance scholars. As music and dance are primarily situated performances, much of the understanding depends upon approaching the event as a main unit of observation and analysis.

NOTE

1.   The argument here is based on Berger and Luckman, 1979; Bernstein, 1964; and Schutz, 1951 [1964].

REFERENCES

Abrahams, R. 1977. Toward an enactment-centered theory of folklore. In Bascom, W. (ed.), *Frontiers of Folklore*. Boulder, Colorado: Westview Press, pp. 79–120.
—— 1981. In and out of performance. *Folklore and Oral Communication* (special issue), pp. 69–78. Published by Zavod za istrazivanje folklora, Zagreb.

Bauman, R. 1975. Verbal art as performance. *American Anthropologist*, 77, pp. 290–311.
—— 1986. *Story, Performance and Event: Contextual Studies of Oral Narrative*. Cambridge: Cambridge University Press.
Ben-Amos, D. 1971. Toward a definition of folklore in context. *Journal of American Folklore*, 84, pp. 3–15.
Berger, P.L. and Luckman, T. 1979. *Kunskapssociologi: hur individen uppfattar och formar sin sociala verklighet.* Stockholm: Wahlström and Widstrand. (Originally published in 1966 as *The Social Construction of Reality: a Treatise in the Sociology of Knowledge*. New York: Doubleday).
Bernstein, B. 1964. Elaborated and restricted codes: their social origins and some consequences. In Smith, A.G. (ed.), *Communication and Culture: Readings in the Codes of Human Interaction*. New York and London: Holt, Rinehart and Winston, pp. 427–41.
Dabrowska, G. and Bielawski, L. (eds), *Dance, Ritual and Music: Proceedings of the 18th Symposium of the International Council for Traditional Music Study Group on Ethnochoreology,* Skierniewice, 9–18 August, 1994. Warsaw: Polish Society for Ethnochoreology, Institute of Art, Polish Academy of Sciences.
Elliott, J. 1995. Who follows whom? The music and dance relationship in Cotswold morris dancing. In Dabrowska and Bielawski (eds), pp. 175–88.
Geertz, C. 1975. Thick description: toward an interpretive theory of culture. In Geertz, C., *The Interpretation of Cultures: Selected Essays*. New York: Hutchinson, pp. 3–30.
Goffman, E. 1967. *Interaction Ritual.* New York: Doubleday Anchor.
Hymes, D. (ed.). 1972. *Reinventing Anthropology*. New York: Pantheon.
Mladenović, O. 1973. *Kolo u južnih Slovena* (Round Dance of the south Slavs). Beograd: Srpska akademija nauka i umjetnosti, knjiga 14 (Serbian Academy of Science and Art). Published PhD thesis.
Nilsson, M. 1991. To sail – a way of dancing. In Buckley, A., Edström, K.-O. and Nixon, P. (eds), *Proceedings of the Second British-Swedish Conference on Musicology: Ethnomusicology,* Cambridge, 5–10 August, 1989 (Skrifter från Musikvetenskapliga institutionen, 26). Göteborgs, Sweden: Department of Musicology, Göteborgs Universitet, pp. 357–60.
Ronström, O. 1992. *Att gestalta ett ursprung: en musiketnologisk studie av dansande och musicerande bland jugoslaver i Stockholm* [Giving Form to an Origin: an Ethnomusicological Study of Dancing and Music-making among Yugoslavs in Stockholm]. Stockholm: Institutet för folklivsforskning.
—— 1994. 'I'm old an' I'm proud!': dance, music and the formation of a cultural identity among pensioners in Sweden. *The World of Music: Journal of the International Institute for Traditional Music*, 36, 3, pp. 5–30. (Published in Berlin by VWB Verlag für Wissenschaft und Bildung).
Schutz, A. 1951 [1964]. Making music together: a study in social relationship. In Schutz, A., *Collected Papers: vol 2, Studies in Social Theory*. The Hague, the Netherlands: Martinus Nijhoff, pp. 159–78.

12 It Goes Without Saying – But Not Always
Brenda Farnell

Mind and action are revealed in an intimate embrace.
(Clark, 1997, p. 33)

INTRODUCTION

In the late 1960s, as an undergraduate student of dance at a women's physical education college in northern England, I was already painfully aware of the extremely tenuous and marginal position held by the study of dance and dancing in the British educational system. There were no departments of dance in universities at that time, a state of affairs that sent a loud and clear message: the academic world completely devalued what I found most meaningful. Imaginative compositions of cultural and artistic value which structured the medium of body movement in space/time apparently did not count as 'knowledge' from the prevailing academic perspective. This dismal situation was not improved by many arts educators of the time, who frequently undermined their case for the educational value of the arts with spurious or muddled philosophical arguments.[1] In the Western world (that is, western European and derived societies) it is widely assumed that what we call 'the arts' are merely for entertainment and enjoyment from which nothing of significance can be learned. The arts in general, and the dance in particular, are regarded as peripheral, expendable, and of no great importance in education as compared to, say, mathematics and the sciences (Best, 1992, p. xii).

One spring day during my final year of study, we were treated to an inspiring guest lecture from an African-American dancer and scholar, Dr Pearl Primus. She had studied the dances of some West African nations, and introduced us to the exciting and complex world of West African dances and music that memorable afternoon. With a naïveté matched only by my enthusiasm, I decided, on the spot, that I was going to go abroad to study dances and dancing in places where such activities were deemed central to the culture and held in high esteem, in marked contrast to my own. I determined that I, too, would go to Africa and study 'primitive dance'.[2]

A few years later, I did indeed finance myself on a journey to West Africa for the purposes of studying 'primitive dance', convinced that all I needed to understand the dances of another culture were my own experiences as a dancer. I had uncritically accepted what was frequently implied, if not explicitly taught, during my modern dance training: that movement and dance were 'universal' and that the language of the body transcended all cultural and linguistic boundaries. Given this assumption, I reasoned that adequate understanding of whatever dances I might come across in Africa, regardless of their cultural context, could be achieved through careful observation and a commitment to learning how to perform the dances in question. How completely naïve and mistaken my reasoning was soon became apparent as I tried to carry out my plans.

One particular hot and humid Nigerian night found me in a remote village on the edge of the Niger Delta, more than two hundred miles from the town of Port Harcourt. There I sat, the only non-Nigerian at the gathering, unable to speak a word of the local Igbo language and without the assistance of anyone who could speak English. I was courteously placed in what I can only assume was a seat of honour, next to a man who was clearly of some importance in the village (I supposed he must be a 'chief'). There followed the most astonishing (to me) and thrilling displays of dancing and drumming that continued all night. I sat there hour after hour, watching intently, smiling at my host occasionally in the hope that it would be interpreted by him as an expression of my pleasure, and I recorded some of the music on my portable tape recorder. I deeply regretted that I did not have a *National Geographic* photographer or a BBC camera crew in tow to film the dramatic events as the dancers, both male and female, leapt and twirled with tremendous agility and power toward and away from the large central fire, their huge shadows amplifying every move against the dark green backdrop of the jungle night.[3] In my notebook I wrote furiously, trying to describe who and what I was seeing, using words and the descriptive terminology of Laban's movement analysis as best I could.

And then it happened: like Saul on the road to Damascus, it suddenly dawned on me that what I was writing down was what I thought they were doing – *I had no way at all of knowing what they thought they were doing*. In other words, I was busy interpreting and making judgements about the meanings of their body movements and their uses of the performance space entirely according to my own language and culture. Without being able to talk to the villagers in their own language, I could not possibly know what it all meant *from their perspective*. What were these steps and movements called in their language, if anything? What choreographic rules did they employ for combining movements one with another? What sorts of gender relations existed between these men and women who danced? What did those actions symbolize in their society and how did they conceive of space/time and the body itself? My naïve assumptions about 'universality' were completely shattered at that point and I stopped taking notes immediately, stunned by my new found wisdom. I realized with considerable dismay that I did not possess the necessary skills to do what I was trying to do.[4]

I preface this chapter with what are now rather embarrassing aspects of my 'personal anthropology'[5] because I continue to encounter similar misconceptions among would-be researchers about what kinds of knowledge and skills are required to understand dances and other systems of body movement in their cultural context. In this chapter, I attempt to show why careful observation and personal experience of dancing/moving are necessary, but not sufficient, for understanding human movement practices from an anthropological perspective. I proceed from semasiological theory[6] and take the position that detailed attention to spoken discourse must enter the research agenda, not because spoken language should act as a model for theories of body movement, but because human beings are language users, and the mind that uses spoken language does not somehow switch off when it comes to moving. Ways of talking with words constitute an integral part of what people do when they 'talk' from the body[7] through visual/kinesthetic modalities such as dances and gestural systems, and there are important connections between these two kinds of semiotic practices at several levels.[8] The human mind is not compartmentalized into separate faculties and so practices that relate concepts of space/time, movement, the body, and action to wider cultural beliefs and values frequently provide sites where visual/kinesthetic utterances and vocal utterances integrate. I call these 'simultaneities' because the term succinctly captures the human capacity to integrate concepts and practices across different modalities as we learn, create and apply knowledge and understanding to the world in which we find ourselves. 'Simultaneities' bring mind and brain back into the world of embodied activity.

THE LIMITS OF OBSERVATION AND EXPERIENCE

Let us start from the semasiological premise that human bodily movement, or 'action-sign systems',[9] in addition to providing the physical
means for embodied activity in the world, are simultaneously a
dynamic expressive medium used by embodied persons for the construction and negotiation of meaning. From an anthropological perspective, the meanings of perceivable actions involve complex
intersections of personal and cultural values, beliefs and intentions, as
well as numerous features of social organization.

> It is social taxonomies of the body and the semantics attached to
> space and time, as they emerge in specific cultural contexts and his-
> torical moments, that create, and are created by, the signifying
> person. (Farnell, 1995b, p. 2)

Such culture-specific resources are 'invisible' in the sense that they
cannot be ascertained or understood simply by watching people move.

Neither can they simply be 'experienced' through active participation. Since action-signs require translation from one culture to
another, two important points emerge: (i) actions that might look the
same will not mean the same across cultural and linguistic borders,
unless borrowed, and (ii) what will be experienced through participation is necessarily filtered through the semantics and structure of the
bodily language(s) one already knows, one's general cultural and linguistic background, and one's imagination. Attempts to perform unfa-
miliar action signs – a new idiom of dance, say, or a martial art – will,
at first, be crude imitations without comprehension, not unlike pro-
nouncing the words of a spoken language one does not understand.
However skilfully copied, without understanding the concepts of the
body and space/time specific to that system, such imitations remain
devoid of their intended meaning and so cannot provide the 'same'
experience for an outsider as they do for a knowledgeable insider.

Some investigators have posited the existence of a pre-cultural, pre-
cognitive, pre-linguistic realm of 'lived experience' to which we can
appeal for instantaneous cross-cultural understanding when it comes
to the body; as if the sheer fact of embodiment allows one to inhabit
the world of the other. Unfortunately, such a view constitutes a
romantic misconception that is, in fact, underpinned by an appeal to
biological determinism. It entails a metaphysics of person that is
extremely problematic from an anthropological perspective, because it
requires a subjectivist separation of body from mind, which in turn

must entail a separation of 'body' from the whole realm of cultural contexts, beliefs and intentions.[10] Some preliminary discussion of such metaphysical assumptions will help clarify the problem.

METAPHYSICAL ASSUMPTIONS

Best succinctly summarizes an important aspect of the prevailing western philosophy of mind and person when he identifies a 'Myth of the antithesis between Feeling and Reason' (1992, p. 7).[11] This involves the common misconception that 'there is necessarily an opposition between, on the one hand, feeling, creativity and individuality and on the other hand, cognition and reason'. This leads to a conviction that the 'creation and appreciation of the arts is a matter of subjective feeling in the sense of a "direct", "inner" subjective feeling, "untainted" by cognition, understanding or rationality' (Best, 1992, p. 3). Best advocates that this unexamined adherence to a subjective/objective dualism be abandoned in favour of the idea that 'artistic experience is as fully cognitive and rational, and as fully involves learning and understanding as any other subject in the curriculum' (1992, p. xii).[12] This over-simple, and ultimately unintelligible, subjectivist account undermines any educational grounds for inclusion of the arts in the curriculum, for how can there be education if understanding and cognition have no place (Best, 1992, p. 4)? Such a position also undermines anthropological investigations because if understanding and cognition have no place, then there is no means by which we can investigate dances and dancing, and no cultural understandings to translate. Even on the subject of feeling and emotions we are silenced, because the subjectivist account ultimately reduces feelings to sensation.

The antithesis between feeling and reason is just one among a number of related pairs of oppositions, often called Cartesian or Platonic–Cartesian dualisms, which have long-standing roots in Western notions of individualism and the subsequent bifurcation of the embodied person into a body plus a mind (see Figure 1). One consequence of this metaphysical doctrine can be seen in the disembodied social theory that has informed mainstream socio-cultural anthropology until recently. It has meant that most anthropologists, socialized according to the mores of western academia, find it hard to imagine what bodily movement might 'mean' at all, far less contribute to our understanding of social and cultural practices (Farnell, 1995b,

mind	body
logic and reason	emotion
thinking	feeling
language	non-language
verbal	non verbal
spirit	matter
culture	nature

Figure 1   Some Platonic–Cartesian Dualisms in Western thought.

p. 4). The traditional method of 'participant-observation' has frequently meant 'to stand aside from the action, take a point of view
and ask endless questions' (Jackson, 1983, p. 340), rather than participate in bodily activities and so discover cultural knowledge through
signifying acts done with bodily movement, in addition to signifying
acts done with words. It is no surprise to find that 'mind' and 'agency'
are associated explicitly with spoken signs and the 'body' stands as a
mechanistic or experiential other.

Unfortunately, the bifurcation of person (mind/body) and communicative practices (verbal/non-verbal) that contributed to this disembodied, objectivist approach to field research has also given rise to an
untenable subjectivism on the part of some western dance educators
and researchers. Ironically, perhaps, instead of rejecting dualistic
thought as untenable, the Cartesian agenda is upheld through an
appeal to the mystique of the dance as a 'non-verbal' activity rather
than a *non-vocal* activity. The opposition between 'verbal' and 'non-
verbal' communication inadvertently separates language and our reasoning minds from the rest of our bodies such that gesture, posture,
facial expression, and the uses of interactional space are reduced to
sensate mechanisms.

What are we to make, then, of statements such as Isadora Duncan's
when she said, 'If I could tell you what it meant there would be no
point in dancing it'?[13] Certainly she is correct, if she meant to reject
the notion that there is a spoken language version of the meaning of a
movement performance that somehow echoes in the mind of the
mover or observer. She may also have been trying to make the point

that her dances involve a symbolic transformation of human experience into a choreographic form with its own structure and semantic
content that had to be understood in its own terms. They were not
necessarily 'about' anything outside that, in the sense of having char-
acters and a narrative storyline such as those found in classical ballets.
It would be a mistake, however, to interpret Duncan's statement to
mean that such non-narrative danced meanings have no cognitive
content, or that they cannot be talked about.

It is instructive in this regard to watch and listen to any dance
teacher or choreographer of modern dance or ballet at work, instruct-
ing dancers in the correct performance of a particular action-sign or
sections of a new work. Students learn the basics of the technique, and
the rules concerning the structure and semantics attached to their
chosen idiom, not in silence, but through the simultaneous use of
speech and action. Successful teachers are often those who put creative spoken metaphors to skilful effect: evoking appropriate imagery
and understanding that results in changes in the student's kinesthetic
concepts and neuro-muscular patterning and so in their physical performance. Likewise, choreographers frequently employ metaphorical
language to explain and demonstrate simultaneously in order to
achieve the desired nuances in a dancer's performance. We cannot be
said to know very much at all about how these kinds of pedagogical
procedures are employed in different cultural contexts, but we can
anticipate that such processes will vary enormously.[14]

If we accept the semasiological recommendation that adherence to
a Cartesian metaphysics of person compromises our anthropological
understanding of dynamic embodiment, how then might we proceed
to investigate such 'simultaneities'? The concept of 'action-sign' brings
a post-Cartesian embodied model of person and agency into the discourse and substantially realigns how we might conceive of relationships between speech and action. This leaves us free to pursue
fieldwork strategies that preserve the simultaneities shared across
expressive modalities as they occur in performed cultural events.

COLLECTION, TRANSCRIPTION AND TRANSLATION OF DATA

In order to illustrate just a small fraction of the ways in which paying
attention to spoken language meanings can be central to understanding action-sign systems, I will draw upon three occasions from my own

field research into Plains Indian Sign Language or Plains Sign-Talk (hereafter PST). The examples illustrate how important indigenous concepts were ascertained through conversational dialogues with consultants during the transcription and translation process.

At the northern end of the Great Plains of North America lies the state of Montana and within it, Fort Belknap Indian Reservation. In this community, traditional Assiniboine stories are told by a few elders who remain fluent in Plains Indian Sign-Talk. PST is a gestural language that was inter-tribal and in use across the entire Plains region, from Canada all the way down to Texas, prior to the gradual imposition of English during the twentieth century. The very existence of this unique movement-based lingua franca initially drew me to this research site, in conjunction with what I had learned about the general import of dancing in Native American ceremonial and spiritual practices. During my initial eighteen months of research, in addition to the usual ethnographic practice of immersing myself in the activities of the community, I spent as much time as possible learning spoken Nakota (Siouan) and PST by paying regular visits to a number of elders who were willing to spend time teaching me, and they generously permitted me to videotape their informal storytelling practices regularly.

Taking Indigenous Concepts of 'Language' into Account

Once a storytelling event had been videotaped, I collaborated with the storyteller and sometimes also with his/her relatives to translate and transcribe (write down) the story. I found that consultants' comments about the video-recordings often provided rich contextualizing information that I could then use as a basis to generate further questions and further elicitation of data. I also made important discoveries about Assiniboine conceptions of relationships between language and the moving body as I encountered problems with my own methods.

On one occasion, for example, when writing down the words of a story from the videotape, I became confused because my consultant's repetition of the spoken Nakota in his story often did not correspond with the words I could hear on the videotape. Fortunately, I taped these transcription sessions as well, and so was able to go over the session again on my own and think about what was going on. I later realized that the discrepancies arose because my consultant was including meanings that in his storytelling were expressed only in the visual PST signs. He saw that I was writing down only the words and translations of the words, and presumably, did not want any of the meaning to be left out. This indicated to me his own sense of the unity of meaning. Clearly, from his perspective, this was not two languages going on at the same time. He was not 'hearing' one language and 'seeing' another: speech and action were integrated so that when asked to repeat to me what he had 'said' on the videotape, he included the signed meanings if they had not appeared in words in the original telling.

Recognizing this compensatory strategy prompted me to change my method. I abandoned my original plan to transcribe the spoken component first and then work on the signs, and began to transcribe and translate the words and signs simultaneously. The process went along much more smoothly thereafter, and the storyteller and I were able to discuss the numerous interrelationships between words and signs as they occurred.

Once theoretically alerted to this integrated conception of what counted as 'language' from the Assiniboine perspective, further evidence began to emerge. On another occasion, for example, in answer to one of my questions, a storyteller demonstrated for me a particular PST sign. I then asked him for a translation into words by saying, 'And how do you say that in Nakota?' He answered, 'Like I just showed you'. As far as the storyteller was concerned he had already said it in Nakota by using the appropriate gestural sign.

I also noticed that sign talkers frequently used the English noun 'word' to refer to either a vocal or a signed utterance. In ways such as this, evidence for an Assiniboine conception of 'language' as constituted by both vocal-signs and action-signs gradually emerged during the course of my research. I would not have learned any of this had I analysed the videotapes from observation alone, or tried to transcribe the visual-signs into Labanotation without asking about the connections between vocal-signs and action-signs.

Taking Indigenous Classifications into Account

Important discoveries about the primacy of movement in Assiniboine classifications also emerged through collaborations with consultants. During the process of analysing the structure of PST signs, for example, I was working towards establishing a kinemic[15] level of transcription in Labanotation, wherein only those differences in performance that altered the meaning of a sign were included in my transcriptions. I began with hand shapes and had come to a provisional conclusion that there were probably 23 distinct hand shapes in PST. I then proceeded to check my analysis with a fluent sign-talker who also had analytic interests. My agenda for our work session was clear – to check the hand shapes – and it was only later when viewing the videotape of our session that I realized my consultant had, with some consistency, been working from a different classificatory scheme altogether, one that I ignored at the time. He had listened and watched my explanations of a particular hand shape, thereafter making a comment or two, either agreeing or disagreeing. In many examples, however, he then proceeded to supplement the example I had given, not with signs that had the same or similar hand shapes, but with signs that used the same movement pattern or path through space. According to his classification system, it was the movement path of a sign that was its most important feature, and movement that linked signs together as being similar or different in their morphology (form).[16]

Having understood the basis of my consultant's classification in contrast to my own predilections, I began to seek further. I found supporting evidence from two further sources: pictographs and Siouan mythology (see Farnell, 1995a, chapter 7). The latter linked the primacy of movement found in Assiniboine classifications of signs with a distinct cultural metaphysics: movement conceived of as an intangible yet powerful principle called 'tákuskąska', 'that which moves' or 'that which gives motion to everything that moves' (see Farnell, 1995a, pp. 248–51).

Incorporating Indigenous Classifications into the Ethnographic Record

The necessity of talking with consultants in order to translate and so understand what can be observed was further confirmed by the following episode. When working on the transcription of a particular story that contained many pointing gestures that seemed ambiguous, I asked for clarification by saying, 'Where does the hand movement in that sign go exactly?' and the reply was not a vocal utterance but a kinesthetic one. The storyteller repeated the action of taking his right hand through space away from his chest and forward. There was no name for that action in words and one was not necessary, because embodied knowledge was being used and shared here, knowledge consisting of kinesthetic concepts, body parts acting in space/time. I then asked, 'When you make that sign, do you think of your hand as moving away from your chest, or is it going toward the front, or toward something?' The reply was a slow, patient, 'No ... it's going east.' No amount of careful observation or experience of doing the sign myself could have revealed that crucial piece of information.

This provides a good example of a 'simultaneity': the same concept of going towards east is shared across two expressive modalities. It is simultaneously a visual/kinesthetic concept about space and a spoken concept about space, and the two modalities inform each other. It would be erroneous to suppose that the action-sign concept is 'in' the word 'east', as if the word was rehearsed and echoed in the story-teller's head as he used the action-sign. Rather the concept is a spatial one. Like spoken language, such spatial knowledge remains out of focal awareness when we use it, because our focal attention is upon the communicative or other semantic task at hand, but when asked, we can bring it into focal awareness and translate the concept across modalities from action to speech. This is a person acting, not a mind thinking while the body experiences, and this point cannot be overstressed.

Further investigation revealed that this entire story, and many others, were structured according to a constant frame of reference based upon the four cardinal directions – north, south, east and west. This situation makes a difference to the transcription of that sign if it is going to be ethnographically accurate. What is constituent to the sign is not the visible movement of going forward middle or away from the chest, but the spatial orientation system which informs us that *from the actor's perspective* what is meant here is that the hand moves towards geographical east. Once informed of this paradigmatic feature of spatial orientation, I saw that it provided geographical referents for all the pointing gestures and I was able to incorporate such indigenous conceptions into the movement score. This transformed the Labanotation transcription from an observationist description of gross physical movement into an ethnographic account of action. Figure 2 illustrates the difference among the three alternatives presented in this example. I have called such an ethnographically informed description an 'ethno-graph'.

The aim throughout the creation of a movement text is to identify such constituent features and describe accordingly. It is precisely this possibility that Williams intends when she describes how a Labanotated text *is* the ethnography (see Williams, 1995, 1996). It is one of the important reasons for researchers becoming literate in the medium and creating texts with the Laban script. Video recordings

(i) hand moves away from chest   (ii) hand moves forward

(iii) 'ethno-graph' - hand moves toward east

Figure 2   Three different action- signs that look identical to an observer. Only (iii) is correct for the Assiniboine story told in Plains Sign-Talk.

are crucial aids when making such texts, but cannot substitute for them, for reasons that should now be clear.[17]

CONCLUSION

I have attempted to show how a critical, reflexive understanding of Western metaphysical assumptions and their effects on our common sense thinking is a necessary prerequisite to ethnographic field research. Without such understanding, we cannot begin to enter into a dialogue with others about what *they* think it means to be an embodied person, and so what it means to dance, or sign, or engage in ritual and ceremonial practices.

I have also suggested that an anthropological understanding of 'talk' from the body requires more than careful observation and movement experience. Understanding the nature and form of dynamic embodiment in social action generally, and in action-sign systems specifically, requires analytic attention to spoken discourse.

Examination of the complex relationships between action-signs and spoken-signs in cultural practices provides the in-depth means necessary to understand and translate complex visual/kinesthetic concepts from one cultural context to another. Field research strategies for investigating these relationships suggested here include (i) investigating 'simultaneities' as cultural sites where speech and action integrate, and (ii) the creation of 'ethno-graphs' – movement texts which record action *in its own terms* and according to ethnographically centred principles.

NOTES

1. See Best, 1978, 1992.
2. The notion of 'primitive dance' was a category already well formed in my mind as a result of some rather confused teaching in the history of dance. I call it confused because it consisted mostly of speculative imaginings about 'the origin' of dancing in some dim and distant 'dawn of civilization'. For example, we were asked to imagine what such ancient conditions might be like and to compose our own 'primitive dances' based on ideas we might have about animal symbolism and worship. This extraordinary exercise, devoid of any historical or pre-historical evidence whatsoever, was bolstered by vague references to contemporary non-Western peoples such as Africans and Australian Aborigines, who were held up as examples of such 'primitive' thinkers. Sadly, this is what passed for undergraduate teaching in the history of dance at that time. To anthropologists, of course, this kind of reasoning is instantly recognizable as a classic example of ethnocentrism, in this instance exacerbated by an uncritical application of theories of social evolution. Although such theories were already long out of date in academic circles, they remained prevalent in the few history of dance texts that were influential at the time. See Williams, 1991 and Kealiinohomoku, 1997 [1969–70/1983].
3. Representations of non-western peoples in popular publications such as *National Geographic* have contributed to the exoticization and distancing of non-western, non-industrialized peoples. Visual representations of scantily clad dancing bodies seem to provide the essence of the 'primitive' for this neo-colonial gaze. See Lutz and Collins, 1993.
4. I was later fortunate and persistent enough to find the means to acquire the skills I lacked. It required extensive training in theories and methods specific to the anthropology of human movement during an MA degree at New York University under Dr Drid Williams. It also required further training in theories and methods of socio-cultural and linguistic anthropology during doctoral studies at Indiana University.
5. For discussion of the notion of 'personal anthropology' and its relationship to reflexivity and new notions of objectivity, see the special issue of

the *Journal for the Anthropological Study of Human Movement* (*JASHM*), 8, 1.

6.   Semasiological theory is an approach to the anthropology of human movement influenced by Saussurian semiotics that was developed by Drid Williams. See Williams 1979, 1982 and 1991.

7.   See Farnell, 1994, for discussion of three complementary discourses of embodiment in contemporary social theory: 'talk about the body', 'talk of the body' and 'talk from the body'.

8.   See Farnell, 1995a; Havilland, 1993; Kaeppler, 1995; Kendon, 1983; McNeill, 1992; Williams, 1994, 1995.

9.   'Action-sign' (Williams, 1982, 1991) marks a fundamental theoretical shift from movement seen as 'behaviour' to movement seen as 'action'. It also provides a much needed hypernym, that is, a classificatory term that refers to any and all kinds of human movement systems. Without it we must resort to lists at a lower level of classification using terms such as dances, sign languages, martial arts, gestures, ritual and ceremonial action and so on. Names such as 'dance' and 'sign language' are derived from western classifications of movement systems, and so become problematic for anthropological investigations when they mask important classificatory differences in other cultures. See Kaeppler, 1978 and Williams, 1997.

10. Reversing the Cartesian centre of privilege, as Merleau Ponty and recent advocates of his work have tried to do (for example, Jackson, 1983; Hanks, 1990; and Csordas, 1989), through appeals to the subjective experience of the body as 'lived', does not offer an acceptable solution. It merely relocates the ambiguous notion of agency contained in the Cartesian 'mind' in an equally ambiguous notion of agency contained in the body. See discussions in Varela, 1994, 1995.

11. Best's discussion is of central relevance to the development of adequate methods in the anthropological study of dance and human movement, because without a thorough examination of the cultural roots of our own metaphysics we cannot be critically reflexive about our own cultural and historical positioning as anthropologists. That is, if the myth is not made explicit and open to critical thought, it remains securely in place as the cultural lens through which we interpret all action-sign systems, wherever they occur. Since we now know that there is no culture-free 'objective' zone from which we might direct our gaze, reflexive awareness becomes the only means by which we can recover a more limited notion of objectivity. It enables us to enter our own metaphysical beliefs into a dialogue with those of our respective others. See *JASHM*, 8, 1, a special issue on the problem of objectivity.

12. The antithesis supports a subjectivist metaphysical doctrine of the human mind as two distinct realms: the Cognitive/Rational realm and the Affective/Creative realm (a distortion of the sciences as well as the arts, both of which require creativity and imagination). As Best explains, this confused myth is sometimes given a pseudo-scientific dress by reference to the different functions of brain hemispheres. It is said that one hemisphere is concerned with the Affective/Creative, the other with the Rational/Cognitive. This myth of separate faculties leads

> to claims that artistic creation and appreciation are matters of feeling not cognition, and thus that the arts consist in having non-rational, noncognitive experiences as opposed to progressively developing understanding.
13. Cited in Bateson, 1972, p. 137.
14. But see Hart-Johnson, 1997, for an excellent description of a typical Graham technique class.
15. A 'kinemic' level of transcription parallels the way in which the distinctive sounds in a spoken language are called 'phonemic' by linguists. For example, the difference between the English words 'bit' and 'bat' is the central vowel sound that is performed with the tongue either higher or lower in the mouth. Although a minor phonetic difference, it is a difference in sound that creates a difference in meaning and so is phonemic. Similar distinctions in movement can be made in action-sign systems.
16. Ironically, one of the reasons I chose the Laban script over other movement writing systems was its greater capacity for recording movement pattern and changing relationships. To have caught myself in the act of momentarily ignoring the very reason for this decision was a most humbling experience. Fortunately, my consultant was not persuaded that my way of classifying was better than his own. The methodological point is that, even with a writing system capable of a sophisticated transcription of movement, I had fallen into a trap set by the metaphysics of my own cultural background and had begun by focusing on what appeared to be the most tangible part of a sign – the hand in a particular shape – rather than the seemingly less tangible movement through space.
17. For discussions of movement literacy and the use of the Laban script in anthropology, see Williams and Farnell, 1990; Farnell, 1994 and 1995a; and Page, 1996.

REFERENCES

Bateson, G. 1972. *Steps to an Ecology of Mind*. New York: Ballantine Books.
Best, D. 1978. *Philosophy and Human Movement*. London: Allen and Unwin.
—— 1992. *The Rationality of Feeling: Understanding the Arts in Education*. London: The Falmer Press.
Clark, A. 1997. *Being There: Putting Brain, Body, and World Together Again*. Cambridge, Massachusetts, and London: MIT Press.
Csordas, T. 1989. Embodiment as a paradigm for anthropology. *Ethos*, 18, 1, pp. 5–47.
Farnell, B. 1994. Ethno-graphics and the moving body. *Man: Journal of the Royal Anthropological Institute*, 29 [n.s.], 4, pp. 926–74.
—— 1995a. *Do You See What I Mean?: Plains Indian Sign Talk and the Embodiment of Action*. Austin: University of Texas Press.
—— (ed.). 1995b. *Human Actions Signs in Cultural Context: the Visible and the Invisible in Movement and Dance*. Metuchen, New Jersey: Scarecrow Press.
Hanks, W. 1990. *Referential Practice: Language and Lived Space among the Maya*. Chicago: University of Chicago Press.

Hart-Johnson, D. 1997. A Graham technique class. *JASHM: Journal for the Anthropological Study of Human Movement*, 9, 4, pp. 193–214.

Havilland, J. 1993. Anchoring, iconicity and orientation in *Guugu Yimithirr* pointing gestures. *Journal of Linguistic Anthropology*, 3, 1, pp. 3–45.

Jackson, M. 1983. Knowledge of the body. *Man: Journal of the Royal Anthropological Institute*, 18, 2, pp. 327–45.

Kaeppler, A. 1978. Dance in anthropological perspective. *Annual Review of Anthropology*, 7, pp. 31–49.

—— 1995. Visible and invisible in Hawaiian dance. In Farnell, B. (ed.), pp. 31–43.

Kendon, A. 1983. Gesture and speech: how they interact. In Wiemann, J.M. and Harrison, R.P. (eds), *Nonverbal Interaction*. Beverly Hills, California: Sage Publications, pp. 13–45.

Kealiinohomoku, J.W. 1997 [1969–70/1983]. An anthropologist looks at ballet as a form of ethnic dance. In Williams, D. (ed.), pp. 15–36.

Lutz, C. and Collins, J.L. 1993. *Reading* National Geographic. Chicago: University of Chicago Press.

McNeill, D. 1992. *Hand and Mind: What Gestures Reveal about Thought*. Chicago: University of Chicago Press.

Page, J. 1996. Images for understanding: movement notation and visual recordings. *Visual Anthropology*, 8, 2–4, pp. 171–96.

Varela, C. 1994. Harré and Merleau-Ponty: beyond the absent body in embodied social theory. *Journal for the Theory of Social Behavior*, 24, 2, pp. 167–85.

—— 1995. Cartesianism revisited: the ghost in the moving machine or the lived body. In Farnell, B. (ed.), pp. 216–93.

Williams, D. 1979. The human action sign and semasiology. In Rowe, P.A. and Stodelle, E. (eds), *Dance Research Collage: a Variety of Subjects Embracing the Abstract and the Practical*. New York: Congress on Research in Dance and New York University, pp. 39–64. *CORD Dance Research Annual*, X.

—— 1982. 'Semasiology': a semantic anthropological view of human movements and actions. In Parkin, D. (ed.), *Semantic Anthropology*, ASA Monograph 22. London: Academic Press, pp. 161–81.

—— 1991. *Ten Lectures on Theories of the Dance*. Metuchen, New Jersey: Scarecrow Press.

—— 1994. The Latin High Mass: the Dominican Tridentine Rite. *JASHM: Journal for the Anthropological Study of Human Movement*, 8, 2, pp. 1–87. JASHM Monograph 1, with foreword by David Pocock.

—— 1995. Space, intersubjectivity and the conceptual imperative: three ethnographic cases. In Farnell, B. (ed.), pp. 44–81.

—— 1996. Ceci n'est pas un 'Wallaby'. *Visual Anthropology*, 8, 2–4, pp. 197–217.

—— 1997. Anthropology and human movement: the study of dances. In Williams, D. (ed.), *Readings in the Anthropology of Human Movement*, 1. Lanham, Maryland, and London: Scarecrow Press, pp. 55–68.

Williams, D. and Farnell, B. 1990. *The Laban Script: a Beginning Text on Movement-writing for Non-dancers*. Canberra: Australian Institute of Aboriginal and Torres Straits Islander Studies, with accompanying workbook.

Part III
Politics and Ethics

13 Fieldwork, Politics and Power
Andrée Grau

The anthropological venture may seem a linear progression from observation to elaboration of theories and writing. Having decided where to do fieldwork, anthropologists go to their chosen area, interact with men and women, collect data and formulate hypotheses. On leaving the field they go home with a variety of 'objects' which they transform through professional concepts, jargon and theoretical models into ethnographic texts.

The reality, however, is not that simple. Kilani, in an elegant essay, demonstrated the complexity of the anthropological construction (1994, pp. 40–62). For him the notion of a reality – the field – existing prior and outside of the anthropologist's work is a naive vision merging the presence of the anthropologist with the present of the ethnographic object.

> L'illusion consiste à croire à une simultaneité entre l'objet 'à voir' et l'acte 'de voir'; autrement dit, c'est amalgamer la 'presence' de l'anthropologue sur le terrain avec le 'present' de l'objet ethnographique. (p. 41)

Such a perspective denies an historical dimension and assumes that being outside an object intrinsically implies objectivity. Indeed, the 'facts' of anthropology are not ready-made, somehow existing out there in the 'real' world, waiting to be retrieved. Rather, as Schultz and Lavenda argue, they are

> first created in the field. They are created anew whenever the fieldworker, back home, re-examines fieldnotes and is transported back into the field experience. And they are created yet again when fieldworkers discuss their experiences with other anthropologists. (1990, p. 69)

Although I had examined the Australian Aboriginal Tiwi kinship dances as part of the infrastructure of social life in my PhD, it took a long time and many discussions with friends and colleagues to make sense of some of my data. I remember, for example, referring in a seminar to my main thesis, which suggested that the Tiwi literally danced their kinship and that dance among them was as much a theory *for* kinship practices as *of* kinship practices. During the discussion that followed, I was asked how I had been adopted into a Tiwi family; a practice common throughout Aboriginal Australia, as an individual cannot exist socially outside of kinship ties. When I answered that after my first practical involvement in the dance, I was named and adopted by what became my Tiwi father, participants felt that it was an excellent example of kinship being invented in dance.

Although the information was not new, through situating myself in the ethnography I re-created my data and it allowed me to reach a new depth of understanding which transformed much of my subsequent writing. It also allowed me to reflect on the many roles I had performed for the Tiwi during fieldwork. My extensive genealogical work, for instance, left a written mark which some Tiwi used. When young people asked about family relationships, for example, they were often sent to me since 'I knew everything'. Similarly, the anthropologist Jane Goodale, the Tiwi expert who has worked with these people since the 1950s (cf. Goodale, 1971), was often referred to as a 'wise woman' and consulted as such by the Tiwi Land Council. In this way our respective work was used by the Tiwi as part of their processes of elaborating local thoughts and of constructing identities. Together anthropologists and Tiwi 'invented' ethnographic data.

Interrogation of the fieldwork process has come to the forefront of theoretical discourse and most scholars include in their monographs a discussion of the format their participation-observation took. By being reflexive about their work and personal involvement, they acknowledge greater responsibility for the construction of their data and its location within different frames of reference. This inclusion of the researcher into the analysis can be enlightening, both furthering and elaborating theoretical thought as in Jeanne Favret-Saada's *Les mots, la mort, les sorts* (1977), in my view one of the best ethnographies ever written. Yet it is true that this exercise may equally lead to ego trips and confessional anthropology.

Examination of terminology and practices can also be illuminating as, for example, the useful distinctions made by some scholars between different types of notes: 'scratchnotes', 'fieldnotes', 'filednotes', and 'headnotes' (Sanjek, 1990; Fernandez, 1993). The 'scratchnotes' are jottings made on the spot, then elaborated on at a quieter, more suitable time into 'fieldnotes'; the 'filednotes' are notes that are organized and reconstructed; and the 'headnotes' all that which never gets written down but remains in ethnographers' heads to inform their writing.

In this chapter, I will focus on some of the facets of the politics of fieldwork both outside the field, in terms of access and representation, and within the field, in terms of interpersonal relationships. These will first be approached generally, then more practically, and will be informed by personal fieldwork experiences on four continents in the past 20 years: South Africa, under apartheid in the late 1970s, Aboriginal Australia in the early 1980s, and India and London in the late 1980s.

ANTHROPOLOGY AS PERSONAL POLITICS

Any viewpoint frames, as much as defines, its field of representation. It is therefore important when dealing with politics and power to situate the perspective taken both politically and theoretically. For me anthropology is grounded in a politics that 'aims to secure a recognition that the non-Western is as crucial an element of the human as the Western and thus is sceptical and critical of Western claims to knowledge and understanding' (Mascia-Lees et al., 1989, p. 8) and my theoretical inclination owes much to the late John Blacking with whom I worked for many years. His vision of humanity inspired me and continues to do so. I am fascinated, like him, in the paradoxes of the human condition, as, for example, the capacity human beings have to perceive themselves as belonging simultaneously to the human species, to specific nations, ethnic groups, classes or creeds, as well as feeling entirely unique (cf. Blacking, 1973, p. 113).

My theoretical concerns arise from a view that anthropology in general, and the anthropology of dance specifically, are concerned with the tension between cultural norms and human creativity, between socio-historical constraints and human agency. Dance is a social fact, conveying meaning through human interactions; thus it reflects ideologies and world views. Yet dance can also be used to explore and manipulate the social reality, with the potential to influence decision-making in other social contexts and occasionally to prefigure political actions.

All discourses are linked to specific motives and the perspective outlined above is no exception. It presupposes the existence of a 'universal nature', in a Chomskian sense: dance, like music, resides at a juncture between the biological and the cultural, encompassing outward forms of culturally patterned movements and an innate, species-specific set of sensory and cognitive capacities which human beings use to make sense of their surrounding world. Thus, the study of dance can afford insights into the root of what it is to be human and contribute to anthropology as a 'science not only *of* humanity but *for* humanity' (Fox, 1973, p. 14).

The ideology underlying my work is fairly typical of a middle-class liberal whose political consciousness took shape in the late 1960s/early 1970s: a mixture of feminism, humanism, Marxism, anarchism and French postmodern philosophy. These different aspects are all evident to a lesser or greater degree in my writings: the realization of a 'human potential' when discussing 'body intelligence' and 'performative modes of thought' (for example, Grau, 1996, 1997b, and in press); the social function of ideologies and the influence which control of the means of production has on social structures, considered in my work on intercultural performance (for example, Grau, 1990, 1992, 1997a) and in my observations of the many competing agendas taking place in Tiwi rituals (Grau, 1994, 1995); the social construction of reality generally and of the body specifically in my writings on the body as world view (cf. Grau, 1997b, in press).

At a political level therefore, the tension between cultural norms and creativity, mentioned earlier, could also be expressed in terms of tension between power and social justice.

FIELDWORK AND THE POLITICS OF POWER

Fieldwork is central to the anthropological venture. It is the experience that characterizes and defines the discipline, guaranteeing the 'truth' of the ethnography. As Pulman argued, fieldwork references in anthropological texts function as a 'truth-making machine' – 'une machine à produire du vrai' (cited in Kilani, 1994, p. 42). As the final phase of anthropological training it acts as the rite of passage that transforms students of anthropology into fully fledged anthropologists. Malinowski, whose writings have acquired the status of 'myths of origin' in the anthropological imagination (Kilani, 1994, p. 42), described it as being to 'anthropology what the blood of the martyr [was] to the church' (Fox, 1973, p. 11). As the gateway to the discipline, fieldwork is inextricably enmeshed with relations of power. Fieldwork methodology courses, if they exist at all, rarely prepare researchers for what is to come. The general assumption in the past and to some extent in the late 1990s is that if you have to ask you cannot be a member of the club: through the mystique of fieldwork anthropologists guard their sacred knowledge.

In a fieldwork situation, the separation of 'work' from 'life' is often difficult and possibly not even desirable. Fieldwork is about dialogue, intersubjectivity, building bridges of understanding between self and other. Both anthropologist and 'natives' are trying to make sense of the other: this requires insight, empathy, imagination, perceptivity and humility on both sides.

Because of the nature of participation-observation, no matter where fieldwork is taking place, dislocation and stress can be expected. Working 'at home' is by no means easier than working in an 'exotic' location. Indeed it can be harder since little attention has been paid to culture shock, the fieldworker assuming there will not be any. During the 1980s, I worked in London with a group of actors with whom I shared much in common, being middle-class, cosmopolitan and 'artistic'. It was, however, a learning experience for me to discover that my dialectical method of fieldwork did not result in the interaction anticipated. The ethnographic approach attempted to create an exchange between analyst and informants so that different kinds of technical knowledge and experience could be confronted, including informant participation in the intellectual process of analysis. The implications of this, however, were never fully understood by the actors despite our commonalities and willingness to share in the research process (see Grau, 1993).

For most fieldworkers the immensity of what they are undertaking is difficult to anticipate. In some instances just surviving the day may seem an enormous accomplishment. Organizing food supplies, coping with climate, insects and disease may seem almost impossible tasks; yet there are also data to be collected and research to do. Dealing with dance one has the added problem of wondering whether one's body will cope with the movement vocabulary of the system under investigation.

Everybody is a potential informant; yet as in ordinary life one may not necessarily be able or even want to engage with everyone; antipathies may exist on both sides. 'Will people want to talk to me?' is one of the many terrors that fieldworkers experience during the first days in the field. Indeed, as more people around the world become accustomed to resident researchers, it appears quite sensible for them to avoid curious anthropologists who will pester them with unending questions for months to come. Nor is the establishment of individual contact straightforward since it may often implicate the researcher with specific factions within the society. Will talking with one kind of dancer, for example, close the door to other kinds? Can I say to a prestigious ballerina that I may juxtapose her statement with that of a stripper? Will she ever want to speak to me again when/if she discovers?

Every step taken during the early days is likely to bear consequences. Although anthropologists appear powerful due to their likely access to greater resources and freedom to leave the field whenever they want, they are also gullible and easily manipulated. The guilt felt by some white researchers in South Africa or Australia, for example, can easily be exploited, even if at first the fieldworkers seem in an obviously powerful position. The premise of my argument is twofold: first, power is an aspect of *all* relationships and second, power relationships are never entirely one-way; there is always a dialectic of control as no agent is ever *totally* powerless in a relationship.

POLITICS IN PRACTICE

Although it would be simplistic to think in terms of three neatly separate periods – pre-fieldwork, fieldwork, and post-fieldwork – it is also true that different dynamics of power develop at different times.

Prior to fieldwork, the politics of funding and gaining access to resources have to be tackled. Class, ethnicity, contacts, gender, affiliations to prestigious institutions and responsibility for children, as well as fashionable theories, all play a role. Diane Bell, for example, recalls how although there were provisions for male anthropologists to claim an allowance for a dependant wife in the field, the category of 'single mother' was non-existent and her dependant children could not be provided for (Bell et al., 1993, p. 32). Similarly, I had to prove that my companion would offer genuine assistance in the field in order to receive a dependant's allowance, even though female dependants could simply be 'wives'.

Prior to fieldwork one is also likely to meet other, usually more senior, anthropologists who may choose to act as gatekeepers, deciding who can work with 'their people'. Although theoretically it is the people themselves who give permission or not to a new researcher to do fieldwork, the world is full of *chasses gardées*. It is not just anthropologists who may influence local councils or other decision-making bodies, but any other type of personnel such as advisers, missionaries or educators. In contrast to such workers, the business of anthropologists appears to involve doing nothing all day except being friendly to the locals, which can be perceived as immensely disruptive and threatening. At a higher echelon one may have to deal with unsympathetic government officials. This is probably one of the few times when to be a *dance* specialist may be an asset: totally against principles and conviction, it may be expedient to talk about dance as something trivial and apolitical, yet so colourful and interesting.

In addition to funding and permission, preparation for the practicalities of fieldwork is essential. Ideally, this would include the acquisition of skills to transcribe foreign languages; to make measurements and draw maps; to learn photographic, film and recording techniques; to gain music and movement notation skills ... the list could go on. More practical skills may comprise how to erect a tent, plant a garden, make a fire or avoid snakes. It is also helpful to seek out good advice from experienced researchers, such as the following, given by Blacking prior to my departure for fieldwork in Venda, South Africa:

> All notes and diaries should be taken using carbon paper and a copy should be send to him for safe keeping. He advised us to take walks at different times of the day (early, middle, late, even at night) to see what people are doing at different times; to go to church, of all denominations, because church services are social events. He also stressed the importance of having one set of 'good' clothes: a suit for Dominique, a smart dress for me, in case we had to attend formal events in Venda such as the installation of a headman. On no account were we to attend such events in informal clothing. Although it might not be obvious to us at first, trousers being often frayed or T-shirts torn, the Venda would be wearing their best clothes and we had to do the same. Neither should we criticise the environment indiscriminately: it is their home and we must always keep it in our minds. He also suggested that we should take every opportunity offered to do anything useful for the Venda, be it teaching Benesh notation or take family photographs, stressing the importance of exchange of gifts and skills. (Grau, 1991, p. 223)

Having seen researchers in jeans or shorts at formal events, heard them criticizing missionaries openly (forgetting that on their return, these people will still be there) and seeing them join in a dance without being invited, I came to realise over the years the wisdom of Blacking's advice.

Within the politics of fieldwork, social survival is at stake and a space needs to be found from which to operate: as Kilani argues 'sur le terrain, l'anthropologue joue son identité' (1994, p. 42). Cherished principles are often discarded: feminists find themselves kowtowing and flirting; non-violents observe individuals being beaten and do not interfere; egalitarians observe exploitation; republicans flatter royalty; and anti-racists loathe the people with whom they work. Ultimately, fieldwork is about exposing our actual selves to our potential selves; this can be unnerving because it questions our very being, highlighting our inability to finalize any single interpretation of human experiences.

Finally, different politics occur when writing up. First, there is the question of ownership of material. Scholars are notoriously possessive of their fieldnotes. I remember the turmoil when Jane Goodale asked for a copy of my notes on the *Kulama* rituals which she had missed. It was like giving my baby away. I am very grateful, however, to have been through the process as it subsequently allowed me to deposit my 'filednotes' at the Australian Institute of Aboriginal and Islander Studies, for the use of Tiwi people and other researchers. As authors, our notes are undoubtedly our construction and as such our property. The knowledge which informed them, however, is not ours; indeed, possessiveness of data is similar to gatekeeping entry to the field. Greater ethical responsibility and development of the discipline of anthropology would result if data were more widely available and open to commentary. Such a policy, however, implies trust that people will acknowledge consultation of material, a procedure that does not necessarily coincide with career building.

Translation of the fieldwork experience into scholarly texts is difficult. As MacClancy and McDonaugh observe:

> It is a commonplace among anthropologists that ethnographies are usually boring, and most of them virtually unreadable ... If anthropologists were not paid to read these weighty tomes, most of them wouldn't. (1996, p. 237)

Anthropologists face an extraordinary conundrum: they have to produce sophisticated and nuanced analyses which will challenge and further knowledge, while being like travel writers and conveying the atmosphere of local life. In addition they have the moral duty to 'inscribe "others" in such a way as not to deny or diffuse their claims to subjecthood' (Mascia-Lees et al., 1989, p. 12).

Postmodern anthropologists such as James Clifford, George Marcus and Michael Fisher have advocated a 'new' reflexive ethnography and the exploration of 'new' forms of writing to address these issues (Marcus and Fisher, 1986; Clifford, 1988; Clifford and Marcus,

1986). Their claim to innovation, however, has been challenged by some feminist writers who argue that 'like European explorers discovering the New World, Clifford and his colleagues perceive a new uninhabited space where, in fact, feminists have long been at work' (Mascia-Lees et al., 1989, p. 14). Although women anthropologists have a history of reflexivity and/or experimentation with the ethnographic style from at least the 1930s (cf. Hurston, 1937; Deren, 1953; Brigg, 1970; Cesara, 1982; Pattie, 1997), their contributions are rarely acknowledged (see Bell et al., 1993 for detailed discussions of these issues). Thus relations of power are not just between the writers and the people about whom they write but they also exist within the scholarly world. How could one ignore for example that 'the postmodern claim that verbal constructs do not correspond in a direct way to reality has arisen precisely when women and non-Western people have begun to speak for themselves and, indeed, to speak about the global system of power differentials' (Mascia-Lees et al., 1989, p. 15)?

The rejection of the 'feminine' could also be linked to the rejection of the 'irrational'. There is no doubt that we choose to ignore certain 'facts' of fieldwork due to their 'difficulty'. In the field we are often directly confronted with extraordinary events, be they instances of telepathy, appearances of ghosts and elemental beings, powers of healing, or alien ways of seeing and knowing (cf. Sperber, 1982, pp. 51–83; Hastrup, 1987). As social scientists we are not normally supposed to include our experience of the irrational in scientific reports except in strictly scholarly terms. Sometimes, indeed, we censure such accounts not only from our public presentations but also from our notes and diaries, because our rational minds refuse to accept the information as scientific data. And yet deep down we know that we have lived a real experience.

Working in dance one is almost constantly confronted with the 'irrational'. The transcendental quality of dancers' experiences, for example, has been documented in different areas of the world: young amateur dancers in London told sociologist Helen Thomas that dance sometimes made them 'black out', 'go to a different place' or 'disappear' (Thomas, 1993, pp. 78–82); a professional dancer wrote about being 'possessed by movements' (Lunn, 1994, p. 27); Greek dancers talked about *kefi*, the high spirit they aimed to experience in dance (Cowan, 1990, pp. 105–12); and in many parts of the world dancers are 'possessed' or 'mounted' by the spirits of gods or ancestors. Anyone who has been involved in intensive dance practice knows too that although not every performance brings such a heightened form of experience, to dance in such a way that the constraints of the technique disappear, to feel that one is literally 'being danced', is the ultimate goal.

I would argue that to realize an adequate and truthful ethnographic account, the admittance of the truth of 'unreality' is essential; only through an implicit internalized knowledge of local cultural standards can meaningful units of analysis can be extracted. Accepting the 'unreal', however, does not mean adopting the 'woolly, supernatural mystery-mongering' which Best argues still exists in parts of the art world (Best, 1996, p. 3). We must move away not only from a so-called 'scientism' where empirical facts alone are seen as valuable, but also from 'subjectivism' which has plagued the arts and the popular imagination for too long (see Best, 1992).

Dance and dance studies, connected to both women and the irrational, have always been marginalized. This situation has been exacerbated by the failure to question deeply held assumptions within the dance profession. To argue that dance could sometimes be oppressive, for example, might be construed as betraying the cause and as politically unsound. Yet it is only through the questioning of beliefs that the full power of dance, with its intertwining of affect and intellect, can be understood.

Working from the margins, however, does have advantages. Without the yoke of the founding fathers of other disciplines, researchers are freer both to question and to experiment (see for example, *Women & Performance* [1992]); as scholars we must not miss this opportunity. We have now reached a time when our results can be heard, when the data from our fieldwork may provide plausible models for challenging power relationships: even, perhaps, for 'changing the world'.

REFERENCES

Bell, D., Caplan, P. and Karim, W.J. (eds). 1993. *Gendered Fields: Women, Men And Ethnography*. London and New York: Routledge.
Best, D. 1992. *The Rationality of Feeling: Understanding the Arts in Education*. London: Falmer Press.
—— 1996. Educating artistic response: understanding is feeling. *JASHM: Journal for the Anthropological Study of Human Movement*, 9, 1, Spring, pp. 1–14. Reprinted from *Curriculum*, 15, 1, 1994.
Blacking, J. 1973. *How Musical is Man?* Seattle: University of Washington Press.

Brigg, J. 1970. *Never in Anger: Portrait of an Eskimo Family*. Cambridge, Massachusetts: Harvard University Press.

Cesara, M. 1982. *Reflections of a Woman Anthropologist: No Hiding Place*. New York: Academic Press.

Clifford, J. 1988. *The Predicament of Culture: Twentieth Century Ethnography, Literature and Art*. Cambridge, Massachusetts: Harvard University Press.

Clifford, J. and Marcus, G.E. (eds). 1986. *Writing Culture: the Poetics and Politics of Ethnography*. Berkeley: University of California Press.

Cowan, J. 1990. *Dance and the Body Politic in Northern Greece*. Princeton, New Jersey: Princeton University Press.

Deren, M. 1953. *Divine Horsemen: the Living Gods of Haiti*. New Paltz, New York: McPherson and Co. Reprinted 1970.

Favret-Saada, J. 1977. *Les mots, la mort, les sorts*. Paris: Gallimard. Published in 1980 by Cambridge University Press as *Deadly Words: Witchcraft in the Bocage*.

Fernandez, J. 1993. A guide to the perplexed ethnographer in an age of sound bites. *American Ethnologist*, 20, 1, pp. 179–84.

Fox, R. 1973. *Encounter with Anthropology*. London: Penguin Books.

Goodale, J. 1971. *Tiwi Wives: a Study of the Women of Melville Island, North Australia*. Seattle and London: University of Washington Press.

Grau, A. 1990. Interculturalisme dans les arts du spectacle. In Pidoux, J.-P. (ed.), *La danse, art du XXe siècle?* Lausanne: Payot, pp. 343–55.

—— 1991. John Blacking: reminiscences. *Popular Music*, 10, 2, pp. 221–8. Published by Cambridge University Press.

—— 1992. Intercultural research in the performing arts. *Dance Research*, 10, 2, pp. 3–29.

—— 1993. John Blacking and the development of dance anthropology in the United Kingdom. *Dance Research Journal*, 25, 2, pp. 21–31.

—— 1994. Dance as politics: dance as a tool for manipulating the social order among the Tiwi of Northern Australia. In *Proceedings of the 17th symposium of the International Council for Traditional Music Study Group on Ethnochoreology*. Nafplion, Greece: Peloponnesian Folklore Foundation, pp. 39–44.

—— 1995. Ritual dance and 'modernisation': the Tiwi example. In Dabrowska, G. and Bielawski, L. (eds), *Dance, Ritual and Music: Proceedings of the 18th Symposium of the International Council for Traditional Music Study Group on Ethnochoreology, Skierniewice, 9–18 August, 1994*. Warsaw: Polish Society for Ethnochoreology, Institute of Art, Polish Academy of Sciences, pp. 89–96.

—— 1996. Dance and everyday experience. *Blitz '96: The Mag*. Supplement to *Dance Theatre Journal*, 13, 1 (Summer), pp. 41–3.

—— 1997a. Dance, South Asian dance and higher education. *Choreography and Dance*, 4, 2, pp. 55–62. Special issue entitled *South Asian Dance: the British Experience*, edited by A. Iyer, published by Harwood Academic Publishers.

—— 1997b. Dancers' bodies as the repository of conceptualisations of the body, with special reference to the Tiwi of Northern Australia. In Rauch, I. and Carr, G.F. (eds), pp. 929–32.

174 *Andrée Grau*

—— In press. On the acquisition of knowledge: teaching kinship through the body among the Tiwi of Northern Australia. In Keck, V. (ed.), *Knowing Oceania: Constituting Knowledge and Identities*. Oxford: Berg Publishers.

Hastrup, K. 1987. *The Challenge of the Unreal*. Copenhagen: Museum Tusculanum Press.

Hurston, Z.N. 1937. *Their Eyes were Watching God*. Philadelphia: J.B. Lippincott. Reprinted by University of Illinois Press in 1978.

Kilani, M. 1994. *L'invention de l'autre: essais sur le discours anthropologique*. Lausanne: Payot, Sciences humaines.

Lunn, J. 1994. Speak up! *Dance Now*, 3, 1, pp. 26–7.

MacClancy, J. and McDonaugh, C. 1996. *Popularizing Anthropology*. London and New York: Routledge.

Marcus, G.E. and Fisher, M.J. 1986. *Anthropology as Cultural Critique: an Experimental Moment in the Human Sciences*. Chicago: University of Chicago Press.

Mascia-Lees, F., Sharpe, P. and Cohen, C.B. 1989. The postmodern turn in anthropology: cautions from a feminist perspective. *Signs*, 15, 1, pp. 7–33.

Pattie, S. 1997. *Faith in History: Armenians Rebuilding Community*. Washington, D.C. and London: Smithsonian Institution Press.

Rauch, I. and Carr, G.F (eds). 1977. *Proceedings of the International Association for Semiotic Studies. Fifth Congress, 1994, at University of California, Berkeley*. The Hague: London.

Sanjek, R. (ed.). 1990. *Fieldnotes: the Making of Anthropology*. Ithaca, New York: Cornell University Press.

Schultz, E. and Lavenda, R. 1990. *Cultural Anthropology: a Perspective on the Human Condition*. St Paul, Minnesota: West Publishing Company.

Sperber, D. 1982. *Le savoir des anthropologues*. Paris: Hermann, Collection Savoir.

Thomas, H. 1993. An-other voice: young women dancing and talking. In Thomas, H. (ed.), *Dance, Gender and Culture*. London: Macmillan, pp. 69–93.

14 Searching for Branches, Searching for Roots: Fieldwork in my Grandfather's Village
Andriy Nahachewsky

I was born into the large Ukrainian community in western Canada where I have been active in the staged Ukrainian dance revival since childhood. During graduate studies, I started a decade of documentation of non-staged Ukrainian dance traditions, mostly in Canada. In this essay I wish to describe my efforts at conducting dance fieldwork in Ukraine. I focus on three key aspects of that endeavour: receiving government authorization, establishing the logistics of the fieldwork and cooperating with local scholars.

GOVERNMENT AUTHORIZATION

My first visit to Ukraine was in 1977. A summer workshop in folk stage dance was organized by the Association of United Ukrainian Canadians, a minority pro-Soviet organization which had recently allowed non-members such as myself to participate. The workshop took place in Kyiv, the capital city in east central Ukraine. All tourist visas at that time were issued in connection with fully scheduled and organized group tours. These programmes were generally limited to large cities. Rural areas and most of western Ukraine were closed to foreigners (with a few exceptions for individuals with the appropriate ideological credentials). We danced in the morning and were expected to participate in a full schedule of tourist activities for the remainder of each day. The political views expressed by our Soviet Intourist guides were very different from those of my home community.

The next summer, I attended a university exchange in the city of Chernivtsi in southwestern Ukraine. Western Ukraine has a history and character quite different from the east and I could feel my own roots much more clearly than I had the year before. My own ancestors hailed from these parts, as did those of 80 per cent of all Ukrainian Canadians. We were still closely attended by our hosts, but we had a bit of free time to walk the streets alone. I had my first views of non-staged dance at a discotheque and when I happened upon a village wedding.

I returned to Ukraine in 1980 for a year-long residency at the Institute of Culture in Kyiv as a special student in a programme designed to train staged-dance teachers for the large staged folk dance industry there. The Ukraine Society had just begun to sponsor students from capitalist countries for study terms, mostly to study the performing arts. I was disappointed that the programme of study included no real discussion of vernacular or village dance. I did manage to gain access to some materials on non-staged dance, which were archived in the Academy of Sciences. I was twice denied permission to go to my mother's cousins in western Ukraine that year. I did sneak out to my grandfather's village, travelling illegally six hours by taxi for a 20-minute visit.

I travelled to Ukraine again several times in the late 1980s and early 1990s as a doctoral candidate and as an assistant professor. By this time, Gorbachev's glasnost had changed many things, including official relations with foreigners. The government required formal letters of invitation and probably continued making security checks before issuing visas, but the communist ideological vigilance against westerners basically collapsed. Given the many political and economic stresses and loss of the old stable infrastructure, the security organs came to place a low priority on the surveillance of visitors. Most of Ukraine was now opened to foreigners with visas. Organizations and individuals other than the ideological watchdogs could now openly make contacts with westerners. The political situation which had practically precluded research on rural dance traditions in Ukraine dissolved with the demise of the Soviet Union.

LOGISTICS OF FIELDWORK

In 1992 I was invited to participate in a fieldwork expedition conducted by the Institute of Ethnology of Lviv, the main city of western Ukraine. The long-established standard format for fieldwork involved a travelling team of six to ten researchers. The goal of this particular expedition was to investigate a particular zone on the margins of the ethnographic region called Pokuttia and to determine whether the traditional lore there should be included in a forthcoming monograph on Pokuttian folk culture. Researchers combined this objective with their own specialization in wedding songs, toponymy, family structure, church architecture, cooperage traditions, textiles and other genres. Typically, the Institute's micro-bus would arrive at a village in the morning and report to the director of the collective farm or other local authority. The team leader introduced the group and presented documents from the Academy of Sciences. Accommodation was arranged, perhaps in a vacant school dormitory or possibly in the team's tents in an orchard. The team carried its own provisions and supplemented them with fresh produce from the village. As soon as the necessary arrangements were made, the researchers spread out on foot in search of informants or artefacts. Most often, the researchers quickly found elderly people resting at home, caring for grandchildren or working in the yard and willing to answer their questions. The local bosses sometimes identified or even summoned specific individuals who were knowledgeable in the given genres. The researchers often worked from a memorized questionnaire, taking notes or recording parts of the interview on tape and taking photographs as necessary. Depending on the topic and the quality of the information, a researcher might conduct one to four interviews in a day. The team leader might poll the researchers and their progress before deciding to stay another day or move on to the next village.

As one of the first westerners to participate in the Institute's expeditions, I was as much a guest as a colleague. The team leader adapted the group's itinerary to suit my interest in dance (we searched specifically for a wedding and stayed in that village for the entire weekend). Evening campfire conversations often included orientational information for me, descriptions of dance traditions, and many questions about Canada and my view of our discipline. My hosts were extremely gracious and were particularly concerned that their spartan living conditions would be unacceptable to me. I was not expected or encouraged to contribute to menial tasks such as putting up the tents or hauling mattresses or washing dishes.

I became familiar with an ongoing project of the Folk Music Programme in the Lviv Conservatory for which literally thousands of wedding and Christmas songs were collected, transcribed and charted on maps to identify patterns and distributions. Project leaders hoped that they would reflect certain historic political and cultural boundaries from the eleventh and twelfth centuries. This massive project involved dozens of fieldworkers and students in hundreds of short expeditions over more than a generation.

That summer I also had the opportunity to go on private field trips with individuals. I travelled for a week with an independent researcher to a specific cluster of villages in an attempt to document the local dance repertoire. Sleeping arrangements were pre-arranged with an acquaintance. We used public transport, hitched rides and walked from our home base to nearby villages each day.

In the summer of 1995 I embarked on a larger field trip, supported by the Social Sciences and Humanities Research Council of Canada and the Huculak Chair of Ukrainian Culture and Ethnography at the University of Alberta. Specifically, the goal was to compare Ukrainian dance in Ukraine and in Canada, and explore the 'Canadianization' and 'ethnicization' in the Canadian experience. My understanding of Ukrainian Canadian dance was that it had changed a great deal in 100 years. I wanted to go to the villages from which my Canadian interviewees and dancers (or their ancestors) had emigrated to see if I could confirm my information on the pre-emigration repertoire and to see how the dance traditions fared in their diverse home lands. I was interested in changes in repertoire and in the forms of the dances, but also in what the dances meant to the people who performed them. I understood that the issue of symbolizing ethnic identity would be a key theme for this comparison.

I hired a graduate student from Alberta and an ethnologist/guide from Ukraine to take care of logistics, provide initial contacts, and participate in the research. Hiring a driver with a van proved to be the cheapest and most reliable option for travel. The research plan included some time in Lviv at the Institute of Ethnology, which served as my host institution. Reflecting emigration patterns to Canada, plans were to visit four particular areas (Borshchiv, Chervonohrad, Terebovlia and Toporivtsi). Plans were to attend as many weddings as possible, since they are the primary multi-generational dance event. Weddings lasted generally from Friday evening to Sunday night. Other days were designated for recuperation (dancing often lasted all night) and for interviews. I pre-arranged side-trips to a Ukrainian area in Romania and another in Poland (the issue of ethnicity and identity in minority situations had been found to be significant in my Canadian materials). I hoped to sample urban and rural weddings, to get some cross-section of wealthy and poor communities, traditionalist and modernist families. I hoped to spend one and a half months in the town of Borshchiv to acquire a better sense of the more subtle nonverbalized meanings that are communicated within a familiar group during dance events. In 1912, my grandfather had emigrated from the village of Mushkativka, 3 kilometres away. I hoped to gain better knowledge of my distant relatives and I hoped that this part of my identity might help people accept my presence more casually.

By 1995, money had become an increasingly significant factor in contacts between North Americans and people in Ukraine as the imbalance of wealth had grown more and more obvious. Soviet wages and consumer prices had been maintained at levels significantly below western averages. In the post-Soviet period, prices rose quickly to international levels while wages did not. A wealthy elite now prospered visibly, while the standard of living of the majority of the population deteriorated. The general attitude towards the new political reality was negative and pessimistic. The unofficial economy remained very large; corruption, racketeering and theft were seen to be rampant and increasing. As it happened, however, we experienced no serious security threats. By North American standards, most areas remained safe.

WORKING WITH LOCAL SCHOLARS

As political interference faded away and as the logistics of research in Ukraine became more familiar, the factor that most strongly coloured my fieldwork experiences was the difference in perspective between myself and my colleagues there. Some of these differences were personal, while others were part of the academic tradition in each area (cf. Pitt-Rivers, 1992; Fahim and Helmer, 1982). In eastern Europe, ethnology developed in the context of romantic nationalism in the nineteenth century (Cocchiara, 1981; Subtelny, 1988, pp. 221–32). In order to justify their aspirations for political independence, leaders of stateless groups needed to demonstrate that their people had a unique and historic culture on a distinct territory. Descriptions of the traditional culture of the peasants served as a key foundation for these movements. An attempt was made during the Soviet period to diffuse the focus on national identity, but nationalism has risen to prominence again as the post-Soviet states work to consolidate their new political status.

I shared some of these sentiments, though my current research project was not so much an attempt to help define Ukrainian culture or to contribute directly to Ukrainian nation-building. Rather, I was using Ukrainian material as a case study in a more general investigation of continuity and change in cultural traditions given differing environments. This difference in orientation was often only implicit but proved to have many implications in my work with colleagues from Ukraine. Specific differences that affected our fieldwork included their interest in collecting texts, concern with geographic borders, origins and purity.

Texts

One of the most striking characteristics of my colleagues' work in Ukraine was their strong tendency to focus on collecting ethnographic texts. Songs, proverbs, textiles, clay pots, dances and other traditional items were collected as objects, counted, compared, classified and preserved in museums, publications or private collections. Researchers' primary focus was on description and quantitative, tangible measurement. Fieldwork performance was often measured by the number of collected texts. I was also interested in documenting dances as texts, though the qualitative aspects of meaning were much higher in my list of priorities. I was somewhat more 'anthropological' in my perspective (Giurchescu and Torp, 1991, p. 1; Kaeppler, 1991, p. 11).

The concern for concrete texts contributes to the low status of dance as a research subject in Ukraine. Given a general unfamiliarity with specialized dance notations, scholars tended to characterize dance as 'pysano vylamy po vodi' (written with a pitchfork on water) – meaning impossible or impractical to research scientifically. Sympathetically, one colleague suggested that I pick a 'real' subject for scholarly study. The large folk stage dance community in Ukraine, for the most part, was notoriously disconnected from ethnology, and functioned exclusively as a theatre art. Larysa Saban, perhaps the most experienced researcher of non-staged dance in Ukraine, works primarily without institutional support.

One of the most obvious practical implications of this concern with texts relates to the use of the tape recorder. Students and researchers in folk music, for example, typically use a cassette recorder for fieldwork. The tape recorder is often placed on pause for most of the interview. Only the actual songs/music are recorded, as well as exceptional excerpts from the conversation if they can be anticipated. In the archive, the songs are copied onto a large reel-to-reel tape and documented with the name, date, performer and other identifying information. The original cassette is generally re-used. Researchers tend to count the specific number of texts they have recorded in each village and in each expedition. Some personal archives include thousands and tens of thousands of texts. In contrast, I tended to let the recorder run continuously from the moment an interviewee agreed to let me tape the conversation until the end, even during the meandering discussions and digressions and my own descriptions. Most of my colleagues considered my interview style slow, ineffective and expensive. I think they perceived my interest in general ambiance and broad descriptions of dance events to be idiosyncratic and a result of poor orientation.

Geographic Borders

Partly because of the connection between ethnography and nation-building, and partly because of Soviet visa regulations, most Ukrainian ethnologists conducted fieldwork entirely within the USSR and often within Ukraine itself. The connections between national borders and culture were reinforced both in the design of ethnographic research projects and in the popular media. My experience with state borders was quite different, as I had crossed state borders dozens of times, researching Ukrainians in Canada, the USA, Poland, Slovakia and the former Yugoslavia.

Within their national borders, the study of regional diversity and geographic distribution tended to be very significant in Ukrainian research. Projects such as the one at the Lviv Conservatory operate on the assumptions of the historical-geographic method, where patterns of diffusion are used as clues in reconstructing historical layers of the culture (Dorson, 1972, pp. 7–12). Again, my own project had a different orientation. I had only fragmentary prior knowledge of the distribution of dance forms around western Ukraine as my Canadian interviewees from different areas were mixed across the prairies. Often, my informants did not know exactly from where their ancestors had emigrated.

Origins

Part of the mindset inherited from romantic nationalism was the idea that a nation's status is connected to the uniqueness and antiquity of its culture. In Ukrainian ethnology then, demonstration of ancient and autochthonous origins of any cultural element was usually seen as desirable. Most ethnographic research emphasized the stability of the given tradition. By contrast, I realized that my research plan emphasized cultural change. Indeed, I was actually hoping to find that the dances had changed in Canada: that would demonstrate that they had become 'naturalized' in their new home rather than remaining foreign.

Differences in concern with origins were very clear when I showed active interest in urban weddings and discotheques. My Ukrainian colleagues on the research team and at the Institute of Ethnology could see little value in recording the dances of these rather unremarkable and culturally bland people. For them, this was a debased culture, something to disdain and apologize for rather than to preserve. To my eyes, however, these events were quite interesting and quite culturally specific. Many of my Canadian weddings were urban, and this experience allowed useful comparisons.

Purity

Cultural and racial purity is conceptually connected with antique origins and is valued very positively in Ukrainian ethnology. Foreign influence is seen as contamination or colonization. International trends are often downplayed by both ethnographers and by experienced informants. Western cultural imperialism is generally acknowledged and valued negatively. Though I felt a pride in Ukrainian culture, I had also been influenced by recent western arguments that many folk traditions around Europe might be much less ancient and much less pure than folklorists and nation-builders had earlier imagined. My cursory knowledge of folk dance around Europe suggested that many features of Ukrainian dance were indeed part of widespread European patterns. For example, since much of western Ukraine was part of the Austro-Hungarian Empire when my great-grandparents lived there, I suspected that the music and dance culture of Vienna in the nineteenth century was likely to have influenced them. Published sources on dance in western Europe reinforced this idea and were often very useful in learning the dance repertoire of my grandparents' generation. I felt that dances and dance elements did not have to be uniquely Ukrainian to be interesting. On the contrary, Ukraine's integration into general European trends was also a satisfying discovery. I know that I irritated my fellow researchers when I voiced these ideas.

I was also suspect of the significance of racial purity and the 'gene fund' which was often cited in explaining the continuity of certain cultural traditions. Unlike my colleagues, I empathized with Benedict

Anderson (1991) that a nation is a political and cultural construction based more on the experiences of its people over the last several centuries rather than in the genetic inheritance of the race.

Ethnographic Authority

Comparisons of indigenous scholars and foreign researchers often suggest that the former have advantages of knowing the culture from the inside and of being sensitive to subtleties which remain unnoticed by people from different cultural backgrounds (Driessen, 1993; Fahim and Helmer, 1982). I certainly appreciated my Ukrainian colleagues who frequently made observations that had eluded my attention. Likewise, they handled the thorny issue of accepting food and alcohol much more successfully than I. On the other hand, 'pure insiders and outsiders do not exist' (Driessen, 1993, p. 3), and my colleagues also operated at some cultural distance from their informants (Jakubowska, 1993, p. 149). A class difference, urban intelligentsia versus rural agriculturalist, was frequently apparent. Perhaps since the days of romantic nationalism, researchers often had an ambivalent relationship with carriers of the traditional culture. On the one hand, this culture was precious and valuable; on the other hand, it needed to be saved from the mud and poverty of the context in which it just barely survived. I felt that the ethnographers generally perceived themselves as situated at a higher level of authority in their culture, conceiving cultural knowledge as familiarity with geographic and historical patterns (Jakubowska, 1993, p. 152). The village farmers might know their local traditions, but their knowledge was limited to one time and place. It would not be unreasonable, therefore, for a scholar to correct an informant on a point that had become forgotten or corrupted in local tradition. Researchers tended to be quite businesslike during interviews, steering the conversation on their own topic, sometimes pressuring them to sing longer than the informant wanted to and dismissing the informant when the information was collected (cf. Pitt-Rivers, 1992, pp. 144–6).

I was not comfortable with the power and hegemony that were at play during the fieldwork trip, though I was in a position of power at least as great as my colleagues. I was male. I was a professor. I had a video camera. I had money and the luxury to travel all the way across the ocean in pursuit of my interests and thoughts about dance. I, too, asked most of the questions and I would be writing up the final reports. I felt morally and ideologically inclined to try to de-emphasize that imbalance in power, to try to interact with other humans as equals. I wanted to believe that I was not superior to my informants (fellow participants? interlocutors? teachers?). Usually I tried to level the playing field as much as possible by giving the villagers voice in directing the conversation, by trying to inconvenience them as little as possible, by attending to their questions, interests and requests. Sometimes I think my approach was successful. On the other hand, I am sure that my colleagues and the villagers themselves sometimes perceived this as clumsy romanticism, condescension or lack of discipline. Again, sometimes I felt that we were actually interesting for the informants, unusual visitors that enlivened an otherwise uneventful day. Indeed, most had rarely spoken to anyone from across the ocean. It was often clear that we were sincerely welcome. By showing interest in them and their knowledge, we validated our interviewees and endowed them with status among their peers.

CONCLUSION

I am generally satisfied with my capacity for fieldwork in Ukraine. The political bureaucracy in that part of the world has dissolved from Soviet antipathy to near unobtrusiveness and even passive support. I am relatively comfortable in the logistics of the fieldwork project, and feel that we did gain access to a rich and striking dance culture. I was pleased with the information I collected on the dances (video records, verbal descriptions, manuscripts from previous researchers and, to a lesser degree, kinesthetic knowledge). We had collected both diachronic and synchronic information, data based on actions as well as thoughts about actions (Jacobson, 1991, pp. 11–16). I was surprised (and pleased) to see the frequency with which certain local and historic forms were confirmed by communities on different continents with practically no contact for eighty years. I am less sure of my knowledge of the meaning of the dances, particularly since meaning is multilayered and intangible. I did not become a near-insider in Borshchiv, as I had originally wished. I did, however, gain many valuable insights on how people experience dance in that culture.

It was the third aspect of the fieldwork – learning to cooperate with local researchers – that comes to the fore most often now that I have returned home from the field. If one measure of the success of fieldwork is the process of 'de-ethnocentrification' and culture shock (Pina-Cabral, 1992, pp. 4, 8; Pitt-Rivers, 1992, p. 142), then fieldwork in Ukraine has been productive for me so far. I continue to grapple with the many ideas and practices of my colleagues in eastern Europe as they to search for roots while I search for branches. In this process, I come more and more to agree with those who value multivocality in cross cultural writing; multivocality which involves the dancers *and* indigenous ethnologists as well.

REFERENCES

Anderson, B. 1991. *Imagined Communities: Reflections on the Origin and Spread of Nationalism*. London: Verso.

Cocchiara, G. 1981. *The History of Folklore in Europe*. Philadelphia: Institute for the Study of Human Issues. (translated by J. McDonald; originally published in 1954).

Dorson, R. 1972. *Folklore and Folklife: an Introduction*. Chicago: University of Chicago Press.

Driessen, H. (ed.). 1993. *The Politics of Ethnographic Reading and Writing: Confrontations of Western and Indigenous Views*. Saarbrücken, Germany: Verlag Breitenbach Publishers.

Fahim, H. and Helmer, K. 1982. Themes and counterthemes: the Burg Wartenstein Symposium. In Fahim, H. (ed.), *Indigenous Anthropology in Non-western Countries: Proceedings of a Burg Wartenstein Symposium*. Durham, North Carolina: Carolina Academic Press, pp. xi–xxxiii.

Giurchescu, A. and Torp, L. 1991. Theory and methods in dance research: a European approach to the holistic study of dance. *Yearbook for Traditional Music*, XXIII, pp. 1–10.

Jacobson, D. 1991. *Reading Ethnography*. Albany: State University of New York Press.

Jakubowska, L. 1993. Writing about Eastern Europe: perspectives from ethnography and anthropology. In Driessen, H (ed.), pp. 143–59.

Kaeppler, A.L. 1991. American approaches to the study of dance. *Yearbook for Traditional Music*, XXIII, pp. 11–21.

Pina-Cabral, J. de. 1992. Against translation: the role of the researcher in the production of ethnographic knowledge. In Pina-Cabral, J. de and Campbell, J. (eds), pp. 1–23.

Pina-Cabral, J. de and Campbell, J. (eds). 1992. *Europe Observed*. Basingstoke: Macmillan.

Pitt-Rivers, J. 1992. The personal factors in fieldwork. In Pina-Cabral, J. de and Campbell, J. (eds), pp. 133–47.

Subtelny, O. 1988. *Ukraine: a History*. Toronto: University of Toronto Press.

15 'Outsider' in an 'Inside' World, or Dance Ethnography at Home
Maria Koutsouba

The pursuit of fieldwork 'at home' has received considerable attention in the field of anthropology in general,[1] but less so within the subfield of dance. An important factor that shaped the outcome of my fieldwork was the opportunity, afforded by my status as a dance ethnographer 'at home', to examine dance from various viewpoints and thus emphasize the multiple layers of potential interpretations. On the one hand, I was a Greek scholar conducting research in my own country and, consequently, an 'insider'. On the other hand, as I do not originate from the island where fieldwork was undertaken,[2] I was also an 'outsider'. Simultaneously, my role was that of a 'dance expert' on the repertoire under investigation, having taught and performed the dances of the particular island for a number of years prior to doing fieldwork.[3] This chapter focuses on ethical and political issues which emerged in that situation and considers the tensions and dilemmas which it foregrounded.

ETHNOGRAPHY 'AT HOME'

What constituted 'being at home' in my situation is not easily defined. I was born and brought up in Athens; yet close ties with both my parents' birthplaces on the mainland of Roumeli and the island of Evia were always maintained, particularly with the latter. This gave me an early opportunity not only to realize that each social institution, such as the family, village, region, country and so on, has its own configuration which provide different degrees of freedom, but that these social constructs carry a high significance in Greek life. A decision to carry out fieldwork in one parent's birthplace seemed 'appropriate' and 'logical'. This would have offered me advantages such as previous experience, easier access or immediate support, with the

186

potential to enhance my family's prestige. It seemed to me, however, that too much familiarity was not beneficial. Consequently, I decided to research the dances of another Greek area on the grounds that such a selection would ensure me a 'safe distance'.

Further reasons for this choice hinged on specific cultural and choreological peculiarities to be found in the area and the fact that an urban folk dance phenomenon coexisted with rural manifestations of dance. I already had established relationships with a number of islanders, particularly those from the village of Karya; my schooldays' friendship with a village resident, for example, had become tighter after I became her son's godmother. Having decided to pursue research on Lefkada, my knowledge of the islanders who had migrated to Athens seemed advantageous as it guaranteed an existing point of reference. Karya was chosen as my place of residence since it was one of the two main villages of the island; because of its northern central position it provided access both to the capital and to a consid- erable number of villages. The village was also appreciated for its long tradition in cultural and dance activities.

Given, as I thought, two great advantages – knowledge, as a Greek, of the various levels of my country's social life and a point of reference through my friend – I felt quite confident starting my research on the particular community. In the field, however, I became conscious of the austerity with which Karsani (inhabitants of Karya village) defined their being and of their insistence in maintaining the borders between these definitions. Karsani identify themselves as Greeks only in con- trast with foreigners, but they are Ionian inhabitants in comparison with the Greeks of other regions. They label themselves as Lefkadians when confronted with the inhabitants of the rest of the Ionian islands, while they form a distinctive population when opposed to the other villagers of Lefkada, let alone the various extended families of the village itself. The magnitude of this austerity was such that, despite my advantages, they considered me to be at the lowest level of the structure of the community's life, since I did not originate from Karya village, was not of Lefkadian nor even of Ionian origin. It was then that my former confidence turned to a feeling of being a stranger in my own country and I experienced what it is to be an 'outsider' in an 'inside' world. But was it really so?

Although this was my first reaction to being in the field, in time, I realized that my acquaintance with rural communities through my parents' birthplaces had placed me in a peculiar situation. Apart from local particularities, I was familiar with the general rules that structured the community under investigation. Yet, I was alien to the people who practised these rules. This realization influenced my behaviour during the research. Thus I rejected the invitation to stay with my friend's parents-in-law living in Karya. I felt quite certain beforehand not only that it was impossible for me to follow their timetable, but also that my work as a dance researcher was going to be 'unusual' for the locals as well. I knew, for instance, that neither sitting inside a *kafenio* (coffee house), a restricted male privilege, nor smoking were 'proper' behaviour for a 'respectable' Greek woman, at least in the periphery of Greece. Yet, I had to do the first as it was one of the best ways to interview men in public circumstances, nor did I intend to give up the second. Similarly, I knew in advance that learning the local famous specific embroidery stitch would pave my way to the female 'implicit'[4] facets of the social life which takes place in the country yards and back streets. I did not, however, pursue the practice of embroidery as I had long ago rejected this Greek female activity because of its gender connotations.

What I did not know was that, at Karya, each *kafenio* is the meeting place of people of the same political party, which was usually indicated by the colour of the chairs and the tables. Nor was I familiar with the villagers' common use of nicknames to distinguish the many families with the same surname. Learning this practice was not only time-consuming but also confusing, as it is common for individuals to have more than one nickname, some of which may be insulting and best avoided when dealing with them. I fell into this trap when in 1993 I interviewed Eleni Stavraka, one of the most important informants, for the first time. My primary weakness was that I had no idea about conflict between villagers, although this ignorance sometimes proved to be helpful. This, at least, was the case with Theodoros Katopodis, a man who was appreciated all over the island as a 'dance person',[5] the previous dance teacher of Karya's dance club, 'Apollon', and founder of the village's folklore museum and embroidery school, but whose oddity had already been mentioned to me by the villagers as a reason for my possible rejection. It was, however, surprising, that not only did he accept me, but he provided much information as to why he felt quite secure with me as an 'outsider' and thus not involved in the various factions. I did not have a similar reception from Pantazis Kontomichis, the main folklorist of the island, when I visited him in the capital. In this case, my origins seemed to be of great importance; indeed, he concealed dance information which I later found in one of his books.[6]

These examples demonstrate a few of the complexities which emerge when practising ethnography at home. Apart from the various practical problems, the most important aspect was the impact of this experience on myself. Through this process I came to question the very concept of 'being at home'. As Strathern wonders, 'how [does] one know when one is at home ... [as] the grounds of familiarity and distance are shifting ones?' (1987, p. 17). Luckily or not, such questions do not end by leaving the field; they are strongly impressed on the memory, following the researcher, perhaps for the rest of his or her life.

'DANCE ETHNOGRAPHY' AT HOME

The study of a community's dance phenomenon is a totally different task from research into the community itself. Once 'in the field' this raises a series of different problems, especially when the community under investigation presents dance complexities, such as the Lefkadian example, and because the concept of dance research is not yet widespread, not only on the island, but generally in Greece.[7] Once in the field, the first problem I faced was how to decide which dance to examine, when I realized that the islanders manipulated the existing dance repertoires in different ways according to the levels of their social life's structure. The dance repertoires which the islanders performed among themselves which appeared to me to be 'Lefkadian', became 'foreign' whenever presented on stage, where another dance repertoire was demonstrated as representative of the 'Lefkadian' dance tradition (Plate 11). Because of this, I received different interpretations of the same kind of dances by the same people in different contexts. The situation was complicated and confusing, particularly in the early stages of the research, until I had elucidated the islanders' way of thinking about dance.

Even then, however, the question of which dance to examine still remained. On the one hand, Lefkada presented an impressive urban folk dance phenomenon: despite its small size, there are six dance clubs, an International Folklore Festival is organized every year and there are also tourist performances. On the other hand, the islanders danced among themselves quite often and in a number of events, such as at village fairs, *horoesperides* (formal evening dances) or family celebrations (Plate 12). Given the former's presentational character, it was liable to processes such as stability, standardization and use of group choreographic devices, whereas the latter's participatory nature was improvisatory, flexible and largely individualized.[8]

Further groupings of the various dance repertoires were articulated by the Lefkadians themselves which made my position even more difficult. Thus, there was a distinction between pre- and post-World War II dance repertoires. The pre-war dances were further divided into urban and rural subcategories. The postwar dance category included dances from the mainland, the Aegean islands and Asia Minor, as these were adopted by the islanders. The coexistence of all these various dance repertoires was not always harmonious. Transformations have created different opinions among the islanders, not only about what dances each dance repertoire consists of, but about Lefkadian dance itself. It was surprising, for instance, to learn that although Eleni Drakatou, a woman in her eighties, was willing to demonstrate a local dance, *barbouni*, which had fallen into disuse, to the dance teachers of the club where her granddaughter attended classes, she never received a positive response from them (Drakatou, 1993); a similarly negative response from the dance club teachers was received by other older people such as Eleni Stavraka (1994) and Vassilis Thermos (1994).

During preliminary research, the totality of the dances performed during the various dance activities all over the island attracted my interest since they formed a multifaceted dance picture that was quite interesting in itself. Yet the quantity and complexity of the material which emerged imposed place and data limitations from the very beginning of the actual fieldwork. Thus, apart from information necessary to clarify the overall dance profile of Lefkada, my main centre of activity focused on the pre-war rural dance repertoire that for a number of reasons (Koutsouba, 1997, pp. 66–7) had been selected for study.

DANCE ETHNOGRAPHY AT HOME BY A 'DANCE EXPERT'?

A final area of enquiry emerges from my existing relationship with Greek dance which began with family activities (attending and participating in village fairs, and dancing at weddings and family gatherings), continued throughout school life (participating in the Greek dance activities and performances of the school) and resulted in my specialization of Greek folk dance as part of my first academic degree in the Physical Education and Sports Sciences Department at the

University of Athens. This transition towards dance from a means of entertainment to a professional career was definitely a turning point in my relationship with Greek dance, which was enhanced in parallel by my involvement from 1985 in 'semi-professional' dancing, as a folk dancer. Starting from Greek dance groups of the Athenian tourist area of Plaka, I became a member of the Theatre of Dora Stratou and of the London Section of the Lyceum of Greek Women, among other dance companies, and I have been teaching dance since 1986 in various places.

Of course, this background meant that once I decided to study Greek folk dance at postgraduate level, I was not 'innocent' of my subject, as I had already learned, performed and taught Greek folk dances, in general, and 'Lefkadian' dances in particular; indeed, I was considered to be a Greek folk 'dance expert'. Perhaps this point may be regarded as a disadvantage at least in terms of objectivity. It was, however, this extensive and intense involvement with dance itself that led me towards its theoretical orientation, particularly from an anthropological point of view. Apart from the fact that the latter inevitably indicates absence of 'absolute objectivity' (Grau, 1983, pp. 4–5), this knowledge proved invaluable in many ways during the research, while raising ethical dilemmas related to dance.

On the one hand, the corpus of knowledge which I had already obtained was constructive in understanding certain aspects of the Lefkadian dance phenomenon including dance itself and dance contexts. It was, for instance, easier for me to recognize the dance patterns from which the local repertoires were built up, to uncover possible relationships among the various dances and to learn those that I did not know before as I was not aware of the entire repertoire. It was also quite uncomplicated to identify the variations of a dance or to notice its transformations over the course of time. Similarly, it was less demanding to outline the dance contexts such as village fairs or family gatherings which, despite local particularities, tend to present a common general structure all over the country.

On the other hand, my status as a dance teacher and dancer had an impact on the ethical problems raised, the strategies adopted concerning my involvement with the local dance teachers and clubs and on my means of gaining inside knowledge of these institutions. A first point concerns my introduction to the teachers of the island's dance clubs. In order to understand the complexities of the situation, a background knowledge of Greek folk dance teachers is essential. In brief, dance teachers in Greece currently come from two different strands.

The majority of them are previous members of a dance club who, after performing in the club for a number of years, later call themselves dance teachers and take up teaching, usually as a second job to earn additional income. Diametrically opposed to this are the few dance teachers who, despite previous engagements in dance, have additionally passed through an official academic dance training to become professional teachers.[9] The two strands have little communication between them, and a latent antagonism is evident.

I was already an official dance teacher before going into the field. Most of the local dance teachers had previously been members of the clubs in which they were teaching; thus, my appearance on the island raised various reactions that required a sensitive approach. First, I had to make clear to the teachers, committee members, particularly of Karya, and myself that I had no intention to teach, not even in the form of seminars as I was sometimes asked. I include myself because the idea of teaching, before going in the field, seemed a good solution to remedy my poor financial situation. Once in Lefkada, however, I realized that this was not a sensible option: not only I was going to lose important informants by taking on the job from the locals, but I was going to disturb the order of things after my departure.

In practical terms, my rejection of the role of dance teacher was relatively easy; morally, however, it was another matter. Through attendence at the dance clubs' performances and lessons, I encountered various elements that were contrary to my official training in terms of dance repertoires, choreographies and musical accompaniment, let alone the methods of teaching. As a dance teacher I felt obliged to interrupt the teaching on many occasions; as a dance ethnographer the only right I had was to observe the *status quo*. Of course, I elected the second option, restricting my input to policies of secondary importance, such as discussing ideas with the dance teachers or giving information about dances whenever I was asked. I still do not know if this was the right attitude, not so much towards the dance teachers but mainly towards the students, children who wanted to learn Greek dance.

Second, a similarly difficult position was created whenever I was asked to criticize the various dance and cultural activities taking place, to make proposals for their improvement or even to participate in them. My first reaction was to refuse so as not to interfere or influence the community. Over time, however, I realized that my continuous rejection to respond to any of them was received negatively, and my presence there was questioned. I had, thus, to find a middle way. In the first case, I made an attempt to restrict my critique to the limits of the contexts in which the activities occurred. The performances of the capital's dance clubs, for example, were much better organized than those of the villages, a reality that I openly admitted. Yet I always took care to emphasize the important contribution that the village dance club made to the local culture.

In terms of proposals to improve activities, whatever this meant for the locals, I was open to discussing my ideas, but only with their organizers since a different attitude might be conceived by them as offensive. With regard to my potential participation in dance performances, the situation was more problematic: although the idea was tempting with its promise of inside information and opportunity to practise the stylistic singularities of the local dance idiom, I again refused since this would automatically have excluded a local girl from the performance.

CONCLUSION

This chapter has examined the perplexities which emerge when a 'dance expert' undertakes dance ethnography at home: dilemmas regarding the selection of place, the particularities of identifying the material of dance ethnography and, predominantly, the strategies adopted in order to facilitate communication with the islanders and the dance scholars/experts. Levels of 'belonging' and issues of representation, shaped during the fieldwork in dance 'at home', were thus revealed. The production of such a text as the doctoral thesis brought into tension the restrictions imposed on a native anthropologist who necessarily must consider ongoing dialogue with the natives after fieldwork together with the demands of the academic world (Mascarenhas-Keyes, 1987). A more dominant tension occurs as a result of 'the paradoxical sense of simultaneous distance and closeness, otherness and oneness' (Danforth, 1982, p. 6) that the native researcher feels when in the field and when translating his or her experience into a text. The 'self as informant', however, can be used not only as a methodological tool during fieldwork as Mascarenhas-Keyes (1987) proposes, but also when included in the ethnographic text, to give new insights into this area.

NOTES

1. This movement is known by a number of terms (see Jackson, 1987; Gefou-Madianou, 1993a). Gefou-Madianou (1993b) emphasizes that 'the distinction of anthropology at home from classical anthropology is of methodological character' (p. 48) and 'anthropology at home is not a new anthropology but an anthropological viewpoint which was created to correspond to particular historical, scientific, ideological and cultural coincidences' (p. 50).

2. Fieldwork was carried out from January 1993 until August 1994; preliminary research for the needs of my doctoral thesis (Koutsouba, 1997) was undertaken in autumn 1992.

3. I place 'dance expert' in inverted commas as the term can take different meanings in various contexts. For instance, a 'dance expert' in a village is someone who masters the local dance repertoire; at a dance club, it means someone who is not only skilful, but additionally aware of stage conventions; and, at a dance class it refers to someone who has the ability to communicate well. I use the term here in order to characterize those who, through an official academic training, have obtained practical and theoretical knowledge of dance.

4. 'Explicit' and 'implicit' aspects of Greek social life (rural and urban) constituted one of the main foci of anthropological research in Greece from its beginning. For an account of a critical examination of the extensive study of this issue in Greece, see Danforth (1983) and Papataxiarchis (1992, pp. 11–98).

5. 'Dance people' refers to members of local families who are appreciated for their dance skills and considered by the islanders to be gifted in this respect.

6. In order to avoid any misunderstanding I emphasize that I refer here to information regarding the Lefkadian dance *tria passa*. During the interview, I was told that there was no information available; yet, in Kontomichis's 1985 publication I found an important reference (p. 243).

7. Greek folk dance has been introduced as an autonomous and worthwhile subject for academic study only in the past ten years in Greece. For more information see Koutsouba, 1997, pp. 22–7.

8. These two conceptual categories have been proposed by Nahachewsky (1995, p. 1) to distinguish dances. In this study, the terms are used in a similar sense to distinguish the dance events as well. For a discussion of the categories see Koutsouba, 1997, p. 84.

9. Folk dancing is currently not considered to be a full-time profession in Greece.

REFERENCES

Danforth, M.L. 1982. *The Death Rituals of Rural Greece*. Princeton, New Jersey: Princeton University Press.

_____ 1983. Introduction: symbolic aspects of male/female relations in Greece. *Journal of Modern Greek Studies*, 1, 1, pp. 157–60.

Drakatou, E. 1993. Personal interview.

Jackson, A. (ed.). 1987. *Anthropology at Home*, ASA Monograph 25. London and New York: Tavistock Publications.

Gefou-Madianou, D. 1993a. Mirroring ourselves through western texts: the limits of an indigenous anthropology. In Driessen, H. (ed.), *The Politics of Ethnographic Reading and Writing: Confrontations of Western and Indigenous Views*. Saarbrücken, Germany: Verlag Breitenbach Publishers, pp. 160–81.

―― 1993b. Ανθρωπολογία οίκοι: για μια κριτική της 'γηγενούς Ανθρωπολογίας' (Anthropology at home: a critique of the 'indigenous anthropology'). Διαβάζω (Read), 323, pp. 44–51.

Grau, A. 1983. Dreaming, dancing, kinship: the study of *yoi*, the dance of the Tiwi of Melville and Bathurst Islands, North Australia. Unpublished PhD thesis, Queen's University, Belfast.

Kontomichis, P. 1985. Δημοτικά Τραγούδια της Λευκάδας (Demotic Songs of Lefkada). Athens: Γρηγόρης.

Koutsouba, M. 1997. Plurality in motion: dance and cultural identity on the Greek Ionian island of Lefkada. Unpublished PhD thesis, Goldsmiths College, University of London.

Mascarenhas-Keyes, S. 1987. The native anthropologist: constraints and strategies in research. In Jackson, A. (ed.), pp. 180–95.

Nahachewsky, A. 1995. Participatory and presentational dance as ethnochoreological categories. *Dance Research Journal*, 27, 1, pp. 1–15.

Papataxiarchis, E. 1992. Εισαγωγή. Από τη σκοπιά του φύλου: ανθρωπολογικές θεωρήσεις της σύγχρονης Ελλάδας (Introduction: from the point of view of gender: anthropological theoretizations of modern Greece)'. In Papataxiarchis, E. and Paradellis, T. (eds), Ταυτότητες και Φύλο στη Σύγχρονη Ελλάδα (Identities and Gender in Modern Greece). Athens: Καστανιώτης, pp. 11–98.

Strathern, M. 1987. The limits of auto-anthropology. In Jackson, A. (ed.), pp. 16–37.

Stavraka, E. 1993. Personal interview.

―― 1994. Personal interview.

Thermos, V. 1994. Personal interview.

16 [Re]Constructing Meanings: the Dance Ethnographer as Keeper of the Truth

Theresa J. Buckland

ETHNOGRAPHY AND REPRESENTATION

The issue of representation in both its epistemological and political dimensions has resounded throughout theoretical literature on ethnography. Yet in spite of Williams's pioneering consideration of reflexivity and objectivity in 1976, the problematics of representation have been slow to percolate dance scholarship. In common with most mainstream anthropologists, dance researchers have been stimulated by the oft-cited collection *Writing Culture* (Clifford and Marcus, 1986) and the more scattered writings of feminist ethnographers published in the 1980s (see Abu-Lughod, 1990). Studies by Sklar (1991) and Ness (1992, 1996) are indicative of the trend to situate the researcher in relation to the people interviewed and observed, to the fieldwork process and to the act of writing. Yet the impact of that writing on the communities and their researcher after publication remains under-investigated in dance scholarship.[1]

In part this can be ascribed to the nascent state of ethnographic publications on dance. It also owes much to the conduct of most twentieth-century dance ethnography within 'scientific' paradigms of European ethnology and folklore studies: discussion of ethnographer/informant relationships before, during and after fieldwork has been minimized in the positivist search for authorial objectivity. In these intellectual traditions, research 'at home' is the norm; yet the ethnographic community is regarded as other to that of the researcher.

Since the classical period of folklore research in the nineteenth and early twentieth centuries, social and economic distances between researcher and researched have lessened: ties of class, gender, ethnicity and shared childhood memories are ever more likely in the wake of increased access to education, social mobility and widespread communications. The chances of members of the ethnographic community reading the academic's representations of them are high. Geographic proximity, shared registers of language and purchasing power mean that the monograph is well within their reach. In any case, the researcher's findings, as a matter of ethical and automatic procedure, should be made available. The ethnographer has responsibilities both to the people studied and to the scholarly community; that much is clear, particularly in a more democratic age. But would that the consequences of this moral imperative were as simple as its initial delivery. This chapter explores an on-going relationship, conducted over 20 years, during which I have published papers read by members of the ethnographic community.

In a post-positivist climate, the researcher recognizes that there is no one stable and overriding interpretation. Voices from the field do indeed compete; there is almost inevitably no consensus of interpretation that the ethnographer can publish nor one truth to be established. Within highly literate and technological cultures, academic responsibility may well necessitate not only the [re]construction of insights from fieldwork but also their relation to previously published and maybe contemporaneously published interpretations. In the case of a distinctive dance ceremonial, regarded as bizarre outside the local community, the profile may constitute long-term interaction and representation through the media. Since the community has not been sealed in a timewarp separate from the rest of the culture, the researcher may be just one in a long line of people and ideas which have had an impact on local interpretations (see Boyes, 1987–88; Limon, 1991). Full cognizance of articles in national and local newspapers, radio interviews, programme notes, local histories, television appearances and the like is essential to identify the sources and application of such material within the local community. How indeed does the researcher, faced with a multiplicity of voices, navigate the 'dilemmas of ethnographic representation ... [which] permeate every stage of the ethnographic process and are certainly not confined between book covers' (Macdonald, 1997, p. 162)? There are, of course, no answers, only stories. This is one telling of my quest for the truth when, as a doctoral student in folk life studies, I began, in 1977, to study the Britannia Coco-Nut Dancers of Bacup, Rossendale in northwest England.

CONCEPTUALIZING FIELDWORK IN THE 1970s

During the late 1970s and early 1980s in England, the emergent academic disciplines of folk life studies and dance were being formulated in response to an inheritance of literature characterized by populism and an anachronistic adherence to evolutionism. The theoretical outlook and procedures of inquiry were consequently propelled by the need to demonstrate an almost scientific credibility within the higher education system. This 'catching up' with other disciplines meant an emphasis on systematic data collection and an implicit functionalism (though selective) as the preferred interpretative framework for 'dance in society'. Such positivist concerns are ironic given the rumblings of collapse of this discourse elsewhere in intellectual thought; yet it should not be lightly dismissed that, in the cultivation of a highly visible and accountable scholarly rigour for both disciplines, such approaches were crucial to their academic legitimization. As a result, my study was shaped by two long-held and interrelated beliefs about the strategies and goals of ethnographic research. The first of these was that a holistic approach will ultimately render 'the truth' as a monolithic entity; the second was that the ethnographer passes from a state of almost complete ignorance to one of omniscience on the cultural practice being studied. Such entwined convictions may position the ethnographer as 'keeper of the truth', frequently as spokesperson for the agents of the cultural practice. This often occurs when the activity not only lies in the domain of public performance but, on account of its unique appearance, is perceived as other to those outside its immediate locality.

My fieldwork typically followed the strategies of folklore studies: unlike classic anthropological participant-observation, which would necessitate living in the town for at least a year,[2] my fieldwork constituted discrete encounters with the community which took place several times annually, staying in pubs and small hotels. Later with personal transport, I was able to make day trips as the need arose. My choice was not only the result of intellectual tradition and economics; there was no obvious role for me as a participant-observer. The custom was strictly performed by adult males, preferably married, who in part viewed participation in the then weekly dance practices and occasional performances at weekends outside the locality as a male space from which wives (and the occasional girlfriend) were excluded. Knowledge of the dance repertoire was jealously guarded by the men, who believed themselves to be the legitimate inheritors of an ancient local tradition which was not open to strangers. Thus I adopted the role of documenter of a unique tradition, arriving at events with notebook and pencil, camera, tape recorder and video recorder. Interested in the processes of change, I documented their selection of the repertoire in different contexts, with different dancers and at different times. Since the repertoire is not large, the dancers were somewhat surprised by my seemingly excessive filming but came to regard this as a bearable obsession and appreciated the videotapes which I later gave them. Not that I handed over unedited video material since I took care to copy only the better performances and filming in order to present my technical competence, the dancers as performers to themselves and to any other potential audience in the best possible light. This role of recording for the future accorded with my other role of detective of the past.

After about a year, the performers of the dance ritual and their immediate community came to realize the depth of my interest and that unlike the attention of previous students (mostly undergraduates) whose study was confined to a few months, my fascination extended over years. They allowed me to attend practices, helped to find old dancers and relatives to interview, patiently answered my questions in their homes, were photographed and videotaped every year, made their personal archives available to me and knew that I was searching local and national archives and talking to local residents in general about the custom of coco-nut dancing. Most of this activity was perceived to be that of an historian and in many respects this was true. As well as bringing personal intellectual biases to the field in regard to history, my training as a folklorist combined the North American school of folkloristics, then dominated by in an interest in contemporary performance, the Scandinavian school of folk life which sought the historicity of contemporary cultural practices and the new British social history which explored popular culture. In the popular realm, however, the term 'folk' signalled and continues to signal tradition, history, the past, mostly with an ultimately undetectable point of origin.

LOCAL MEANINGS

I have presented my focus upon recent history as largely a matter of expedience and as contingent upon the importance of diachronic perspectives in the theoretical viewpoint of contemporaneous English folklore study. Yet it was evident that the past loomed large in the local community's account of itself and of the Britannia Coco-Nut Dancers.³ I was often directed to the Bacup Natural History Society; though in fact most of the ephemera associated with their history were held by individual dancers. In interviews, frequent references were made to Bacup's former prosperity, of times when the Rossendale Valley was known as the 'Golden Valley' on account of its inhabitants' wealth. Comparisons were also made with the previously large population and the high number of pubs in the town. Certainly, I was conducting fieldwork throughout a period of economic recession which hit northern England badly, but the decline in Bacup was already long established. A stable and positive element throughout the twentieth century, however, has been the tradition of coco-nut dancing, epitomized by the Britannia team, whose regular annual appearance since the 1920s has been interrupted only by the Second World War. Local inhabitants also perceived their town to be quite distinctive, a common view among residents in neighbouring towns, who often regarded Bacup as possessing peculiarly conservative patterns of behaviour, social values and an almost incestuous preoccupation with its own families and localized culture so as to render it 'backward'. Many Bacupians appeared to relish this image which coincided with pride in the representation of the Britannia Coco-Nut Dancers as a unique tradition. Not that the community was unanimous in responding favourably to the custom. Some people whom I interviewed had little time for the dancers, pointing to what they regarded as the dancers' excessive alcohol consumption, or complaining of the overcrowding in their local pubs owing to the large influx of crowds; some just preferred to holiday away from the town at Easter. Yet others welcomed the visitors, spoke warmly of an annual event with which they had grown up and pointed to the celebrity which the dancers' activities brought to the town:

> We've got what no one else has got. Well, they're world famous for it, aren't they?
> Well, they're marvellous to watch, you know, they're unique really. I mean they haven't them anywhere else.
> It's just something for Bacup, isn't it? It's a Bacup ... it *is* Bacup.⁴

Meaning is, of course, conceptualized according to the needs and discourse within which the question is framed. For the inhabitants of Bacup, the phenomenon of the Coco-nutters or Nutters as they are popularly known in the Valley requires no rationale beyond that of tradition. I have written elsewhere (Buckland, 1991) of how the team came to be recorded and championed from the late 1920s by the English Folk Dance Society (later the English Folk Dance and Song Society [EFDSS]) and how the dancers successfully retained independence and control of their own custom. That independence can similarly be witnessed in the dancers' responses to inquiries about the meaning of the tradition. Outsiders often construed the custom as a folk activity and, following evolutionist rationales of classical folklore theory, equated meaning with ancient origin. The dancers certainly do not slavishly adopt the latest analysis presented to them by scholars; they select elements of alternative interpretations according to their audience and circumstances. For the dancers, there are two dominant exegeses: the local aetiological legend (see Buckland, 1986, p. 146) which relates how the dance was brought by Cornish tin miners to the nearby locality, and the official explanation, provided by the EFDSS which interprets the custom as a survival of a primitive spring ritual. Space precludes the rehearsal of exactly how this latter explanation evolved to dovetail with variants of the more localized explanation, and how both are now used in piecemeal fashion to address a variety of contexts.[5] In pursuing the meaning, alias the origin, of the dance, however, considerable attention was paid by outsiders to the dancers' unusual costume, especially their black faces (Plate 13). To those growing up with the Coco-nutters, the necessity to interpret only arises when visiting spectators ask. It is perhaps best exemplified in an old lady's response in the late 1970s when I pursued the question of why the dancers blackened their faces. 'Only to look like Coco-nutters, I suppose,' was her puzzled response to my inquiry.[6] Meanings for the local community relate more to local identity, continuity, pride and, more pragmatically, entertainment, particularly for the children. Why the dancers should dress in such a particular manner and when and where they originated concern most people in Bacup only in so far as they symbolize the town to the outside world and herald a holiday which a number of people spend in the pubs and clubs.

Growing fame for the Coco-nutters over the twentieth century has occasioned more numerous performances at national and indeed international levels, thereby generating a need for exposition to new audiences. Championed by the EFDSS as a rare survival of primeval folk culture, the Britannia Coco-Nut Dancers are officially explained as a mystical spring fertility ritual, which pushes their supposed origins to lie beyond written history. This Tylorian slant, which brought the

Bacup tradition into line with interpretations of more widespread
English ceremonial dance forms such as morris and sword dances, was
embellished by Douglas Kennedy, successor to Cecil Sharp, doyen of
English folk dance scholarship, as director of the Society. In his role as
patron, as early as the 1930s, Kennedy informed the Britannia team
that their black faces were part of an ancient means of disguise for
ritual performers (see Buckland, 1984, pp. 704–5). Such a feature was
certainly unusual in most English ceremonial dance teams known to
the Society at that time, but Kennedy was following typically Frazerian
modes of analysis. This interpretation, though, accorded well with the
dancers' own experience (see Buckland, 1990, p. 2) and there is considerable evidence, prior to the twentieth century, of blackened faces
in England to preserve anonymity in anti-establishment and ludic
behaviour (see Thompson, 1975, 1993). It was not, however, the only
interpretation available. Not only did black faces correlate well with
the local legend of miners (some of the Britannia dancers in the 1930s
were coal miners) but there were also local nineteenth-century
customs of pace-egging and niggering which involved black faces (see
Buckland, 1990, pp. 2–4). Yet the official explanation, totally unsub-
stantiated in terms of historicity, bestows a mystique and kudos of age
upon the activity. As memories of the Victorian Easter customs have
receded so has the exegesis of the folk dance revival movement gathered momentum. The black face *is* a disguise, both literally and
symbolically.

PUBLICATIONS IN THE FIELD

During fieldwork, I discovered, not surprisingly, that those participants in the custom who had closest and longest contact with the
Society and its influences gave me fuller versions of the official origin
theory. I regularly witnessed key members such as the leader or
secretary rehearsing its variants to the media. As time went on,
however, the expectation to present my own findings to the dancers
grew. Given my pioneering zeal to critique the speculative, evolutionist legacy in folk life and dance studies, it was hardly surprising that
my own account of the team's provenance should emphasize written
rather than mythological history. My first publication was descriptive
of the local history which I had uncovered (1986) and copies, given to
the team as thanks, were circulated. As a result, I occasionally found
myself asked by the dancers to speak to the media, indeed to act as

their official historian. I possessed other historical information, however, which I delayed publishing. My wider research revealed a theatrical tradition of coco-nut dancing that had probably travelled through amateur blackface acts to Bacup in the mid-nineteenth century. The custom's prehistoric roots were undoubtedly in question. When I finally published these findings in an American specialist dance journal (see Buckland, 1990), I again presented copies to the team. By this stage, admittedly, I was no longer in frequent contact with the dancers (my doctoral research was completed in 1984); yet I maintained annual contact at Easter. There was little discussion of the article's content with me or in my hearing but this was not dissimilar from the reception of the 1986 publication. Interestingly, my nineteenth-century origin theory was largely ignored and the dancers continued to reiterate variants of the two local legends, favouring the explanation of the black face as an ancient form of disguise. I may have conceived of myself as a keeper of the truth but the dancers made it clear that they were in control of their own interpretation and its dissemination.

My apprehension about publishing the known historical context of coco-nut dancing went beyond that of its relative youth and theatrical precedents. In the later twentieth century, the black face could be interpreted by folk cognoscenti or historians of English social history as a means of disguise; but in a post-imperialist England coming to terms with its racist inheritance, the black face was being increasingly construed as representative of a person of African derivation. Nor indeed as my 1990 article pointed out is such an interpretation at odds with the known history of the practice of coco-nut dancing. Its parallels with amateur black face acts stimulated in England by the arrival of the North American minstrel shows from the 1840s are clear, even though the English practice of minstrelsy and its socio-cultural meanings are distinct and decidedly complex to decipher (see Pickering, 1997). For the Coco-nutters, the black face has been part of their costume since at least 1857. There is little apart from the black face to suggest any representation of people of African derivation, although an historian of theatre costume might suspect an attempt to depict Moors through the turban-style hat and skirt. Nothing in the dancers' repertoire suggests anything other than an English nineteenth-century provenance with possibly older roots in north-west English processional dance styles. In the now politically correct world of the media, the black face of the Coco-nutters has recently become an issue. Whereas in the past, there has been complete acceptance of the argument of the black face as a disguise, television producers and festival organizers have now become anxious about potential audience reaction.[7] The Coco-nutters have lost television appearances through their refusal to appear without black make-up. In such a climate, my 1990 article could exacerbate the situation for the dancers if used by unsympathetic and sensation-seeking media.

RESOLUTIONS, STORIES AND TRUTHS

I believe that I have paid my dues to dance scholarship by publishing the information in a specialist journal and made the information available to the dancers; how they use it is their own concern. To casual inquirers and the media, I underplay the theatrical minstrelsy connections and point out the correspondences with blackface pace-egging and amateur minstrelsy in nineteenth-century Rossendale, but underline the distinctive nature of the coco-nut dance for which few comparable notations of the choreography exist. I do know one truth and that is that I have no concrete point of origin for the tradition in Bacup. It remains a mystery and one which I believe many would prefer never to be totally solved.

When I began studying English ceremonial dances, a revival morris dancer told me that when asked by the public where the tradition came from, he frequently asked them which they would prefer – the truth or a story? But the truth is a story, of course, and just one of many tales to tell which reveals our interpretation at any particular moment. I cannot deny the links between representations of African people performing coco-nut dances on the nineteenth-century stage, of course, but there is the question of how much significance I accord them. In the early 1990s, I came across an ex-dancer with the Coconutters whom I had frequently interviewed when he was a member of the team but had not seen for a number of years. At the end of the day, he asked me: 'Well, did you ever find out the origin of these dances?' I tried the multiple possibilities approach, the potential many truths, the evasive ethnographer reluctant to put words for future delivery into my interviewee's mouth. He cut straight across me: 'Shall I tell you what I think?' I barely had time to nod. I thought I already knew his opinion having, on numerous occasions in the early 1980s, heard him deliver the usual mix of local and official EFDSS legends. He went on:

I've been out of them a few years now – I'll tell you what I think and you can tell me if I'm right. I don't think it's very old at all – all this talk of it being ancient – I think it dates from the Boer War. A few drunks got together and said remember that dance we saw in South Africa? We could do something like that and that's all it is!

He supported his hypothesis by referring to the African style of the dress and the fact that a local club was known as the Kimberly which suggested South African connections to him. I persisted in my stance that its origins may be older, given the discrepancies in dates between the Boer War and written records of coco-nut dancing in the area earlier in the nineteenth century. Following his accusation that I was a romantic, I pointed out that when interviewed several years before he had professed an ancient origin for the custom. He responded that he was now older and wiser. Yet it was clear that he understood the romance of mysterious origins as he advised me: 'If you ever find out the truth, suppress it!'[8]

Here was another version of the truth; having published my 1990 article the year before I was in no position to act upon his request. As the next storyteller in a line of interpreters of the custom, my academic credentials undoubtedly give me power as a truth keeper, but it is a responsibility which is never stable. 'The truth' is a kaleidoscope of possibilities and, in the field, it depends who is lifting that kaleidoscope to his or her eye, when and in which direction it is pointing. As historians and ethnographers of dance, we must obviously acknowledge the many constructions of narrative and account for our own; but it also remains our responsibility to aim to distinguish stories from fantasies.

NOTES

1. For examples in the anthropology literature see Brettell (1993); see Grau and Koutsouba in this volume for examples on dance.
2. See Edwards (1999) for an anthropological approach to the same community. I would like here to record my thanks to Jeanette Edwards for discussion and generous sharing of her research.
3. A similar response was experienced by Edwards; see her monograph (1999), chapters 2 and 7 for details.
4. Fieldnotes, 17 July 1979 and 19 July 1979.
5. See Buckland (1984, pp. 703–11) for a detailed examination of historical sources and their ethnographic use in this context.

206   *Theresa J. Buckland*

6.   Fieldnotes, 18 July 1979.
7.   See, for example, Taylor (1997). Some morris dancers reviving tradi-
     tional dances from memories of groups which certainly in the 1930s
     blacked their faces now use colours such as red and green to minimize
     offence. The controversy is not restricted to dancers. Some traditions
     with a more overt origin in nineteenth-century minstrelsy, such as
     'Darkie Day' in Padstow, Cornwall and impersonators of the theatrical
     blackface act, Al Jolson, have received similar press coverage: see *The
     Guardian*, 20 January, 1998, p. 6; *Daily Mail*, 20 January, 1998, p. 35;
     and *The Guardian*, 16 July, 1998, p. 4. I am grateful to Derek Schofield
     for assisting with these references.
8.   Fieldnotes, 30 March 1991.

REFERENCES

Abu-Lughod, L. 1990. Can there be a feminist ethnography? *Women &
    Performance: A Journal of Feminist Theory*, 5, 1, pp. 7–27.
Boyes, G. 1987–88. Cultural survivals theory and traditional customs. *Folklife*,
    26, pp. 5–11.
Brettell, C.B. (ed.). 1993. *When They Read What We Write: the Politics of
    Ethnography*. Westport, Connecticut and London: Bergin and Garvey.
Buckland, T. 1984. Ceremonial dance traditions in the south-west Pennines
    and Rossendale (3 vols). Unpublished PhD thesis. Institute of Dialect and
    Folk Life Studies, School of English, University of Leeds.
—— 1986. The Tunstead Mill Nutters of Rossendale, Lancashire. *Folk Music
    Journal*, 5, 2, pp. 132–49.
—— 1990. Black faces, garlands, and coconuts: exotic dances on street and
    stage. *Dance Research Journal*, 22, 2, pp. 1–12.
—— 1991. 'In a word we are unique': ownership and control in an English
    dance custom. In Buckley, A., Edström, K.-O. and Nixon, P. (eds),
    *Proceedings of the Second British-Swedish Conference on Musicology:
    Ethnomusicology, Cambridge, 5–10 August, 1989* (Skrifter från
    Musikvetenskapliga institutionen, 26). Göteborgs, Sweden: Department of
    Musicology, Göteborgs Universitet, pp. 361–9.
Clifford, J. and Marcus, G.E. (eds). 1986. *Writing Culture: the Poetics and
    Politics of Ethnography*. Berkeley: University of California Press.
Edwards, J. 1999. *Born and Bred: Idioms of Kinship and New Reproductive
    Technologies in England*. Oxford: Oxford University Press.
Limon, J. 1991. Representation, ethnicity, and the precursory ethnography:
    notes of a native anthropologist. In Fox, R.G. (ed.), *Recapturing
    Anthropology: Working in the Present*. Santa Fe, New Mexico: School of
    American Research Press, pp. 115–35.
Macdonald, S. 1997. The museum as mirror: ethnographic reflections. In
    James, A., Hockey, J., and Dawson, A. (eds), *After Writing Culture:
    Epistemology and Praxis in Contemporary Anthropology*, ASA monograph 34.
    London and New York: Routledge, pp. 161–76.

Ness, S.A. 1992. *Body, Movement and Culture: Kinesthetic and Visual Symbolism in a Philippine Community.* Philadelphia: University of Pennsylvania Press.

—— 1996. Dancing in the field: notes from memory. In Foster, S.L. (ed.), *Corporealities: Dancing Knowledge, Culture and Power.* London and New York: Routledge, pp. 129–54.

Pickering, M. 1997. John Bull in blackface. *Popular Music,* 16, 6, pp. 181–201.

Sklar, D. 1991. Enacting religious belief: a movement ethnography of the annual fiesta of Tortugas, New Mexico. Unpublished PhD. dissertation, Department of Performance Studies, New York University.

Taylor, P. 1997. TV goes politically correct – and blacks out the coconutters. *Manchester Evening News,* 11 July, p. 3.

Thompson, E.P. 1975. *Whigs and Hunters: the Origin of the Black Act.* London: Allen Lane.

—— 1993. *Customs in Common.* Harmandsworth, Middlesex: Penguin.

Williams, D. 1976–1977. An exercise in applied personal anthropology. *Dance Research Journal,* 9, 1, pp. 16–30.

17 Textual Fields: Representation in Dance Ethnography

Georgiana Gore

INTRODUCTION: WRITING DANCE CULTURE

Writing dance culture, to borrow from the title of Clifford and Marcus's landmark text, *Writing Culture: the Poetics and Politics of Ethnography* (1986), is conventionally thought to be the final stage in the production of dance ethnography. Indeed this phase is commonly referred to as 'writing *up*' as if the act of presenting dance through textualization was a practice distinct from the lived experience of fieldwork. The notion of 'writing up' also implies that the messy, open-ended and often confusing business of negotiating with other cultures can be tidied up and neatly packaged into an authoritative and fully comprehensive account of the dance culture in question. Such ethnographic accounts often effect a form of closure, thus circumscribing the other within a set of paradigms which do not necessarily represent that other's concept of his or her own culture. The intellectual status of both the dance ethnography and its author is assured, but little or no room remains for the negotiation of alternative meanings. These forms of textual representation gain a status denied to those deployed in situations of face-to-face interaction, where the 'results' of fieldwork are merely written *down* (see Fabian in Okely, 1992, p. 3), in a manner usually conceived of as unproblematic because author and reader are one and the same person. Field notes are thus construed as 'subjective, spontaneous, private, unpublishable narratives [which] ... include failures of objectivity, states of confusion, excessive pleasures that are traditionally excluded from published accounts' (Ness, 1996, p. 129); and, as such, their publication constitutes both a professional and performative risk. Writing up, however, is but one privileged moment in the ethnographic enterprise, this privileging being related to the very constitution of the discipline of anthropology during the late nineteenth century as the scientific study of human beings,

208

and to its professionalization within academia. (See Turner's brief critique and proposal for the development of ethnodramatics [1982, pp. 89–101].) It may also be that the construction of a narrative account of the other is related, as Ricoeur suggests, to the fact that 'action is already articulated in signs, rules, norms: it is already always symbolically mediated'[1] (1983, p. 113), a phenomenon evident, no doubt, to the dance ethnographer.

In this chapter I propose that representational practices inform all stages of dance ethnography, including fieldwork, from the conception of a *field* research project to its execution and completion (if, indeed, fieldwork can ever be construed as a process with a definite ending, or even beginning). This notion that representation imbues all social practices has found its extreme manifestation in the context of interpretive anthropology, with the Geertzian proposition that all social events must be regarded as texts or rather 'textualized', a proposition derived from and in turn influencing Ricoeur's hermeneutic philosophy.[2] (For evidence of the intertextuality of Geertz's and Ricoeur's writings, see Clifford, 1988, pp. 38–40; Adam et al., 1995, p. 90; and Ricoeur, 1983, pp. 113–15, 151.) In an interpretive framework, therefore, representations of dance begin to be constituted in the field through the juxtaposition of local versions of events with the inferences produced by the ethnographer (see Geertz, 1973; Marcus and Fischer, 1986, pp. 17–44; Watson, 1992, p. 137). The researcher's danced and spoken representations are compared with local versions of dancing and talking about dance. Even in a more contemporary dialogical conception of fieldwork relations, this shuffling between 'experience-near' and 'experience-distant' representations of dance culture characterizes the production of ethnographic knowledge.

> Hopping back and forth between the whole conceived through the parts that actualize it and the parts conceived through the whole that motivates them, we seek to turn them, by a sort of intellectual perpetual motion, into explications of one another. (Geertz, 1983, p. 69)

Metaphoric use of movement to describe intellectual processes becomes realized in dance ethnography through the conscious implication of the body and actual use of movement to construct interpretations of local dance practices *in situ*.

Despite the many caveats which currently exist about using the reificatory term 'culture' (see for example Clifford, 1988, pp. 230–6; Hastrup, 1995, pp. 16–17, 154–7), I have chosen to retain it. I use it alone or in the expression 'dance culture' because it situates the products of human social activity, that is, dance, as contextually or co-textually constructed. A dance culture, which, following Hastrup, is not an 'empirical entity' but an 'analytical implication' (1995, p. 17), may include 'Dance', 'a dance', 'dancing' or 'dance event' for example, depending on who is doing the dancing, why, where and when, and who is talking about it. It is precisely because the expression evokes a certain vagueness that I retain it and because it challenges the Eurocentric theatre dance connotations of the word 'dance' which, as I have outlined elsewhere (Gore, 1994, pp. 59–60), misrepresents commonly held conceptions in Nigeria, the site for my fieldwork. Moreover, it actually provokes discussion of some of the very problems which its use invokes.[3]

Throughout the chapter, examples will be drawn from my ten-year experience of living and working in Benin-City, capital of the ancient kingdom of Benin and of the Southern Nigerian Edo State, which for the duration of my stay, between 1980 and 1990, was then part of the larger Bendel State.

REPRESENTING THE FIELD

That the distinguishing feature of dance ethnography is fieldwork remains a truism. What, however, is often eluded is that the field is a conceptual and not an empirical space, the location and boundaries of which are ethnographically generated. The manner in which the field is represented defines the modes in which the dance culture is construed, as field and culture are often conceived as coterminous in several if not in all their dimensions. The conventional anthropological view of culture is that this defines both a linguistic and geographically locatable entity (see Clifford on Said, 1988, pp. 271–6), a typification which may bear no relationship to the shifting realities of those who supposedly belong. Benin-City, for example, is a city of half a million ethnically diverse inhabitants, most of whom now speak two if not three languages (Pidgin, one of Nigeria's 420 languages, and sometimes English) and who negotiate daily between different and, sometimes, competing cultural contexts, each of which solicits different linguistic and social skills.

The centrality of fieldwork to dance ethnography refers not only to its epistemological and methodological status (that is, as initiatory rite of passage [Marcus and Fischer, 1986, p. 21]), but also to its positioning in both time and space within the totality of the ethnographic enterprise. Fieldwork may be regarded conceptually as the prerequisite for dance ethnography, that is, its starting point; but, in the conventional narrative which structures how an individual should undertake dance research in the field, the fieldwork period 'abroad' is framed by two phases at 'home', a preparatory period of conceptualization and a time 'writing up'. Ness describes this as the

> classical ethnographic score ... dual movement processes [which] create an arrangement in which acts of embodying cultural knowledge (gathering culturally novel forms of lived experience) are positioned in complementary geographic and historical distribution with reading and writing-'up' – literary activity. (Ness, 1996, p. 141)

Representations of fieldwork (a term which conventionally implies an activity occurring in a defined space and time) inevitably deploy metaphors of place and displacement to define an activity which has been historically constituted as occurring somewhere *other* than the researcher's place of origin, his or her 'home'. Distance between researcher and field is intrinsic to the activity whether this distance be construed as geographical, cultural, subjective or epistemological. As Segalen (1995, pp. 745–81) proposed as early as 1908,[4] exoticism (from the Greek *exo* meaning outside and therefore conveying the process of making strange) is the inevitable consequence of, or rather precondition for, the study of other practices. For without this capacity to render even the familiar strange there may be no discourse on otherness, since complete identification renders analytical practice impossible (Kilani, 1994, pp. 11–14). If we accept, therefore, that distancing is an epistemological condition of ethnographic research,[5] the question is how best to acknowledge this without returning to the reificatory stance of positivist anthropology where 'we' and 'they' are constituted as separate categories, implicitly in relations of inequality; nor indeed, without, thus, reinstating the colonial context. (See Fabian [1983] for an analysis of the problematics of spatial conceptions of the relations between other and ethnographer, these being constituted through fieldwork as observational practice as separate from representational practices.)

If the field is construed as a geographical location bounded in space, how do we decide where it begins and ends? Is it indeed coterminous with the location of an area on a map (region, city, village), with the location of a group of people, with the location of a specific form of activity? And who defines the boundaries of this location? Or is the field rather that space (defined by de Certeau as 'practiced place' [cited in Hastrup, 1995, p. 57]) constructed by the researcher in a dialogical relation to otherness, and therefore a space the creation of which begins 'at home' with the first encounter with the other through all forms of representation (including textual, visual, aural, performed, multimedia, and so on)?

CONSTRUCTING THE FIELD

Was my first encounter with the Benin kingdom to shape future research in ways difficult to foresee? In late 1978 or early 1979, I chanced upon Attenborough's 1976 BBC documentary on the Benin kingdom – seemingly my earliest memory of Benin bronzes and the spectacular ritual and ceremonial practices of divine kings in an African kingdom. Did this somehow alert me to the newspaper advertisement which I came across later in 1979, and provide an unconscious representational blueprint for future research on palace rituals? Or is this juxtaposition merely the historical reconstruction, the contextualization, of events which were discrete in time and space?

It was in January 1980 that I finally set off to undertake an initial two-year contract as a Lecturer/Research Fellow in Choreography in the Department of Creative Arts, University of Benin.[6] Despite a certain initiation into the politics of the country, a glancing knowledge of the traditional culture and dance, my ignorance and naivety were considerable. Given the romantic and stereotypic representations of traditional Africa with which I set out, what I had failed to anticipate was the curious effect of British colonialism, which had imbued many aspects of life with a peculiar, and, to me then, quaint, Victorian Britishness, which rendered the environment simultaneously familiar and doubly strange. In dance terms, this meant that during a middle-class social dance event in Benin's post-colonial leisure/sports club, we would invariably be treated to a medley of British ballroom dancing (waltz, foxtrot, and so on) and African popular dancing (*juju*[7] and highlife,[8] for example) and also sometimes entertained with a staged version of a traditional dance from a local cultural group. Such syncretism or creolization is characteristic of many Bini socio-cultural events as was witnessed in 1989, the year in which the palace staged the Tenth Coronation Anniversary Celebrations to mark the Oba (king) of Benin's accession to the throne in 1979, and his ten years' successful reign. During that year, numerous were the events which included dance and music as a central feature, as these are intrinsic to local notions of celebration.

Cultural heterogeneity thus challenged any purist conceptions I might have had of a contemporary West African kingdom (as presented for example by Attenborough's [1976] film). Benin-City is, in its own way, as cosmopolitan as London in terms of the diversity of its peoples and dances, and as culturally sophisticated, a fact attested to as early as the sixteenth century by Portuguese explorers and traders (Ryder, 1977).

To my hosts of a certain age, educated during the colonial régime, I suspect that I was less of a curiosity than I might have sometimes felt myself to be. A tradition of single, childless, white, female, British teachers was already well established within the school system. I thus entered the field as 'Miss Gore', an appellation bearing little or no social status, offset, however, by my professional designation as a university lecturer. Despite, or perhaps because of their immanence to social relations, and because dances are often performed for someone of a status higher than one's own, that I was teaching and researching into dance did little to contribute to my local standing, although it did bring me into contact with a community of practitioners who were flattered by my interest in local dance culture. On acquiring my PhD two years later, my academic status was immediately enhanced; and by becoming 'Dr Gore' I began to gain increasing social credibility, as I now had a title of some distinction. This social ascription and that of *oyinbo* or *ebo* (white person) remained throughout my stay as did all the other aforementioned social attributes, although, as I became incorporated within diverse social networks, I gained other public and private appellations, usually defined by my affiliations in a given context. My gender, race, age, childlessness and single family status (and professional middle-class background) in many respects determined my social position in the community and were to have multiple effects upon my research, as regards access to events, contacts with particular people, my fields of interest, sources of funding, and so on (see, for example, Caplan [1992] on the position of women researchers in Africa).

PRESENT IN THE FIELD

My presence in 'Africa' was not therefore framed by traditional ethnographic conventions. I had not come with the specific intention of initiating a field project, although my appointment explicitly indicated that I undertake dance research. My stay was not restricted in time to the conventional one calendar year cycle of ritual events, the ethnographer's timescale for accurate observation. Although I would live like a 'native' academic of my grade, my stated purpose was not to experience native life from the inside. The moment that I stepped off the plane I was 'at home'. Not only did I have nowhere to which I must return, but I also felt in some sense 'grounded'. I was present in the field, and yet had to actualize it through the simultaneous construction of social space and subjectivity. My position as lecturer ensured that I was already situated within a network of social relations, and as already stated, my social attributes conferred an identity of sorts. The others' representations of who I was and what my needs might be determined the contacts proffered. Access was facilitated to specific dance cultures, a number of discrete 'fields' were soon made evident and yet, paradoxically, these were determined by local conceptions of what seemed appropriate for a foreign academic lecturing in dance. By having an already constituted identity, I could shortcircuit the time cycle usually required to make contacts, but the scope of the field was thus reduced. For example, an introduction, during my first month, to the director of the performing arts section of the Bendel Arts Council, and to its dance troupe and choreographer (whose job it was to document and restage local dances) led to my appointment, during the course of that first year, as Chief Judge of Maiden Dance for Bensfac '80, the Bendel State Festival of Arts and Culture, a competitive festival of dances, held in December 1980. One of its avowed aims was to discover and improve the standard of Nigerian dances (Imoru, 1980, p. 7), and the Arts Council therefore wanted 'professionals' involved, who would assist in defining the criteria for evaluation, already framed within Eurocentric performance conventions and enshrined in a score sheet. My participation allowed me privileged access to document on film and photograph the festival's 80 or so traditional dance performances, divided into the five categories of 'maiden', 'ritual', 'ceremonial', 'acrobatic' and 'masquerade', and culled from the 19 Local Government Areas of the State, each of which, after local selection, could bring one dance for each category. After this event, I was overwhelmed by the sheer volume of dance in Bendel State, as well as by its aesthetic diversity and quality. I felt guilty that, apart from visual records, I had not made better *use* of the 'ethnographic' material on offer, and was still uneasy about doing the 'salvage ethnography' (even in its contemporary manifestations) which seemed to be required of me. That available traditional dance material should be somehow exploited, mined and preserved for posterity, like dead museum pieces is but one representation of dance ethnography. (See Buckland's chapter in this volume on the constitution of the dance ethnographer as custodian of tradition.) However, this representation of 'doing fieldwork in an African kingdom' (Nevadomsky, 1980) haunts me today as it did then, as it does not conform to a more reflexive approach in which bodily passions and actions are implicated.

How then were my 'fields' constructed? Acculturation to any new context requires mediation between self and other, that dialogic relation which characterizes fieldwork. This was therefore the relation with my students, although my hierarchical position as a choreography lecturer was perhaps more explicitly defined than the unequal relations instituted by the dance ethnographer. Practical dance teaching in a contemporary improvisatory mode, being more dialogic than conventional theatre dance training, facilitated intercultural discussion with my students, if sometimes only indirectly through comments on the work in hand. The initial framing of classwork within Euro-American conventions of theatricality enabled me to test, somewhat unconsciously, local performance conventions. Eurocentric conventions of staged dancing (including bodily training and choreographic production), even in its most popular or experimental manifestations, articulate, I remain convinced, notions about how the body and movement are constructed following a Foucauldian diagram of disciplinary technology, which privileges the scopic (Foucault, 1977) and aims to produce a malleable and creative body as instrument. Strategies include constructing an internalized consciousness of the body, visualizing bodily gesture in relation to the whole, dissecting and recomposing movement sequences according to a progressively difficult arrangement, which conforms to stereotypically linear and serial spatio-temporal configurations, framing movement (for example, with a marked beginning and ending), and so on. From student reactions, it became evident that local conceptions of rehearsal and performance were different. For the duration of my stay, my students, who came from all parts of the country but were predominantly Bendelites, taught me much about 'Nigerian' conceptions of dance, representations which were assimilated as I reconfigured my teaching strategies and which provided a conceptual framework for further research.

Two formal research contexts eventually became privileged not through strictly rational choices related to 'research design',[9] but, as is often the case, through the ritualization of social practices and the hazards of fortuitous encounters motivated by my particular interests. Moreover, once I could no longer envisage a future in Benin, the knowledge of limited time intensified the research process and sharpened my focus. The two contexts are unsurprisingly both located within Bini culture, the hegemonic culture of Benin-City because of its history as an empire and therefore ideologically and statistically the most likely context for research. These were the public performances of the ceremonial rituals enacted in the palace of the Oba of Benin (some of which feature in Attenborough's [1976] documentary), and a specific 'village' shrine to the god of the sea and fertility, Olokun,[10] now located in the heart of the city. I later realized that these two are related in a number of significant ways and have provided me with interestingly contrastive material, given that the former context represents official Bini discourse and ideology as authorized by the monarchical institution and 'tradition', and the other, the 'commoner's' popular version of events.

Admittance into Bini society was marked formally by my presentation at court around 1986, which, however, set official limits on my research: the Oba authorized me to observe and write all that I wished, but forbade the kingdom's chiefs from revealing any 'secrets'. This process of incorporation can be mapped through the transformations in the positions from which I was permitted to document the central rites of divine kingship, *Igue*, now held annually in the palace grounds during the Christmas holidays. These are ceremonial rituals staged in honour of the Oba and his ancestors, the culmination of which occurs when the Oba dances around a sacrificial cow and tosses the *eben*, one of two ceremonial swords.

From a position as outsider in 1980, when I stood and discreetly watched from behind several rows of local and foreign dignitaries, seated in the shade of a canopy directly flanking and framing the performance arena, I gravitated, in 1989, to the arena itself for my last *Igue*, and a 'full' one, as it marked the Oba's ten-year successful reign. Observational distance and a framed view of the action, which constructed *Igue* as a spectacularly staged ritual, were replaced by my participation as an officially sanctioned researcher, permitted to document from the inside. The ceremony was spent squatting, camera in hand, at the feet of chiefs, who, in a row with their *eben* resting on the ground and demarcating the performance space, awaited their turn to dance before the Oba prior to his own electrifying performance. The narrative thread of the dance event and the spectacular scopic vista, so clearly captured from a distance, thus dissolved in the tangible bustle of 'onstage' activity and in the threat of danger immanent in all such rites of passage: for if a chief drops the *eben* or falls while dancing, he is said to die during the coming year (Plate 14).

With the shift in orientation from periphery to centre, from outside to inside, the dance ethnographer's subjectivity becomes fully constituted within local discursive practices, both social and danced. Social acceptance as marked through dance indicates that one has found one's place in the other's world, a socio-spatial reorientation constructed in danced dialogue over time between dance ethnographer and other.

CONCLUSION: DANCING IN AND OUT OF BENIN

Dance like power in Benin-City is ubiquitous and invisible to the newcomer, unlike the soundscape of musical and conversational rhythms, both human and animal, which fill the atmosphere. For a long time when I first arrived I lay awake half the night listening to the deafening electrified live band music which invariably graced most neighbourhoods on a Saturday night, and I felt excluded, marginalized from what was obviously a major dance event. I eventually discovered through invitation and participation that this represented either grand parties during the waning of the oil boom years, or more likely one of the many 'second burials', the grandest and most elaborate of which are generally performed in Benin by the eldest son for his father (Bradbury, 1973, pp. 213–28). Indeed, if I were to retain one kind of dance event as the most widely frequented by all social strata, irrespective of creed, class, age, gender, religious affinities or ethnic affiliations, it would be these second burials, elaborate mortuary rituals, the prominence of which is explained by the fact that death rather than birth is the most celebrated event of an individual's life in Benin as this, paradoxically, ensures the person's status in life as well as in death.

The oscillation between past and present in the writing of this text begins to slow as I start defining dance in Benin within the contours of a fixed frame in present tense – the time of now in which I have recast my ten-year stay as 'fieldwork', time 'out' of my European life experience, but time shared in the constitution of common representations (Fabian, 1983 and Hastrup, 1995). It seems, also, that use of the present indicates that I am nearing the end of this journey in which I have attempted to map the representational conditions of my fieldwork in Benin. Were I to start again from the beginning I have no doubt that the trajectory taken would be different since the body's memories would assemble into an alternative narrative. Moreover, if the hallmark of anthropology is 'to experience the force of detail in practical life and to recast it in a theoretical mode that transcends it' (Hastrup, 1995 p. 22), does this means of organizing knowledge not situate our own subjectivity in the way that ancestral knowledge situates that of the Bini? As I dance the discourse of the past, as I dance in and out of Benin, so I make sense of my world, a world past in becoming, which, like the *ehi*, a person's guardian spirit and 'Destiny', maps a potential trajectory for the future.

NOTES

1. My translation.
2. See Ricoeur's (1971) article 'The model of text: meaningful action considered as text'.
3. Wright (1998) has recently addressed how the concept of 'culture' has been transformed from that of a 'thing' into that of a 'political process of contestation over the power to define key concepts, including that of "culture" itself' (p. 14). Moreover, she produces a succinct account of its 'old' and 'new' meanings.
4. See Clifford (1988, pp. 152–63) on Segalen's 'aesthetics of the diverse' and concept of exoticism.
5. See Martin (1997, p. 340) on Blau concerning the arguments for the maintenance of distance between audience and performer in the theatrical context.
6. The Department of Creative Arts later became a faculty, and dance, which I established and ran, became a section in the Department of Theatre Arts.
7. Throughout the text, tone marking is not included in the orthography of Nigerian languages.
8. For further information on these West African popular music and dance styles, see, for example, Waterman (1990) on the Yoruba *juju* and Coplan (1978) on Ghanaian *highlife*.
9. Hammersley and Atkinson's *Ethnography: Principles in Practice* (1995) is a useful, reflective beginner's manual.
10. I have begun to write about these two elsewhere (for example, Gore, 1995 and Wierre-Gore, 1998); see, also, Charles Gore (1998), who inevitably includes references to dance in his work on urban shrine configurations and rituals.

REFERENCES

Adam, J.-C., Borel, M.-J., Calame, C. and Kilani, M. 1995. *Le discours anthropologique: description, narration, savoir*. Lausanne: Payot.
Attenborough, D. 1976. *The Tribal Eye*. London: BBC. (Book based on the film series directed by David Collison and Michael Macintyre.)
Bradbury, R.E. 1973. *Benin Studies*. London: Oxford University Press for the International African Institute.
Caplan, P. 1992. Spirits and sex: a Swahili informant and his diary. In Okely, J. and Callaway, H. (eds.), pp. 64–81.
Clifford, J. 1988. *The Predicament of Culture: Twentieth-century Ethnography, Literature and Art*. Cambridge, Massachusetts: Harvard University Press.
Clifford. J. and Marcus, G.E. (eds.). 1986. *Writing Culture: The Poetics and Politics of Ethnography*. Berkeley: University of California Press.
Coplan, D. 1978. Go to my town, Cape Coast!: the social history of Ghanaian highlife. In Nettl, B. (ed.), *Eight Urban Musical Cultures: Tradition and Change*. Urbana, Illinois and London: University of Illinois Press, pp. 96–114.
Fabian, J. 1983. *Time and the Other: How Anthropology Makes its Object*. New York: Columbia University Press.
Foucault, M. 1977. *Discipline and Punish*. Harmondsworth: Penguin.
Geertz, C. 1973. *The Interpretation of Cultures*. New York: Basic Books.
———— 1983. *Local Knowledge: Further Essays in Interpretive Anthropology*. New York: Basic Books.
Gore, C. 1998. Shrine configurations in Benin-City, Nigeria. In Hughes-Freeland, F. (ed.), *Ritual, Performance, Media*. London: Routledge, 1998, pp. 66–84.
Gore, G. 1994. Traditional dance in West Africa. In Adshead-Lansdale, J. and Layson, J. (eds), *Dance History* (2nd edn). London: Routledge, pp. 59–80.
———— 1995. Rhythm, representation and ritual: the rave and the religious cult. In Adshead-Lansdale, J. and Jones, C. (compilers), *Border Tensions: Dance and Discourse, Proceedings of the Fifth Study of Dance Conference*. Guildford: Department of Dance Studies, University of Surrey, pp. 133–9.
Hammersley, M. and Atkinson, P. 1995. *Ethnography: Principles in Practice* (2nd edn). London: Routledge.
Hastrup, K. 1995. *A Passage to Anthropology: Between Experience and Theory*. London: Routledge.
Imoru, A. 1980. Foreword. In *Bendel State Nigeria Festival of Arts and Culture Programme*. Benin-City: Bendel Arts Council.
Kilani, M. 1994. *L'invention de l'autre: essais sur le discours anthropologique*. Lausanne: Payot.
Martin, R. 1997. Dance ethnography and the limits of representation. In Desmond, J.C. (ed.), *Meaning in Motion: New Cultural Studies of Dance*. Durham, North Carolina: Duke University Press, pp. 321–43.
Marcus, G.E. and Fischer, M.J. 1986. *Anthropology as Cultural Critique: an Experimental Moment in the Human Sciences*. Chicago: University of Chicago Press.

Ness, S.A. 1996. Dancing in the field: notes from memory. In Foster, S.L. (ed.), *Corporealities: Dancing Knowledge, Culture and Power*. London: Routledge, pp. 129–54.

Nevadomsky, J. 1980. Doing fieldwork in an African kingdom: a methodological Badaeker in the Kingdom of Benin. Unpublished paper.

Okely, J. 1992. Anthropology and Autobiography: Participatory Experience and Embodied Knowledge. In Okely, J. and Callaway, H. (eds), pp. 1–28.

Okely, J. and Callaway, H. (eds). 1992. *Anthropology and Autobiography*. London: Routledge.

Ricoeur, P. 1971. The model of text: meaningful action considered as text. *Social Research*, 38/39, pp. 529–62.

——— 1983. *Temps et récit, tome I: l'intrigue et le récit historique*. Paris: Seuil.

Ryder, A. 1977. *Benin and the Europeans 1485–1897*. London: Longman.

Segalen,V. 1995. *Oeuvres complètes*. Paris: Robert Laffont.

Turner, V.W. 1982. *From Ritual to Theatre: the Human Seriousness of Play*. New York: Performing Arts Journal Publications.

Waterman, C. 1990. *Juju: a Social History and Ethnography of an African Popular Music*. Chicago: Chicago University Press.

Watson, C.W. 1992. Autobiography, anthropology and the experience of Indonesia. In Okely, J. and Callaway, H. (eds.), pp. 134–46.

Wierre-Gore, G. 1998. Le festival d'Igue: danses, parades et hiérarchies au Royaume du Bénin. In Montandon, A. (ed.), *Sociopoétique de la danse*. Paris: Anthropos, pp. 27–38.

Wright, S. 1998. The politicization of 'culture'. *Anthropology Today*, 14, 1, pp. 7–15.

Index

221